a STATE in DENIAL

a
STATE in
DENIAL

Pakistan's Misguided and Dangerous Crusade

B.G. Verghese

RUPA

Published by
Rupa Publications India Pvt. Ltd 2016
7/16, Ansari Road, Daryaganj
New Delhi 110002

Sales centres:
Allahabad Bengaluru Chennai
Hyderabad Jaipur Kathmandu
Kolkata Mumbai

ISBN: 978-81-291-3598-8

First impression 2015

10 9 8 7 6 5 4 3 2 1

Typeset by SÜRYA, New Delhi

Printed at Replika Press Pvt. Ltd., India

Contents

Preface

And ye shall know the truth, and the truth shall make you free.

—St John 8:32

A nation in denial, Pakistan is in a state of deep crisis. Its fledgling, born-again democracy is threatened by internal dissension, self-made jihadi extremism, provincial rivalry and the looming presence of an army that remains a state within the state. Yet, there are emerging and increasingly articulate forces that recognize that Pakistan must reimagine and reinvent itself from the Indian 'other' to restore the identity it foolishly abandoned at birth. Muhammad Ali Jinnah so wanted to distance his 'nation' from the parent state that he abandoned its soul and defined it emphatically, solely and negatively as 'not India'—India being a permanent, existential Hindu enemy.

His famous 11 August 1947 speech to the constituent assembly of Pakistan[1] revealed his utter confusion. It was virtually censored and later withdrawn by his own government, as he had not merely repudiated the two-nation theory on the basis of which Pakistan had been born but had also, astonishingly, confessed in plain terms that he had little to say about the future of Pakistan as he had not thought about it sufficiently!

The denial by Pakistan of its history, geography and culture has caricatured reality. Pakistan has proclaimed itself an Islamic state, but has defined Islam in narrow sectarian terms. It has moved from being Muslim to becoming increasingly radical, trying hard to establish that it is 'Muslim enough'. It has dedicated itself to something called 'the ideology of Pakistan'[2]—a strange constitutional term—and is committed to defending 'the ideological frontiers'[3] of Pakistan, whatever and wherever they be. The Constitution it conferred on Pakistan-administered Kashmir (PAK) in 1974, and modified in 1990, ordained that fundamental rights shall be subject to the 'ideology of accession to Pakistan',[4] and made acceptance of this ideology a part of the oath of office of all leading functionaries and members of the legislative assembly (MLAs). Such actions are—and there's no mild way of putting it— pure gobbledygook.

Based on this, official Pakistani textbooks in state schools distort, omit and reconstruct the country's social and political history in an extraordinarily brazen manner. The Jinnah Institute, Islamabad, reviewed these textbooks in 2012 and described them as filled with a 'curriculum of hate'[5]—hate of India and of Hindus. To reinvent itself, Pakistan at one time tried to describe itself as West Asian and contemplated a confederation with Iran and Turkey in the abortive USA-sponsored Regional Cooperation for Development (RCD). It joined the Central Treaty Organization (CENTO) or the Baghdad Pact and has since been the sword arm of a number of West Asian, especially Sunni monarchies, crowning this position with possession of the 'Islamic' bomb.

Having denied its identity ab initio, Pakistan has been a state in constant denial ever since. This is documented in cast-iron terms in the record of Indo-Pakistan diplomatic correspondence between 1947 and 2007.[6] More damning have been the self-confessions of Pakistani actors, military and civil, in graphic and unapologetic terms. The plea always is, 'Let's move on, never mind the repeated perfidy and innocent lives lost. After all, we are today the worst victims of terror anywhere.' Maybe. But these are Pakistan's terrorists—raised, trained, armed, supported, launched, funded and shielded by it, to strike India and others. Now, some of these monsters, more Islamist than Pakistan bargained for, have turned against it; Islamabad dare not get off the tiger's back. Much of this has happened with the most perfidious American and British assistance—damn the collateral damage.[7]

War, tensions and cross-border terror have alternated with talks to manage or prevent conflict and seek a peaceful settlement. There have been such contrapuntal exchanges since 1947. India too has erred on occasion. But it has, by and large, sought to be accommodative and reconciliatory. It is not irredentist. It makes no claims on Pakistan. But Pakistan, alas, has an undefined ideology and ideological frontiers to defend. For it, Kashmir is the 'core' issue, together with the Indus waters. Everything else is hostage to a settlement of these two issues on its terms, irrespective of the UN (United Nations) Resolutions on Jammu and Kashmir (J&K), now effete, and the Indus Waters Treaty.

Kashmir and the Indus waters are, however, far from being the 'core' issues. They are consequences, not causes, of the endless stalemate. The real core issue is Pakistan's lack of identity or anchorage. Edward Lear, in his collection, *Complete Nonsense*, asks, 'Who, or why, or which, or what,/ Is the Akond of Swat?'[8] The same question may be addressed to Pakistan. The last 'akond', Minagul Aurangzeb, was incidentally in school with me in united India and remained a loving friend till the end. We often met and exchanged greetings, the last time on the occasion of Eid in August 2014. He was an ill man and tragically died a day later. With men and women like Aurangzeb—and there are many others—all proud Pakistanis, but dedicated to secularism, peace and cooperation with India—we shall overcome.

Pakistan has also to come to terms with its true Islamic heritage—a soft, humanistic, syncretic, Sufi-infused Islam, rather than the narrow, revivalist and fundamentalist Wahhabi Islam that has been imposed on its people as 'the ideology of Pakistan'. World Islam is in crisis. It is sorely in need of another renaissance imbued with the spirit of 'ijtihad' (or innovation, and an 'independent or original interpretation of problems not precisely covered by the Quran, Hadith and Ijma'[9]), which the Prophet himself ordained and which, not so long ago, heralded a glorious era of Islamic civilization, science and culture.

It is argued by some of the severest Pakistani critics that Pakistan has been there for sixty-eight years and is here to stay. It cannot be wished away. True enough. But it is, with Israel, the only ideological state in the world and continues to be chained to an ideology that is confused, illiberal and ill-suited to a modern state. This is truly Pakistan's core issue.

India cannot afford to sneer at or stand aloof from such an inference. It must assist in change. This is the challenge. Even incremental success could be transformative. If the right efforts are made, the issues of Kashmir and waters could be resolved.

I have cited many foreign authors and responsible Pakistani sources, so as not to make it possible for anyone to dismiss this text as an Indian rant and pure propaganda. Indians, too, must know the truth, and understand that India is arguing and acting from a position of strength—so that this nation can make those concessions that are necessary.

Peace has its victories, no less renowned than war.

HISTORICAL CHURNINGS

1
Blood and Mistrust

The Indian union's reluctance and structural inability to communicate inhibits governance in the country. For truth to prevail—as the national motto, 'satyameva jayate' demands—the facts must be known in a timely, complete and objective manner. It is cause for celebration, therefore, that much archival material from the official records of Indo-Pakistan relations has been compiled in collaboration with the public diplomacy division of the ministry of external affairs.[1]

Gaps remain and not everything has been placed in the public domain. Many official papers have remained in private hands; the few deposited in the Nehru Memorial Museum and Library find a place in the volumes edited by Avtar Singh Bhasin.[2] Considerable material has otherwise come to light over the years through memoirs and other sources, Indian and foreign. I have cited some of these to flesh out the Indo-Pakistan story. Yet, there are interesting nuances and nuggets in the present narrative that offer a better and deeper insight into the anxieties, hostilities, mistrust, hopes and yearnings that have gone into shaping what has been a tormented relationship between India and Pakistan—a relationship that awaits healing four generations after the huge trauma of Partition, one of the greatest tragedies of human history.

Why all has not been revealed even at this distance of time remains a teasing question. One must only hope that whatever else is locked away in private or official archives will come tumbling out. Other nations are opening their archives, leading to events directly and vitally bearing on India being recorded through foreign eyes.

The Indo-Pakistan story makes sad reading—freedom being born in blood. Even as the story unfolded, mistrust ran deep. In a letter dated 30 December 1947 to India's prime minister, Jawaharlal Nehru, Pakistan's prime minister, Liaquat Ali Khan, charged India with never wholeheartedly accepting the 'Partition scheme', being 'out to destroy the state of Pakistan', and indulging in a 'systematic sabotage against the implementation of Partition' through economic strangulation, the withholding of financial assets, 'the wholesale massacres of Muslim population', and the 'forcible' and 'fraudulent' accessions of Junagadh and J&K.[3] In 1951 it drew attention to Shyama Prasad Mukerjee's speeches, widely reported as stating that India must regain East Bengal—a statement that Nehru deplored.

This same theme of unfair accessions was vehemently recalled by Zulfikar Ali Bhutto in his *Myth of Independence*.[4] Here, he claimed that Assam and the entire Northeast of India had been grabbed by expelling Muslims. If Jinnah had received a 'moth-eaten travesty'[5] called Pakistan, Bhutto's lament was that all that survived was a truncated and traumatized nation, even as its eastern wing was ultimately severed by Hindu India. The Indian grudge has remained a constant refrain.

On 26 January 1950, the Constitution proclaimed the new republic of 'India, that is Bharat', denoting both its ancient civilizational and more recent territorial personality. *Dawn* editorialized that 'the use of the word "India" to denote the part of the subcontinent not included in Pakistan is justified by neither history nor geography'. It claimed that the Constitution had:

> [...] elongated the name to "India, that is Bharat" [...] This is jugglery designed to exploit the old name which belonged as much to the people of Pakistan as to the people of Bharat—for propaganda advantages exclusively for one section of the now divided population [...] From today, the words 'India' and 'Indians' will therefore be replaced with the word 'Bharat' and 'Bharatis'. We shall call that country henceforth by its proper, not the improper, name![6]

The government of Pakistan followed suit with a similar refrain. Nehru was greatly concerned about Pakistan's constant denigration of India and the vicious propaganda unleashed against the fledging nation by the media and otherwise. A Joint Press Code was drawn up and adopted on 28 April 1950 by the All-India Newspaper Editors' Conference and the Pakistan Newspaper Editors' Conference.[7] But it was observed in the breach.

Underlying Pakistan's charade was a tragic malaise. As author Avtar Singh Bhasin observes, Pakistan believed that the legacy of the Mughal Empire and preceding Muslim dynasties had fallen on its shoulders; it abandoned its languages, culture, heritage and even its geography, pretending to be part of West Asia. It discarded its history and invented a new one that denied its past and poisoned its future. From its very birth, as highlighted in the preface, Pakistan failed to adopt a positive identity. Moreover, it turned its back on India (read Hindus), which it treated as 'the other', a permanent enemy. This is truly its core problem, and Kashmir is only a territorial expression of Pakistan's constitutionally confused and warped Islamic identity (referred to as 'Nazariya-e-Pakistan'), which stretches to something called 'the ideological frontiers of Islam'.[8] Today, this truth is slowly dawning as Pakistan tears itself apart.

Even earlier, a group of fourteen eminent Muslim Indians—in a memorandum dated 14 August 1951 to Dr Frank P. Graham, the former UN representative for India and Pakistan—had this to say:

> The concept of Pakistan was vague, obscure and never clearly defined, nor its likely consequences foreseen [...] When Partition took place, Muslims in India were left in the lurch [...] Pakistan leaders proclaimed that they would convert Pakistan into a land where people would live a life according to the tenets of Islam. This created nervousness and alarm among the minorities living in Pakistan. Not satisfied with this, Pakistan leaders went further and announced again and again their determination to protect and safeguard the interests of Muslims in India. This naturally aroused suspicion among the Hindus against us and our loyalty to India was questioned. [...However] we are convinced that India will never attack our interests [...while Pakistan] is willing to sell us into slavery—if only it can secure Kashmir.[9]

In 1953, Nehru had occasion to allude to the debates on Pakistan's Constitution (not finally adopted until 1974) and feared its 'medieval concept'[10] of an Islamic state would affect the minorities by creating two classes of citizens in law. Further, 'inevitably, certain elements in India, which are communally inclined, will take advantage of this to spread their wrong policy and wrong arguments and create ill will when we want goodwill'.[11]

The Partition riots displaced millions, who became hapless refugees. Unspeakable brutalities and atrocities were committed on families on both sides. There was particular concern about abducted women. The problem of the safe evacuation of populations wishing or forced to migrate to the other side was delicate and daunting.

Settlement of evacuee property issues dragged on interminably, causing Nehru to write to his counterpart, Pakistan's secretary general, and later, prime minister, Mohammad Ali, that there was an apprehension on the part of Pakistan that 'if the matter were pursued logically and any kind of inquiry held, this could lead to Pakistan being made liable for a very large sum of money'.[12] Non-official estimates placed the respective values in the range of Rs 300 crore for Muslim property and Rs 3,000 crore for Hindu–Sikh properties. Pakistan wished to keep the matter in suspense until the canal waters' dispute was settled. As for Pakistan's complaint of India withholding from Pakistan its legitimate financial dues on Partition, Nehru replied that making payments while an undeclared war was being waged against India in Kashmir would only help fund that jihad. This apart, Nehru expressed deep distress at reports of the manner in which the Khan brothers (Khan Abdul Ghaffar Khan and Dr Khan Sahib) and the Khudai Khidmatgars—Congress stalwarts wholly dedicated to non-violence—were being treated in the North-West Frontier Province (NWFP). He also had occasion to complain bitterly to Mountbatten about the negative role of Francis Mudie, the governor of West Punjab, in 'creating friction' and disruption and gathering around himself for the purpose some other retired British civil servants from the United Provinces and Punjab with 'unenviable reputations'.[13]

Both sides debated for years the merits and modalities of signing a no-war declaration or non-aggression pact. India preferred a wider 'peace and friendship treaty'. At the same time, referring to Pakistan's constant threat of military support for 'freedom fighters' in J&K, Nehru said 'peace is not offered with clenched fists or with threatened aggression and resounding cries of jihad'.[14]

The situation has scarcely changed.

2
Integration: Bahawalpur, Kalat

Few today remember that a quarter of India's population and a third of its territories were under princely rule. These 562 (or so) states ranged from large entities like Hyderabad, Kashmir and Mysore to tiny feudal estates, each with a given number of gun-salutes. During the hundred years before Independence, the British had taken over states under Lord Dalhousie's Doctrine of Lapse, whereby a state whose ruler died without a male heir would 'lapse' to the Raj. Otherwise it was provided that should a ruler wish to join British India, he could do so through an Instrument of Accession, as embodied in the 1935 Government of India Act, under the headings of defence, external affairs and communications. So a mechanism for formally absorbing princely India into the Raj was already in place well before 1947.

With Independence looming large, the future of Indian princely states attracted anxious attention. To deal with the problem, the existing political department was broken into the state departments of India and Pakistan—the Indian one being headed by Sardar Vallabhbhai Patel, with V.P. Menon as the secretary.

As for the tribal territories of the Northeast, at least four schemes were floated—the first authored by Governor of Assam Sir Robert Reid, conceptualizing a crown colony for the northeast of India and the hill region of Burma. His successor, Sir Andrew Clow critiqued this and suggested some variations, following two papers by principal secretaries, James Mills and Philip Adams. These were later endorsed by Reginald Coupland, a British constitutional adviser. The proposal, now known as the Coupland Plan, envisaged that the governments of India and Burma would have a treaty with the British government to share responsibility of the Naga-inhabited areas as 'trust territory'. The Nagas and Mizos shot down the idea and preferred to cast their lot with India.[1]

Under Mountbatten's June 3 Plan, British paramountcy would lapse with the end of the Raj at midnight on 14-15 August 1947. Technically, the states would become independent but, the viceroy added, compulsions of geography, demography, viability and ground realities would compel accession to one dominion or the other. Nehru favoured some form of popular consultation, especially where the ruler was of a different faith from that professed by a majority of his subjects. Jinnah differed; in his view, the ruler was sovereign and his word must be final.

In the case of smaller states and feudatories with compelling commonalities, it was considered prudent to encourage them to group together in larger entities to facilitate negotiations and an orderly transition. Thus, many rulers, Junagadh included, joined the Kathiawar States Union, and indicated they would jointly accede to India. The princes bargained for greater autonomy— some like Bhopal, Travancore and Hyderabad even for independence, their dewans and constitutional advisers often playing a major role.

Other plans were also being canvassed. According to Penderel Moon, writer and the British resident in Bahawalpur:

> […] a plan had also been mooted—and had received some backing from the Political Department—for combining the States or a large number of them, into a kind of third Dominion. [M.A.] Gurmani [a senior Muslim League leader] occasionally seemed attracted by the idea. It was not, in my view, a practical proposition; but a few of the larger States forming a compact area […] might have successfully stood aloof both from India and Pakistan, if they had acted together in unison.[2]

Mischief was afoot. It was India, not Pakistan, that was in danger of being Balkanized. The maharaja of Jodhpur, a Hindu-majority state with deep cultural and economic ties with India, was handed a blank piece of paper by Jinnah, asked to set out the concessions he wanted from Pakistan and assured him that they would be approved. Nongstein and another little state embedded in Assam's

Khasi Hills were admitted into Pakistan, which also made efforts to absorb Tripura.

Unlike Pakistan—which sought to inveigle ambitious princes to accede to it on any terms—India was not for territorial aggrandizement at any cost. When a preponderantly Muslim-majority border state like Bahawalpur sought to parley with India, it was sternly told by the Indian states ministry that by popular inclination and geographical compulsion it should join Pakistan. No Standstill Agreement was signed with it.[3] Just then, the nawab of Bahawalpur decided to visit the UK while accession loomed. This encouraged some notables to suggest that in the same manner that Pakistan had dangled concessions to several Hindu princes to join Pakistan, the nawab might be able to extract a better deal from Pakistan were he to appear to be in conversation with India. The gambit failed; India was not interested in the nawab's games, and he acceded to Pakistan in October 1947.

The Congress-affiliated Khudai Khidmatgars under the Khan bothers had won the popular mandate to rule the NWFP after the 1937 and 1946 elections. But with the approach of Independence, it was considered desirable to hold a referendum to test whether popular opinion now favoured joining India or Pakistan. Since the NWFP would not be contiguous with India, Khan Abdul Ghaffar Khan argued in favour of a third choice, namely, independence. The Congress had strongly ruled against the princes opting for independence with the lapse of paramountcy, so Nehru regretfully demurred. The Khudai Khidmatgars thereupon boycotted the referendum that followed which delivered the province to Pakistan. Khan Abdul Ghaffar Khan was greatly embittered by this 'Indian betrayal'.

Kalat saw itself as an independent Khanate. Decades back, the British had got a perpetual lease of Quetta and certain other Baloch areas from the Khan to carve out British Balochistan. According to the *Jinnah Papers*,[4] on 11 August 1947—as a result of a series of consultations between the Khan of Kalat and Jinnah in the presence of Lord Mountbatten—a press communique was issued stating that 'the Government of Pakistan recognizes Kalat as an independent sovereign State, in treaty relations with the British Government, with a status different from that of Indian

State'.[5] Further, 'legal opinion will be sought as to whether or not agreements of leases between the British Government and Kalat will be inherited by the Pakistan Government'.[6] A Standstill Agreement was signed between Kalat and Pakistan.

Prior to this, on 8 August 1947, Lord Mountbatten had told the secretary of state, Lord Listowel:

> I was invited by the Khan of Kalat to add to the communique that I also recognised he was an independent sovereign ruler. I replied that so far as H.M.G. was concerned they considered Kalat to be an Indian State, but since the two interested parties both agree I did not propose to interfere with the agreement.[7]

It was on receiving this note that the government of Pakistan released the 11 August communique.

With the creation of Pakistan, Kalat's dewan-i-am or lower house decided to send a deputation to Karachi on 25 February 1948 to negotiate and formalize future treaty relations between the two states. Jinnah, the Khan of Kalat's legal adviser but now governor general of Pakistan, played along, since he was confident that with the lapse of paramountcy, the Quetta lease would come to Pakistan. According to some sources, he even informally suggested a plebiscite.

On 17 March 1948, Pakistan 'accepted' the accession of Kharan, Lasbela and Makran, reducing Kalat (to which these feudatories belonged) to a landlocked entity. The Khan of Kalat protested in vain. On 20 March 1948, he received a message on behalf of Jinnah, stating that the governor general had decided to cease dealing with Kalat personally and that future negotiations should be conducted directly with the government of Pakistan.

Another blow to the Khan of Kalat was an All India Radio broadcast of 27 March 1948 that referred to a press conference by V.P. Menon, in which Menon had purportedly announced that Kalat had been pressing for its accession to India instead of to Pakistan; however, the government of India would not have anything to do with a state within or contiguous to Pakistan.

Deeply angered, the Khan of Kalat issued a communique in response:

> It had never been my intention to accede to India [...] It is, therefore, declared that from 9 p.m. on March 27—the time when

I heard the false news over the air—I forthwith decide to accede to Pakistan, and that whatever differences now exist between Kalat and Pakistan be placed in writing before Mr Jinnah, the governor general of Pakistan, whose decision I shall accept.[8]

Significantly, the 'government of India sought to put the record straight',[9] first in a cabinet meeting, and next, through the prime minister's statement in parliament on 30 March 1948. It was suggested that there was an error in reporting by All India Radio, and V.P. Menon had been misquoted. The clarifications did little to undo the damage already done. On 30 March 1948, *Dawn* commented editorially on Menon's 'naivety'. It wrote:

After having accepted the accession of Tripura state which is much more contiguous to Pakistan than to Indian territory, and having not only engineered the Maharaja's accession but also started a war of conquest of Kashmir, such a pose ill becomes India!

However, *Dawn* also had a warning for the Khan. So-called Kalat nationalists were known to be in touch with anti-national elements in India. Therefore, the Khan's first duty was to put down with an iron hand the disrupters who were talking of 'Balochistan for the Balochi', stirring 'Baluch nationalism' and poisoning the minds of innocent tribesmen with misinformation. Such propaganda was the negation of the very ideal of 'one God, one religion, one people'.

Pakistan's war on Balochistan had commenced, within a framework of charges of Indian complicity. Kalat's accession to Pakistan was formally accepted on 31 March 1948.

A decade later, Prince Karim Aga Khan purchased Gwadar, an enclave on the Makran coast with a population of 85,000 people, from the Sultan of Oman for $3 million and gifted it to Pakistan. It had originally belonged to Kalat, but had been transferred to Oman. It is being developed by Pakistan as a strategic port, currently under Chinese management.

3
Doublespeak: Junagadh, Hyderabad

Well before Mountbatten set out the modalities of accession by the princely states, options were being discussed in the chamber of princes and outside. Junagadh was an overwhelmingly non-Muslim Kathiawar principality not contiguous with Pakistan. Pockets of its territory were islanded in the neighbouring states of Bhavnagar, Nawanagar, Gondal and Baroda, and it shared with them common railway, postal and telegraph services operated by the government of India.

Early in 1947, the dewan of Junagadh invited Shah Nawaz Bhutto, a staunch Muslim Leaguer, to join the state council of ministers. Press speculation regarding future developments caused the Junagadh durbar to issue a press note on 11 April 1947, stating:

> What Junagadh pre-eminently stands for is the solidarity of Kathiawar and would welcome the formation of a self-contained group of Kathiawar States. Such a group while providing for the autonomy and entity of individual States and their subjects would be a suitable basis for cooperation in matters of common concern generally and coordination where necessary.[1]

Such a Kathiawar States Union was indeed formed. The Junagadh constitutional adviser, Nabi Baksh informed both Mountbatten and Patel separately that he proposed to advise the nawab to accede to India. On 15 May 1947, the dewan announced: 'We have officially informed our attached units [presumably the feudatory entities of Mangrol, Babriawad and Manavadar], that they will be at liberty to adopt any course for their preservation and progress after the termination of paramountcy in June 1948 or earlier.'[2]

Later, in May 1947, on the dewan's going abroad, Shah Nawaz

Bhutto was appointed his successor, and on 15 August 1947, announced Junagadh's accession to Pakistan, which formally accepted it on 13 September 1947. India learnt of this from the newspapers some days later. It protested against this development 'in utter violation of the principles on which Partition was agreed upon and effected' and offered to hold any democratic test, such as a plebiscite.[3]

Mangrol, Babriawad and Manavadar were all coerced and stampeded into acceding to Pakistan. Mangrol, actually, first acceded to India, but renounced this in quick measure. Junagadh forces moved into these territories, causing terror among the local population.

Jinnah rejected India's protestations as 'misconceived and untenable' and accused Nehru of 'trying to import fresh criteria' into the matter of accession, 'limiting free exercise of choice by States'.[4] He mocked the suggestion of a plebiscite as 'a matter between [the] ruler-constituted authority and the people'.[5] Further, he accused the jamsaheb and other Kathiawar rulers of inciting violence within Junagadh.

Meanwhile, Samaldas Gandhi, nephew of the Mahatma and a nationalist leader, gathered around him refugees and other state subjects from Junagadh domiciled in India. He then went on to announce the formation of a Junagadh provisional government in Bombay on 25 September 1947 and its decision to accede to India. The provisional government soon moved to Rajkot, tightening the noose around Junagadh and rendering it increasingly difficult for Shah Nawaz Bhutto to administer the state. An imminent breakdown of state governance compelled the dewan to request the Indian government to take over the administration. This was peacefully done on 9 November 1947. No Indian troops had entered Junagadh before this date, despite provocation.

Pakistan had taken the matter to the United Nations which was informed of India's promise of an impartial plebiscite. Prime Minister Liaquat Ali Khan remained defiant and refused to recognize 'your occupation of Junagadh', adding that 'a free and fair Plebiscite can only be held after your forces are withdrawn, the administration of the ruler is restored and normal conditions prevail'.[6] Gratuitous advice this in unwarranted circumstances, but soon to be brazenly defied and denied in J&K!

This was followed by an official press note from Karachi that Pakistan had no intention of recognizing India's 'military coup d'etat [...] Neither the Dewan nor [...] the Ruler himself has any authority to negotiate any settlement, temporary or permanent, with the Indian dominion'.[7] Good but irrelevant advice, again blatantly ignored by Pakistan when it took over Gilgit and the Northern Areas by a military coup that overthrew the maharaja's governor, Ghansara Singh, in late 1947.

The Junagadh plebiscite was held by India on 28 February 1948. Of 2,01,457 registered voters, 1,90,870 exercised their franchise; only 91 individuals cast their vote in favour of accession to Pakistan.[8] India offered a second plebiscite if requested, under international auspices. The offer, as expected, was never pursued as even Pakistan knew that the result would be no different.

As a footnote, the Indian high commissioner in Pakistan, Sri Prakasa, informed Delhi on 4 December 1949 that Shah Nawaz Bhutto and others had approached him more than once with 'piteous appeals to restore them to Junagadh on the promise of accession to India and full responsible government for the State's people'![9] Delhi's tart reply was that the nawab had fled Junagadh 'taking with him all the realisable assets of the State'. Should he return, 'we have no doubt there will be a major communal flare-up [...] and he will not be tolerated for twenty-four hours'.[10]

A final irony. An elaborate note was recorded in November 1947 by Governor General of India Lord Mountbatten in a one-to-one meeting with his counterpart, Jinnah, in Lahore. The quaid-i-azam:

> [...] admitted that there was no sense in having Junagadh in the Dominion of Pakistan. He had been most averse to accepting this accession. He had in fact demurred for a long time, but had finally given way to insistent appeals of the Nawab and his Dewan.[11]

Nehru, likewise, confessed at an Indo-Pakistan meeting presided over by Mountbatten in Delhi on 8 December 1947 that 'India had in some ways been wrong about Junagadh'[12] in the matter of its handling of the provisional government. But there was no parallel with what had happened in Kashmir.

Apart from Junagadh and Kashmir, the only princely state to hold out against accession was Hyderabad. The obvious fact was its geographical compulsion to join India as it was wholly enclosed by the Bombay and Madras Presidencies and the Central Provinces, all of which constituted part of India. Even in political theory it had nowhere else to go. Aware of this, its representative, the nawab of Chhatari, urged the Cabinet Mission in 1946 to retrocede to it territories ceded to the East India Company, with an additional claim to an outlet to the sea. V.P. Menon recalls that when asked by Lord Wavell (the governor general of India before Lord Mountbatten took over) what port he had in mind, he mentioned Goa[13] (though the state subsequently also bargained for an outlet via Berar and Vizianagaram to the Bay of Bengal). Chattari added that Hyderabad would not require a territorial corridor but only an 'easement' to enable it to import by rail, across British India territory, goods received in their own port.[14]

Despite Hyderabad's landlocked position within India and its predominantly non-Muslim population, the nizam was adamant about holding out for independence. He saw this as the only alternative to risking riots if he acceded to India and recognized the impossibility of joining Pakistan even if he was able to forge close relations with it. India's offer of a plebiscite was refused. The nizam's prime minister, Laik Ali and, increasingly, the Razakar[15] leader, Kasim Rizvi, dictated terms. Pakistan encouraged the obduracy of the nizam who finally appealed to the United Nations. The international community was less interested in the hard facts than in preventing an Indo-Pakistan war.

Its patience exhausted and in view of the growing depredations of the Razakars, India took police action. The 108-hour operation concluded on 17 September 1948 with the surrender of the Hyderabad forces. The nizam withdrew his case before the Security Council six days later.

Years later, on 21 September 1960, Nehru met President Ayub Khan in Murree and recorded a note of their conversation. Talking of Kashmir, Ayub Khan said that mistakes had been made on both sides:

> Pakistan had raised some issues which the President thought were not justifiable. Thus there was the case of Hyderabad and

Junagadh, etc. It was clear that these places could only go to
India. They were surrounded by Indian territories and they
could not separate themselves.[16]

But he seemed to indicate that Pakistan was justified in regard to
its claim on Kashmir, though he did not actually say so.

More recently, in his *The Destruction of Hyderabad*,[17] A.G. Noorani
suggests that India was both legally and morally wrong on
Hyderabad, and its 'invasion' of that princely state severely
damaged, if not destroyed, its rich composite culture. This is a
wholly exaggerated view. Noorani himself admits that Hyderabad
was never independent and was embedded in India without access
to the sea—something it had desperately sought to make good by
securing a port in Marmagoa (now Mormugao, Goa) or
Masulipatnam (now Machilipatnam, Andhra Pradesh) and transit
rights to either territory. The nizam had spared no effort over
many years to achieve this goal, but to no avail. In the
circumstances, Hyderabad had nowhere to go but India. The nizam
could have bargained for better terms regarding cultural
guarantees, more property, higher personal status and so forth,
but was in no position to demand independence or even special
relations with Pakistan that would almost vest it with co-
sovereignty.

Noorani writes of the Arya Samaj and various Hindu atrocities,
but pays little attention to an illegitimate Hyderabad 'sovereignty'
that would have disrupted the Indian union and created a second
Pakistan in its heartland. Nor does he dwell in any detail on the
depredations of the Razakars and the violent communist uprising
in Telengana that was only put down after the police action. Could
India have waited and negotiated until the nizam was worn down?
Jinnah, on his part, was negotiating with several other princes,
seeking to bribe them with concessions that were not his to give.
This would have been a recipe for the Balkanization of India.

As for the pious objections of others, what would be the reactions
of the great powers and of the United Nations were Colorado,
Lancashire or Multan to demand sovereign independence despite
being completely islanded within the USA, the UK and Pakistan?
Who would tolerate this nonsense? No such state has ever existed
in any part of the world at any time. The proposition is both
mischievous and absurd.

4

The Kashmir Unfolding

Pakistan had set its eyes on J&K well before Partition. Jinnah had sought to woo Sheikh Abdullah, admittedly the tallest popular leader in the state. The sheikh was later to remark that all the quaid-i-azam had to offer was Islam, which was already extant in the state, its Sufi underpinnings embodied in a unique, syncretic Kashmiriyat that culturally united both Muslims and Hindus.

However, the Muslim League believed that J&K was naturally part of Pakistan on grounds of contiguity and a Muslim majority, apart from being a 'lifeline', as it controlled the headwaters of the Indus and gave the nation strategic depth. The Muslim League's steadfast principle—that with the lapse of paramountcy, the princes were sovereign—gave way to the argument that Dogra tyranny and the maharaja's policy of exterminating Jammu Muslims had led to a huge exodus of refugees to Pakistan and an uprising in Poonch which was aided by Second World War ex-servicemen from the region and their fierce warlike tribal cousins from the NWFP. This had led to the formation of an Azad Kashmir government on 22 October 1947, days before Maharaja Hari Singh's 'forced and fraudulent' accession to India. All this was after India had unfairly intervened in Junagadh, set up a provisional government and then taken over the state.

What are the facts? Although Pakistan had signed a Standstill Agreement with J&K to maintain the status quo and ensure the movement of all essential supplies and services, on 4 September 1947, Major General Scott, the long-term chief of staff of the J&K state forces, wired the state government at Srinagar, warning them that armed infiltrators had entered J&K from Kahuta in

Rawalpindi district 'looting and attacking minority communities'.[1] When confronted by India, the deputy commissioner of Rawalpindi denied these facts, and sought specific details. On 27 September 1947, Nehru alerted Sardar Patel that the Muslim League in West Punjab and the NWFP was preparing to send in large numbers of lashkars to J&K before winter snows cut it off. He thought that the maharaja should be advised to release Sheikh Abdullah from detention for his 1946 Quit Kashmir call,[2] and rally the National Conference behind accession to India.

Events moved fast. On 3 October 1947, J&K sent an SOS to the government of Pakistan highlighting the violation of the Standstill Agreement and asking it to restore the movement of supplies to the state. A few days later, Maharaja Hari Singh cabled the British prime minister, Clement Attlee, protesting the blockade. He added that with the 'obvious connivance of the Pakistan Government the whole of the border from Gurdaspur side up to Gilgit is threatened with invasion which has actually begun from Poonch'.[3] Pakistan denied such 'manufactured' reports and made counter allegations.

On 22 October 1947, the tribal raids commenced, and two days later, the commander-in-chief of the Indian army received information that tribesmen had seized Muzaffarabad.

On 25 October 1947, Nehru sent a cable to Attlee, stating that the maharaja had appealed for assistance, which India was favourably disposed to provide. J&K's northern frontiers marched with Afghanistan, Russia and China and its security and tranquillity were vital for the security of India, which remained willing to abide by the wishes of the people.

Lord Mountbatten urged Nehru not to lend assistance until an instrument of accession was signed by the maharaja of Kashmir. The maharaja's letter of accession was obtained by V.P. Menon in Srinagar on 26 October 1947 and was formally accepted by the cabinet on his return to Delhi post haste. Indian troops were flown into Srinagar at first light the following morning and Sheikh Abdullah, who was released, was sworn in as head of a popular government.

Liaquat Ali protested and argued that the failure to send essential supplies to J&K 'was due to dislocation of communications and disturbances in Punjab.'[4] The tribal raid was provoked by the killings of Muslims in Poonch and elsewhere, and it was India that had invaded Kashmir. He cabled Attlee denouncing Abdullah as a 'quisling'. As a 'paid agent of the Congress for the last two decades and with the exception of some gangsters he has purchased with Congress money, he has no following among the Muslim masses'.[5] He further accused India of seeking to change the demographic composition of J&K by eliminating or driving out Muslims in order to frustrate a free plebiscite.

At a subsequent meeting with Mountbatten, Nehru and others, Liaquat Ali denied supplying trucks and petrol to the raiders to traverse hundreds of kilometres through Punjab to enter J&K. He said he could not stop the tribals. Any effort to do so would mean going to war with the tribes, which he was not prepared to do.

On 1 November 1947, Mountbatten had a marathon meeting with Jinnah in Lahore, after which he recorded in an elaborate note:

> Jinnah's first observation was that it was redundant and undesirable to have a plebiscite as the states should go accordingly to their majority population. If we [India] would give him accession of Kashmir, he would offer to urge the accession of Junagadh direct to India.[6]

On Mountbatten's insistence that the first order of business must be to stop the fighting in J&K, Jinnah said that both sides should withdraw at once. Asked how the tribesmen were to be called off, Jinnah replied that all he had to do was to give them an order to come out and they would do so. Mountbatten 'expressed mild astonishment at the degree of control that he appeared to exercise over the raiders'![7]

The fact is that Pakistan had mobilized, armed and officered the raiders to wage an undercover war of conquest. The story was later told in *Raiders in Kashmir* by Akbar Khan, then the director of weapons and equipment at Rawalpindi. In the beginning of September 1947, Akbar Khan was asked to prepare a plan for the accession of Kashmir and was soon thereafter called to Lahore for a meeting with Liaquat Ali Khan, Finance Minister Ghulam Muhammad, Mian Iftikharuddin (a leading Muslim Leaguer), Major Khurshid Anwar and some others.

Two sets of plans were prepared by Akbar Khan and Khurshid Anwar, who had gathered a lashkar of tribesmen. The invasion of Kashmir was on track. On 20 October 1947, the commander-in-chief of India received a telegram from the general headquarters in Pakistan (commanded by General Frank Messervy) stating that some 5,000 tribesmen had attacked and captured Muzaffarabad and Domel and were advancing on Baramula and Srinagar via Uri.

The evidence was precise and overwhelming. Pakistan's plea that India had triggered the Poonch revolt that caused the tribesmen to intervene was hollow. Indeed, even Christopher Snedden—an Australian scholar sympathetic to Pakistan, who repeats the charge that tribal intervention followed Dogra repression and atrocities in Poonch—makes note of the Azad Kashmir census of 1998 marked 'for official use only' and therefore considered 'reasonably accurate'; this carries a history of the events of 1947, but makes no mention of the Poonch uprising.[8] Rather, it states that it was the maharaja's accession to India that sparked the liberation movement of the Muslim population of the state against Dogra and India forces in Kashmir.

At a meeting taken by Mountbatten in Delhi on 8 December 1947 with Liaquat Ali, Nehru and their senior advisers, Pakistan was for an immediate ceasefire and withdrawal by the armed forces of either side followed by a plebiscite conducted by an impartial administration under the joint supervision of Jinnah and Mountbatten. The invaders and the aggressed were neatly equated! Nehru angrily ruled out a plebiscite until the raiders and outside elements were ejected from the state. 'If necessary, he would throw up his prime ministership and take the sword himself […] against the invasion. Nothing else mattered—until Kashmir was cleared, though it might take five years or ten'.[9]

Akbar Khan's *Raiders in Kashmir* merits closer attention.

> Since the British declaration about the forthcoming partition, we had assumed that Kashmir would naturally join Pakistan. In fact, the very concept of Pakistan had included it as an integral part, the letter K in the name Pakistan standing for Kashmir […] Kashmir had to be in Pakistan because three-fourths of its four million inhabitants were Muslims, and its territory of 84,500

square miles had no effective road, river or rail links, nor direct economic ties with India.[10]

That was totally misplaced logic. A group of Pakistani military officers had waited on Jinnah while he was still in Delhi.

> The Quaid-e-Azam had assured the delegation [...] that the idea of Pakistan had swept over Kashmir as it had over the rest of India and thus, in spite of Sheikh Abdullah, the Kashmiri Muslims would want to join Pakistan—and secondly, Kashmir had geographically no choice but to join it.[11]

He was disproved on all counts. Jinnah was fully involved in the conspiracy and plans to invade J&K from the start, his pious disclaimers nothwithstanding. Akbar Khan notes that 'as we came to know some years later, Jinnah himself ordered an attack on Jammu',[12] and launched what was to be Pakistan's coup de grace across the international border with the aim of severing J&K's vital lifeline at Akhnoor.

Yet, there is a tinge of disappointment in Akbar Khan's writing:

> It was because of fear that during the 1947-48 Kashmir war, not even a single one of our leaders entered Kashmir to visit the troops or see the situation at the front. On the opposite side, Nehru, Abdullah, as well as their ministers and generals were regularly visiting the front. On our side no one crossed the border. Not even at night. Not even in the dark [...][13]

There is now no dearth of evidence that the British, behind a cloak of military neutrality under the commander-in-chief, Claude Auchinleck, were supporting Pakistan from both sides. Akbar Khan writes that the Pakistan commander-in-chief, General Frank Messervy 'by December 4, 1947, appeared to have been taken into confidence'. He had earlier told Akbar Khan that he could not confront India only with sticks. Now, in December, he told Khan:

> 'Well, you will not have to do it with sticks alone any longer, I am going to help.' He allotted me one million rounds of ammunition which would keep us going for another month— and also permitted me to take twelve volunteer officers from the Army for a period of three weeks.[14]

As the Second World War came to a close, British thinking revolved around the strategy it should adopt were India to be partitioned. The British chiefs-of-staff committee met in London in May 1947 and recommended this:

> From the strategic point of view there were overwhelming arguments in favour of West Pakistan remaining within the Commonwealth, namely, that we should obtain important strategic facilities, the port of Karachi, air bases, and the support of Muslim manpower in the future; be able to ensure the continued integrity of Afghanistan; and be able to increase our prestige and improve our position throughout the Muslim world […][15]

This has remained the steadfast goal of the Anglo-American alliance whatever the collateral damage to India—which has been immense.

5
UN Scorned, Gilgit-Baltistan Seized

Mountbatten had privately persuaded Liaquat Ali to accept UN intervention to resolve the Kashmir issue. He now asked if Nehru would go along with the proposition. Nehru wondered how Pakistan entered the picture and under what section of the UN charter a reference could be made. At a tripartite meeting (involving Nehru, Liaquat Ali and Mountbatten) in Delhi on 21 December 1947, Nehru said India had, three months ago, unilaterally offered a plebiscite under UN auspices after the raiders had gone and peace was restored. That offer had been repeated to no avail. India now intended to make a reference to the UN charging Pakistan with acts of aggression in Kashmir. Liaquat welcomed third-party intervention but expressed disappointment at the 'single-point reference to Kashmir' rather than 'all the fundamental differences between the two Dominions', epitomized in India's determination to 'destroy Pakistan'.[1]

Apart from the tribal raiders, Liaquat had told Nehru that an 'international brigade' was fighting alongside the 'Azad' Kashmir forces.[2] Other reports indicated the presence of American mercenaries, including a certain Haight Russell who assumed the rank of brigadier. Robert Trumbull, *The New York Times* correspondent in Delhi, reported on 27 October 1947 the presence of US intelligence agents in Kashmir as part of a mission to fill 'gaps' in western defence and containment plans in Central Asia and stave off communist inroads.

At their meeting on 28 December 1947, Nehru and Liaquat had also agreed that the legal position of Hunza, Nagar and Chitral (all feudatories of J&K) should be examined. These territories had been taken over by Pakistan following a coup against the maharaja's governor, Ghansara Singh, by the Gilgit Scouts[3] and its commandant, Major William Alexander Brown, a serving British military officer seconded to J&K. Brown later reverted to the British army in India and was promoted.

On 1 January 1948, India filed a complaint before the Security Council under Article 35 of Chapter VI of the UN charter pertaining to the pacific settlement of disputes through mediation—rather than under Chapter VII that relates to 'acts of aggression'. India brought to the Security Council's attention 'a situation whose continuance is likely to endanger the maintenance of international peace and security'.[4] Nehru later explained that a plaint under Chapter VI was preferred 'as we were anxious not to humiliate Pakistan in any way and to keep a way open for a friendly settlement'.[5] Within weeks, Pakistan filed a counter complaint and the title of the agenda item was amended from 'The Jammu & Kashmir Question' to 'The India-Pakistan Question', altering the content and context of the original Indian suit.

Later, in 1951, Girja Shankar Bajpai, secretary-general in the ministry of external affairs, said he had informed Dr Miguel A. Marin (the UN representative, Frank Graham's legal adviser) that the infiltration into Ladakh 'of Kazakhs and other elements from China was now presenting a real problem for us. We do not, however, wish to confuse the Kashmir issue with this new development'. Could this have been a first inkling of China's intrusion into Aksaichin?

Islamabad, to this day, invokes the Security Council resolutions of 13 August 1948 and 5 January 1949 and the principle of self-determination inscribed there. These resolutions took note of the reports of the UN Commission for India and Pakistan (UNCIP) and its special representatives. The representatives saw through the prevarications of Pakistan, but failed to follow the logic of their own findings. Nehru wrote to the UK prime minister Harold Macmillan on 18 September 1957 expressing his frustration at the total lack of progress on India's complaint in the Security Council on account of Pakistan's intransigence that was being encouraged by 'great countries' (read the US and UK). The Security Council's resolution of 13 August 1948 had found Pakistan guilty of aggression twice over (the tribal invasion and the induction of its own forces) and had called for a complete withdrawal as a first step, but to no effect. In 1957, Nehru lamented: 'Nine years have passed since this Resolution, and the facts are patent that Pakistan has not carried out its obligations even as regards Part I [ceasefire].'[6]

In 1959, M.C. Chagla, India's ambassador in Washington, protested that a state department map showed J&K as 'disputed'. How could this be the US position when on 4 February 1948, Warren Austin, leader of the US delegation in the UN had told the Security Council:

> [...] the external sovereignty of J&K is no longer under the control of the Maharaja [...] This is an affair between nations, and with the accession of J&K to India, this foreign sovereignty went over to India and is exercised by India, and that is how India happens to be here as petitioner.[7]

Nehru felt that the British, in particular, and the US were hostile to India. They favoured Pakistan as an anti-communist western ally that had joined Central Treaty Organization (CENTO) and the Southeast Asia Treaty Organisation (SEATO) and had long provided the Americans an air base in Peshawar, while receiving US military aid. Even earlier, the attitude of certain British officers such as Generals Auchinleck and (Douglas) Gracey, the British commanders in India and Pakistan respectively, had been unhelpful. In November 1952, Vijaya Lakshmi Pandit, India's UN representative had informed Nehru that the British Security Council delegate, Gladwyn Jebb had informed her of a joint UK-US resolution, that the UN proposed to move, in which both India and Pakistan had to reopen direct negotiations at the UN headquarters regarding the size of the forces to be left behind during a potential plebiscite. The two nations were to report back within thirty days. In case action could not be taken on this resolution within thirty days, the UK and US would feel 'compelled' to take the Kashmir question to the UN General Assembly where no (Russian) veto would apply. The increasing military collaboration between Pakistan and the US was also militating against progress on the question of demilitarization in Kashmir.

The UN resolutions were subverted as emphasis passed from a

ceasefire and truce (as under the UN resolution) as the first priority, to the holding of a plebiscite under a plebiscite administrator, Admiral Chester Nimitz of the US Navy.

Though firm on India's position with regard to J&K, Nehru was also worried about certain 'foolish' and 'irresponsible' statements' by Sheikh Abdullah in 1949, with the maharaja pulling in a contrary direction.[8] It can be assumed that the Sheikh's statements hinted at independence, casually referred to during conversations with the American statesman, Adlai Stevenson and others.

Be that as it may, Nehru was also exploring alternatives. In a personal and secret letter to Krishna Menon, a close confidante and high commissioner in London, he envisaged 'the possibility of Kashmir being considered more or less independent and guaranteed as such by India, Pakistan and possibly the UN' or, alternatively, 'some kind of partition either by previous agreement or as a result of the vote'.[9] He did not fancy either option, but did not wish to rule them out altogether.

With the Kashmir question stalemated in the UN, the J&K constituent assembly concluded its deliberations and adopted a new Constitution ratifying its accession to India and unfolding a scheme of partial integration under the terms of the special relationship under Article 370 of the Indian Constitution. The union home minister, Govind Ballabh Pant, gave a first hint of future thinking in Srinagar when he virtually ruled out a plebiscite in Kashmir on account of Pakistan's intransigence. The constituent assembly had taken definite decisions and 'the tide cannot be turned now'.[10] There was a furore in Pakistan and among its Baghdad Pact partners.

In 1957, Gunnar Jarring, the UN representative, opined that a plebiscite might no longer be possible because of 'changing political, economic and strategic factors surrounding the whole of the Kashmir question, together with the changing pattern of power relations in West and South Asia'.[11] Soon thereafter, Frank Graham added an amen with his remark that the UN could not reconstitute the status quo required under the UNCIP resolutions and hence a plebiscite was not a practical proposition in the existing conditions. Kashmir had moved on.

Since then the Kashmir question has never come before the Security Council, though Pakistan makes ritual references to it at every annual meeting of the General Assembly. The secretary-general once recommended removing the matter from the UN agenda; but Pakistan protested and Kashmir still remains inscribed there. The Shimla Agreement of 1972 stipulated that the J&K question would be settled bilaterally. Notwithstanding that, Pakistan continues to harp on 'self-determination' for Kashmir (though not for PAK and Gilgit-Baltistan) and a plebiscite in accordance with the UN resolution of 13 August 1948, which has been a dead letter following Pakistan's intransigence over the years in implementing any part of it.

6

New Factors and Options

New factors had intervened by the 1960s. Pakistan had come under military rule, China had bared its fangs in Tibet and along the Himalayan border, and a liberal J.F. Kennedy had moved into the White House. India's second five-year plan was in the doldrums with a foreign-exchange crisis and food scarcity. Its takeover of Goa in 1961 anguished and angered the West. With the cold war still hot, the US continued to need Pakistan as an ally and believed it might both befriend and build pressure on India to settle Kashmir. B.K. Nehru and John Kenneth Galbraith, the Indian and American ambassadors respectively, were both close to the political leadership in their own country and country of representation.

Anxious to get his aid to the India programme through the Congress and facilitate the work of the new aid consortium that had been created, Kennedy was keen to stave off another Security Council meeting, for which Pakistan was pressing. The stratagem was to dangle the aid carrot and prevail on both Nehru and Ayub Khan to use the good offices of Eugene Black, the president of the World Bank—who had steered the Indus Waters Treaty to a successful conclusion—to break new ground on Kashmir. Nehru, however, was hesitant to have a plebiscite that would resurrect an 'obscurantist political [two-nation] theory of religion as the basis of the state'.[1] He instead proposed an Indo-Pakistan summit after the forthcoming 1962 Indian general elections. Kennedy was disappointed, but B.K. Nehru told him that Jawaharlal Nehru had hinted that it might be possible to settle on the basis of the status quo.

The Indian Commonwealth secretary, Y.D. Gundevia, carried

the conversation forward with Galbraith, suggesting a solution along the ceasefire line (CFL), with some modifications. Galbraith's mention of a proposed Chenab line was negated by Gundevia who replied that that would mean re-negotiating the Indus Treaty.

Ultimately, the US and UK sent out Averell Harriman, assistant secretary of state, and Duncan Sandys, Commonwealth secretary, respectively, in late November 1962 to secure agreement on another high-level meeting between the leaders of India and Pakistan.

The six rounds of Indo-Pakistan talks that followed opened in Rawalpindi on 27 December 1962. Swaran Singh, the Indian railway minister, and Zulfikar Ali Bhutto, minister for industries, natural resources and works, and their advisers discussed a whole gamut of issues, but the principal focus was Kashmir. Bhutto was adamant regarding a plebiscite in J&K—which Swaran Singh said Pakistan had aborted and was now not possible in the changed conditions. The ice was broken with the Indian high commissioner in Pakistan, G. Parthasarathy, suggesting a political settlement, with the two sides delineating an international boundary in the state. It was accordingly agreed to consider three older proposals, namely, a revised demilitarization plan prior to a plebiscite made in 1949 by McNaughton, the regional plebiscite plan proposed in 1950 by Owen Dixon, and the ideas exchanged in 1955 during talks between Nehru and Mohammad Ali, prime minister of Pakistan, pursuant to an initiative to reopen talks taken by the governor general of Pakistan, Ghulam Muhammad.

Ghulam Muhammad, through an intermediary, had mooted that a large piece of territory in Jammu, including Poonch, Riyasi, Udhampur, etc., should be transferred to Pakistan; and Skardu to India. Kargil would be attached to Kashmir with some joint control of the Kashmir area where a plebiscite might be held five to twenty-five years hence. Nehru had rejected the scheme as impracticable (and suggestive of a communal divide) but thought a line along the Kishanganga and the transfer of part of the Poonch area and a bit of the territory adjacent to Mirpur might be considered.

At the second round of discussions in Delhi (16–18 January 1963), the Indian side presented a memorandum affirming that a settlement must be 'practical, realistic and final'.[2] Any territorial adjustments should cause the least disturbance to the life and

welfare of the people. If an agreement was reached on these points
and on the disengagement of forces, measures to facilitate freer
movement of persons, development of trade, etc., could be
considered. The settlement also had to embody a solemn
declaration by both parties to live side by side in peace and
friendship. Pakistan proposed modifications. It pressed for
inclusion of a reference to its basic position with regard to a
plebiscite. Further, account had to be taken of the composition of
the population, control of rivers and the requirements of defence.
A final draft was agreed upon incorporating all these ideas.

At the third round in Karachi in February, Swaran Singh mooted
transfer of certain areas west and north of the Valley, including
rich forests on both sides of the Kishanganga. Bhutto professed
shock and said only a little more than Kathua district on the
Punjab border, in the extreme south of Kashmir, could be conceded
to India as Pakistan was entitled to the entire state of J&K!

A special secretary to the ministry of external affairs (later)
said that Pakistan had magnified the Kashmir problem out of all
proportion:

> If it needed defence in depth, so did India. The Indus Waters
> Treaty had resolved the question of the headwaters of the Chenab
> and Jhelum. Pakistan had developed a psychological complex
> and no national ethos. She has not set for herself worthwhile
> national goals, does not know what she stands for, has only
> negative policies and reveals negative trends. Hate and Islam
> are the only cohesive forces in the state.[3]

The fourth and fifth rounds of talks in Calcutta and Karachi
respectively (12–14 March 1963, and 22–25 April 1963) proved
infructuous. Differences had widened.

The sixth and final round concluded in Delhi on 16 May 1963
with the two ministers, Swaran Singh and Zulfikar Ali Bhutto,
recording with regret that no agreement could be reached on
Kashmir.

Contrary to received wisdom in India, B.K. Nehru warned
policy-makers in Delhi that:

> [...] the Americans do believe that Pakistan has a good case on
> Kashmir—though the Administration is very careful not to say

so. The sympathy with Pakistan is not only because it is an ally but because it is regarded as the wronged party.[4]

After the 1962 border conflict between India and China, the US had sent out General Maxwell Taylor to discuss India's military expansion and re-equipment plans to meet potential Chinese threat. Numbers and budgets were discussed. However, matters got complicated by India's military purchase plans to meet the Chinese menace, with the Lockheed F-104 Starfighter, the English Electric Lightning, the French Mirage and the Soviet MiG-21 being in contention. India believed the Lightnings were expensive and not easy to maintain; it favoured the Soviet MiG-21 on considerations of price and the offer of transfer of technology and manufacture to India. However, Kennedy was worried about the implications of any Indian MiG deal in preference to the F-104, not only because it could lead to an arms race between India and Pakistan (which had purchased the F-104), but also because of the access the Soviet Union would then obtain in India to Western-made military hardware. Kennedy also wished to keep Ayub Khan in good humour as America needed the Peshawar air base and Pakistan's continued participation in CENTO and SEATO. However, in informal diplomatic exchanges with US spokesmen, a query as to why the Americans were so sensitive about the MiG deal fetched the reply that the MiGs had taken such a toll on their GIs in Vietnam that the very name was anathema to many! However, ultimately, the MiG deal went through.

China and Pakistan were meanwhile drawing closer and had commenced talks on a China-Kashmir boundary settlement, which was concluded in March 1963.[5] Speaking on the treaty, Zulfikar Ali Bhutto, then the foreign minister, had this to say:

> An attack from India on Pakistan is no longer confined to the security and territorial integrity of Pakistan. An attack by India on Pakistan involves the territorial integrity and security of the largest state in Asia [...] Therefore a subjugated or defeated Pakistan [...] also poses a serious threat to other countries in Asia and particularly to the largest state in Asia.[6]

Pakistan was also stepping up incidents along the CFL and seemed to be planning to act in concert with the Chinese on the northern border. As a riposte and a deterrent to China, the US, at this time, decided to extend the operational area of the Seventh Fleet to the Indian Ocean.

Sheikh Abdullah had meanwhile been released from prison[7] and immediately went to see an ailing Nehru on 8 May 1964 to seek a fresh approach for a Kashmir resolution. This, it was premised, should promote Indo-Pakistan friendship and cooperation, not weaken the secular ideal or the position of minorities in either country, and bring about greater security and welfare to the region. Abdullah said he was not seeking revenge for his ouster.

At the time he was arrested in 1953, a special committee he had set up—which included Bakshi Ghulam Mohammad and G.M. Sadiq—had evolved various alternative solutions to the Kashmir imbroglio. Bakshi, who would become the prime minister of Kashmir once Abdullah was arrested, had suggested giving the Valley an independent status guaranteed by India, Pakistan, the USSR and China, while 'Azad' Kashmir could go to Pakistan, and the Jammu area to India.

B.F.H.B. Tyabji, secretary to the ministry of external affairs, held informal discussions with the Sheikh in his personal capacity and refined these proposals, while G. Parthasarathy was requested to examine the idea of an Indo-Pakistan confederation with Kashmir. Abdullah proceeded to Rawalpindi with Mirza Afzal Beg (among others) and met Ayub Khan, who scoffed at the absurd notion of a confederation as a ploy to undo Pakistan and 'lead to our enslavement'.[8] Undaunted, the Sheikh proceeded to Muzaffarabad to meet Abdul Qayyum Khan, the 'Azad' Kashmir premier. No sooner had talks begun when news came of Nehru's demise. Abdullah returned post haste to Delhi and the initiative stalled.

For many years prior to this, India and Pakistan had discussed signing a no-war pact. Nehru had been keen to proceed with this to allay Pakistan's fear of a permanent threat from India. His concept embraced a treaty of peace, friendship and cooperation. Pakistan had, however, paid lip service to the idea as its intent was that this should be conditional on delivery of Kashmir to it as a right on its own terms. While Pakistan insistently described Kashmir as the core issue, Nehru averred that the Kashmir problem was the consequence and not the cause of the Indo-Pakistan conflict.

7

Division of J&K Spurned; War

Western ire over India's assimilation of Goa, the Sino-Indian conflict and corresponding Sino-Pakistan entente, and the death of Nehru taken together gave Pakistan the impression that India was down and now was the time to strike.

Pakistan had augmented and modernized its air force and armoured strike force with Lockheed F-104 Starfighters and Patton tanks with US aid after joining CENTO. India saw no external threat to Pakistan to warrant such armament. Nehru had told US President Dwight Eisenhower that US arms aid to Pakistan would inevitably be used against India, while its own re-armament drive was to augment its defences against a hostile China.

Responding to mutual fears in Rawalpindi and Delhi of adverse consequences following US military aid to the other country, the American ambassador in Pakistan, Walter Patrick McConaughy issued a statement in December 1963 recalling the US commitment to take action against either violator—a stance reiterated by Kennedy. However, Zulfikar Ali Bhutto, as foreign minister, continued to rail against the US and the UK for upsetting the military balance in the subcontinent. Pakistan now saw a new belligerence in India on the issue of the influx of infiltrators into Assam.[1] The Americans, in turn, railed against the leader of the Indian delegation to the Security Council, M.C. Chagla, and his plain talk, which they felt was undue needling.[2]

However, India's fears were soon realized. The western boundary between the princely states of Kutch and Sindh had been settled in 1912, from the mouth to the top of Sir Creek. This was demarcated and boundary pillars erected. The boundary east of this point ran along the northern border of the Rann of Kutch and was not contested from 1936—when Sindh was granted provincial status and separated from the Bombay Presidency—until 1947. Nonetheless, in July 1948, Pakistan claimed that the Kutch-Sindh boundary ran along the Rann of Kutch—a salt marsh wedged between the Arabian Sea, Gujarat and the province of Sindh that it termed a 'dead sea'—by which definition half of it belonged to it under international law. The area contested extended over 3,500 square miles. Since it was undemarcated, it created problems for Sindhi cattle owners.

In 1956, there had been skirmishes around Kanjarkot Fort and Chad Bet, about eight miles inside the Indian border. There had since been contestations and confrontations. Matters came to a head with border incidents, leading to a major border war, precipitated by a Pakistani offensive in mid-April 1965.

Pakistan sought support from Iran and Turkey at a CENTO meeting. On 4 May 1965, the Chinese official news agency, *Hsinhua* criticized the 'big nation chauvinist and expansionist logic of the Indian ruling circles' and expressed full support to the Pakistani government in opposing 'the Indian policy of military expansion'.

The US and UK were alarmed at the prospect of escalating Indo-Pakistan conflict. India supplied incontrovertible evidence—that the Americans themselves confirmed on the ground—that Pakistan had used Patton tanks and other US equipment in Kutch. When the Indian ambassador to the US, B.K. Nehru took up with the US Secretary of State, Dean Rusk, the complete breach of solemn American assurances in this regard, he was told that the US had taken up the matter with both sides and the important thing now was to end the fighting. The ambassador replied that US military observers had visited the battleground on both sides and ascertained the facts on the ground. Why then this eternal equation of both sides, when one was clearly in breach of the law and the other had clearly observed it? Rusk and, subsequently, other ranking state department officials, assured the ambassador that the matter had been pursued with Pakistan vigorously and this was one reason hostilities had ceased. B.K. Nehru had, however, as we know, earlier warned policy-makers in Delhi that the Americans were biased in favour of Pakistan, whom they considered the wronged party.

On 30 June 1965, an agreement was reached on a ceasefire and the restoration of the status quo ante as of 1 January 1965. This implied vacation of aggression by Pakistan. Thereafter, if negotiations for a settlement proved inconclusive, the matter would be referred to an impartial tribunal. A three-member Kutch tribunal was set up in due course under a Swedish judge nominated by the UN secretary general, U. Thant and representatives of Iran and Yugoslavia as members. On 19 February 1968, on the conclusion of the 171st meeting, the tribunal awarded parts of the northern border region, including Kanjarkot and Chad Bet, to Pakistan. By September 1969, the boundary, as awarded, had been demarcated and implemented on the ground.

Altaf Gauhar, Ayub Khan's secretary for information and his alter ego, was later to reflect on the Kutch war. He was reasonably confident that the Rann of Kutch accord might serve as a model for settlement of the Kashmir dispute. He, in fact, declared that 'in all cases where a peaceful means for settling the Indo-Pakistan dispute proved unavailing, the sensible answer is to have recourse to independent arbitration.'[3] Ayub was probably encouraged in this belief by British Prime Minister Harold Wilson, with whom he discussed the possibility of resolving the Kashmir dispute through arbitration during his stay in London in 1968.

The feeling in army circles in Pakistan was summed up by Gul Hassan, then the director of military operations:

> The setback in Kutch proved immeasurably disconcerting to the Indian Army. As a result the government of India was in a quandary. On the other hand, ours was in a state of euphoria. The high command of our army was intoxicated by our showing and our morale could not possibly have been higher. We were ready for any task that may be assigned to us and without any question.[4]

Author Abdul Ghafoor Bhurgri says:

> In senior army circles and in the Foreign Office, Ayub Khan came under criticism for letting the Indians off the hook. There was great disappointment within the GHQ [general headquarters] that when the Indians were withdrawing, their retreat could have easily been cut off, but unfortunately, Ayub Khan did not allow it.[5]

Ayub's judgement did get impaired by the Rann of Kutch in one respect: his old prejudice that 'the Hindu has no stomach for a fight' turned into belief, if not a military doctrine, which had a decisive effect on the course of events.

Altaf Gauhar is of the view that Ayub blundered into a war with India in 1965. Ayub was cautious, but the hawks around him kept pressing for war. The Kutch episode and the assumed victory in arms created a sense of triumphalism. While the Hazratbal agitation on the loss of the Prophet's hair had been resolved,[6] Kashmir was astir. Sheikh Abdullah had been arrested in May 1965 for meeting Chou En-lai abroad. This was the time to strike. It was in these circumstances that Operation Gibraltar was planned, pushed along by an ambitious megalomaniac, Zulfikar Ali Bhutto. Another adventure was launched to 'defreeze'[7] the Kashmir issue, as Ayub put it.

8

Operation Gibraltar

Even as the Kutch imbroglio was being resolved, Pakistan was up to more mischief. The Soviet premier, Aleksei Kosygin, on 20 August 1965 wrote to Lal Bahadur Shastri, who had succeeded Nehru as prime minister, expressing concern at the outbreak of fresh hostilities in J&K. Shastri responded, exposing Pakistan's perfidy. He stated that the two countries had signed a ceasefire agreement in Kutch on 30 June 1965. However, even before the ink was dry, Pakistan mounted its thinly disguised but large-scale infiltration into J&K on 5 August 1965, with its armed forces dressed as civilians. Equipped with automatic weapons, hand grenades and wireless sets, and trained in guerrilla and sabotage techniques, the 'Gibralter forces' crossed the CFL, with instructions 'to destroy bridges and vital roads, attack police stations, supply dumps, army headquarters and important installations, inflict casualties on Indian forces, and attack VIPs in Jammu and Kashmir.'[1] They hoped to incite local people to rise up against the government. Worse still, according to the evidence of captured infiltrators, their training had started on 26 May 1965 at Murree under Pakistan's 12th infantry division commander, Major General Akhtar Hussain Malik.

'Operation Gibraltar', as it was named, was masterminded by Aziz Ahmed, foreign secretary and Zulfikar Ali Bhutto, who was soon made foreign minister. The operation was kept secret, with even the corps commanders being kept out of the loop. Among civil officials only the foreign secretary and defence secretary were in the know. The air force was excluded from the joint planning. According to Altaf Gauhar (Ayub Khan's information secretary), they were not considered sufficiently 'security minded'![2]

Operation Gibraltar was a total disaster. Local shepherds raised the alarm and led the Indian security forces to the enemy columns infiltrating along five multi-directional axes, where they were scattered with considerable losses. The Indian army took the strategic Haji Pir pass and nothing stood between it and Muzaffarabad.

In desperation, in May 1965, Pakistan launched Operation Grand Slam, to attack the vital Akhnoor Bridge in J&K. This operation, too, ended in a failure for the Pakistan army. However, one casualty of the 1965 war was Pakistan's closure of the Indo-Afghan land route for trade and personnel.

Within Pakistan, Ayub had kept away from Islamabad as a cover-up, but the directive he sent the foreign minister and army chief was boastful. As Altaf Gauhar records, Ayub said that 'as a general rule, Hindu morale would not stand more than a couple of hard blows at the right time and place. Such opportunities should, therefore, be sought and exploited.'[3] Gauhar goes on to say that this directive conclusively shows that:

> Ayub did not know, even on August 29 [...] that Gibraltar had failed, that not one of its major objectives had been achieved, and that the enemy forces were in a commanding position with Muzaffarabad, the capital of Azad Kashmir, within their reach.[4]

Ayub's absence from the capital gave Bhutto and Aziz Ahmed the freedom to take control. With a change in command, Yahya Khan and Bhutto made Ayub the fall guy.

Meanwhile, U Thant had written to both heads of government appealing for a return to the status quo ante as of 5 August 1965, when, according to the US military observers, Pakistani intruders transgressed the CFL. Ayub feigned surprise at the charge of 'so-called 'infiltration'[5]. He said:

> You seem to consider Aug. 5–when the so-called 'infiltration' is alleged to have taken place—as the date when the cease-fire agreement of 1949 between India and Pakistan began to be so widely disregarded by unprecedented acts of violence along or in the vicinity of the cease-fire line as to have reduced that

agreement to little consequence. If the cease-fire in Jammu and Kashmir was reduced to a nullity, this process has taken place over a long period of time as a result of Indian designs and provocations.

Ayub claimed that India was now engaged in 'genocide' against 'the Muslim population' in response to which 'freedom-fighters'— not raiders, but sons of the soil—had taken to arms against Indian tyranny. On 15 August 1965, Indian forces again crossed the CFL 'to take over three unoccupied posts near Kargil, which they had earlier been made to vacate upon your intervention'.[6] In quick succession thereafter, the Indians had, between 24 August and 1 September, taken two Pakistani posts in the Tithwal sector and the Haji Pir Pass. Ayub continued that it was to prevent further aggression that, in exercise of the right to self-defence, Pakistani and 'Azad' forces crossed the CFL in the Bhimber (Chhamb) sector (across the Pakistan-J&K international boundary). India had, thereafter, escalated the conflict by using its air force, and it seemed it was doing all this to avenge its reverses in Kutch.

The UK and US, however, were satisfied that Pakistan had clearly violated the CFL on 5 August 1965, as indicated by the UN Military Observer. But they turned against India on 6 September 1965, when, in order to avert the loss of Akhnoor, and the line of communication to Poonch, Srinagar and Ladakh, the Indian army launched a counter offensive in the Lahore sector and, subsequently from Rajasthan into Sindh. Pakistan invoked US assistance under CENTO and SEATO, but was snubbed.

While Pakistan sought a permanent Kashmir solution, with a UN force in interim control, the Indian high commissioner in London, Jivraj Mehta, told the British government that acceptance of U. Thant's appeal for a ceasefire must be accompanied by 'some condemnation of Pakistan's acts of aggression against India and Kashmir.' India had consistently drawn world attention to recent Pakistan violations 'only to be ignored or fobbed off'.[7]

L.K. Jha, secretary to the prime minister's office, told John Freeman, the British high commissioner in India, on 5 September that Shastri insisted that further UN action must be based on 'full recognition of the Nimmo [chief military observer to the United Nations Military Observer Group to India and Pakistan between

1950 and 1966] report', failing which 'a counter offensive [would if necessary] be launched against West Pakistan.' The prime minister's own solution for Kashmir was rationalization of the CFL:

> [We need a] little more room [to India] in the north around Kargil [...] and straightening of the line from Uri to Poonch [...with] equivalent concessions of tactical convenience to Pakistan and cession to it of a respectable amount of territory [...] towards the southern end of the ceasefire line.

Freeman reported a 'somewhat reckless mood of the Indian cabinet'[8] to London.

The US felt sanctions might help. Pakistan had supplies for only three weeks' fighting, but India could carry on longer. Shipment of arms to both sides was suspended. U. Thant visited India and Pakistan and Bhutto appealed to the African nations. On 16 September 1965, the Chinese sent a note alleging Indian transgressions across the Sikkim-Tibet border and the presence of Indian military structures across the line of control (LoC); they accused India of seizing Tibetan livestock and kidnapping Tibetan personnel. These were immediately rejected as baseless and all references to Kashmir dismissed as interference in India's internal affairs (in support of Pakistan).

In a sharp note in response to a subsequent Chinese demarche and a three-day ultimatum, the ministry of external affairs noted the People's Liberation Army had already started firing along the Sikkim border, intruded across Dongchui La and Nathu La and massed troops at Demchok in Ladakh. It rejected Beijing's new doctrine of assuming a 'role of guardianship and hegemony over Asian countries [...] and its claim to advise the Government of India on how to resolve its differences with its neighbour Pakistan over Kashmir or any other matter.'[9]

The Americans and British were concerned at this not unexpected turn of events, but felt it could have a sobering effect on India, which could hold its own against limited Chinese intervention—though it would increase Chinese influence in Islamabad. They believed Ayub Khan had been led astray by Bhutto. Ayub Khan had, in fact, appealed to the Chinese to avoid any aggravation.

The Soviets had all this while been counselling India and Pakistan to end hostilities and enter into fresh talks. Kosygin offered Soviet good offices and mentioned Tashkent as a venue on 17 September 1965. Five days later, India and Pakistan both accepted a UN-mandated ceasefire and withdrawal of 'all armed personnel back to the positions held by them before August 5, 1965'[10] no later than 25 February 1966. India's stance was tacitly vindicated. Pakistan's extravagant conditions were ignored. These were that India must withdraw its forces from all of J&K; an Afro-Asian force must be inducted under UN supervision; and a plebiscite should be held within three months of the ceasefire!

Yet, a week later India had to draw U. Thant's attention to numerous violations of the ceasefire by Pakistan and stated that Indian withdrawals could only take place once these violations had completely ceased. During the period of the Indo-Pakistani war, members of the Indian mission in Pakistan were abominably treated and the Indian chancery was occupied and searched. India protested, as did Pakistan, about misdemeanours against its staff in Delhi.

John Freeman noted in a despatch to London that Pakistan's attempt to secure a military solution had 'decisively failed'. On 27 November 1965, Kosygin wrote to Shastri informing him that after prolonged discussions in Moscow, Bhutto had agreed to a meeting in Tashkent without any preconditions. Shastri responded immediately and suggested a date in the first week of January 1966.

9

Tashkent and After

Shastri, Ayub and Kosygin met in Tashkent along with their advisers with the avowed objective of establishing enduring peace across the subcontinent. Shastri said India wished to live in harmony and friendship with Pakistan and respected its territorial integrity. Ayub remarked that wishing peace did not establish peace. It was necessary to 'face the problems, which endanger peace'.[1] Kosygin hoped Tashkent could be a turning point.

The Tashkent Declaration was signed on 10 January 1966. Both sides agreed that troop withdrawals to the 5 August 1965 positions would be completed by 25 February. Ceasefire terms would be observed. There would be mutual non-interference in the internal affairs of the other and hostile propaganda would be eschewed. Diplomatic relations would be restored, prisoners repatriated and economic and trade relations resumed. Both sides agreed to set up joint bodies to determine the next steps.

Sadly, Lal Bahadur Shastri passed away the day after signing the Tashkent Declaration, to be carried back home to a grieving nation that etched in its memory his battle cry of 'Jai Jawan, Jai Kisan'.

In a broadcast to the nation, Ayub said the basic issue of Kashmir remained. Bhutto however expressed his misgivings over the Tashkent Declaration and launched a tirade assuring Pakistan's support for the Kashmiri people's inalienable right to self-determination.

> Peace and justice are inseparable in the creed of Islam. Peace without honour is indeed inconceivable and repugnant to the tenets of our ideology. History is not deficient in instances

where mere professions of peace have been overtaken by events resulting from the continuance of injustice and inequity. Words are no substitute for intents. If, in reality, injustice should persist, then peaceful declarations by themselves would not prevent tension or avert conflict. The Tashkent Declaration has to be judged in its totality and against the historic background of our struggle for justice in Jammu and Kashmir. [...] The spectre of war and conflict can vanish only when a lasting peace is achieved by allowing the people of Jammu and Kashmir their right to freely determine their future. It would be a fitting tribute to the Soviet Union if its initiative were to result in a significant contribution to the realisation of the legitimate aspirations of the people of Jammu and Kashmir who have waged such a valiant struggle for liberty.[2]

In India, criticism largely turned on its decision to give up its hard-won gains at Haji Pir and Kargil.

Military commanders met to discuss withdrawals and a reduction of forces in Kashmir. It was agreed to work towards a reduced quantum of regular troops, irregulars and armed civilians, as specified in the 1949 Karachi Agreement, by 1 April 1966. Desultory discussions continued at other levels on other aspects of the Tashkent normalization agenda.

In the meantime, Ayub and Bhutto were drifting apart. Bhutto continued to rage. The Indian Foreign Office recalled his savage outburst some months earlier when he stated:

We cannot allow peace to be settled on India's terms. We who have ruled India for 800 years, we who have dominated India for 800 years and who are responsible for much of India's civilization, for the Delhis and the Taj Mahals and for the grandeur and glory of India, are we today in the twentieth century to accept peace on India's terms? One hundred million people to accept peace on India's terms? It is out of the question. It is for you to know that we will never accept peace on India's terms. It is preposterous, it is scandalous, it is a dishonour to us, to accept peace on India's terms [...][3]

Bhutto also affirmed and demanded 'complete equality' between the people of India and the people of Pakistan in response to B.K. Nehru's remark that Pakistan must accept its unequal size vis-à-vis India.

On 4 February 1966 the two sides exchanged views on the agenda for talks. The Indian high commissioner, Kewal Singh met Ayub and Bhutto at the Bhutto home in Larkana to iron out differences. His impression was that Ayub was reasonable, but Bhutto and others, like Aziz Ahmed (foreign secretary) and Altaf Gauhar (information secretary) were hawks.

The two official delegations led by Swaran Singh and Bhutto met in Rawalpindi on 1 and 2 March 1966 without an agreed agenda. Bhutto reiterated that movement on Kashmir must precede everything else. The foreign secretary, C.S. Jha briefed the Soviet ambassador on his return to Delhi and told him of his misgivings, which were shared by a number of heads of the Indian mission. He felt Pakistan's new tactics were 'seriously denigrating and damaging to the Tashkent Declaration'.[4]

East Pakistan had been left vulnerable during the 1965 war as Bhutto had virtually left its defence to Chinese assurances of intervention. There was now a strong move for complete autonomy in that province, provoking stern measures on the part of Ayub. By this time, the Indian consulate in Rajshahi had been closed down as it was said to have become more 'a centre of espionage, subversion and activities prejudicial to the security of Pakistan' than a visa or a diplomatic office.[5] Growing unrest in East Pakistan led to the announcement of a six-point plan for autonomy in 1966 by Sheikh Mujibur Rahman, leading to a charge of sedition and secession with Indian assistance. What came to be known as the Agartala Conspiracy case was later aborted by strong protests.

Chou En-Lai visited Rawalpindi in June 1966 and Bhutto was sacked soon after. There was a marked crescendo in Pakistani propaganda against India. On 23 September 1966, Pakistan Radio broadcast:

> Pakistan has told India that no useful purpose will be served by continuing exchanges on holding an Indo-Pakistan meeting at the official level, without a change of heart on India's part towards the Kashmir dispute.[6]

Ayub, on his part, responding to a question asked to him at Chatham House, London, in November 1966, on M.C. Chagla being appointed India's minister of external affairs, said:

It does not look as though they [India] are looking for an opportunity to make up with us. What is needed is a powerful political personality with firm views about a settlement and able to give effect to them. A Foreign Minister representing a minority is not in that position! [7]

Little did he know Chagla! The Indian foreign secretary noted that 'by its actions, statements and military preparations, Pakistan has as good as buried the Tashkent Declaration.'[8]

More broadsides followed. At a banquet in honour of the Shah of Iran, a Regional Cooperation for Development partner along with Turkey, Ayub said: 'Pakistan did not fight the war merely to defend her own sovereignty and integrity but the war was as much fought in the cause of other Muslim countries.'[9] Iran had aided Pakistan in 1965. Here was but one example of Islamabad activating its strange doctrine of defending 'the ideological frontiers of Pakistan.'[10]

An arms build-up had by now started in Pakistan with Chinese and American assistance, ostensibly in view of Indian's re-armament against China. The American policy 'was modified in 1967 in favour of Pakistan and spares for previously supplied lethal equipment were allowed.'[11] India warned the US that a resumption of arms supplies to Pakistan would once again be only used against this country as before. In the meantime, Defence Minister Yashwantrao Chavan informed parliament that China was supplying Pakistan aircraft, tanks and foreign exchange to purchase arms from elsewhere. India's offer of a mutual and balanced reduction of forces was spurned. Rawalpindi insisted on parity with India. Consequently, Chagla told the Pakistani foreign minister, Sharifuddin Pirzada, in May 1967:

> The question of arms reduction is [...] inseparably linked with what you describe as a settlement of the Jammu and Kashmir dispute. I must confess to You Excellency our disappointment [...] The question of arms reduction by both countries patently stands on its own merits. Any such reduction is good in itself and is bound to have a wholesome effect on the economies of both countries and to create a better atmosphere all round between the two countries. We are unable to accept the contention that a reduction in arms expenditure can only come about with

or after the settlement of the Jammu and Kashmir question. Such a view does not seem to us to be helpful. It has the inevitable connotation that Pakistan is interested in escalating its expenditure on arms for the purpose of achieving its aim in Kashmir. Any such implication is unacceptable to us, it negates the Tashkent Declaration in which both Pakistan and India have pledged to settle all their disputes and differences by peaceful means.[12]

Pakistan's anti-Indian propaganda never ceased and Naga and Mizo insurgents received sanctuary in and transit through East Pakistan.

On 9 November 1970, Swaran Singh, the minister for external affairs, informed the Lok Sabha that the US government had informed India of its decision to make a 'one-time exception'[13] to the arms embargo to India and Pakistan. It had offered to sell Pakistan six F-104 Starfighters, 300 armoured personnel carriers, seven B-57 bombers and four maritime patrol aircraft. US military assistance to Pakistan from 1954 to 1965 was of the order of US$1.50-2 billion. 'But for American arms aid to Pakistan, the sub-continent might have been spared more than one destructive war.'[14]

This 'one-time exception' was to be the subject of a conversation between Indira Gandhi and the US secretary of state, William Rogers in New York in October 1969. Henry Kissinger, to whom Rogers relayed his conversation, dismissed Indira Gandhi's concerns as 'paranoia', and said Indians were 'suffering because they were the leading non-aligned country and now they're just another undeveloped one.'[15] Indira Gandhi, on her part, was told by Rogers that 'Congress feels India is non-aligned against us, though I have tried to defend it.'[16]

Separately, as a footnote to Pakistani insistence on 'self-determination' in J&K, the Swedish ambassador in Delhi reaffirmed to the Indian foreign secretary that the UN General Assembly had accepted self-determination as an essential first step prior to the achievement of independence by a colonial territory. The foreign secretary said that self-determination was inapplicable to sovereign states or parts or minorities therein. This would be contrary to the spirit and purpose of the UN Charter, which upholds the territorial integrity and sovereignty of member-states.

10

Towards 1971 and 'Joy Bangla'

Ayub Khan's growing unpopularity and Zulfikar Ali Bhutto's scheming led to Ayub's replacement by General Yahya Khan. Indira Gandhi tried to recall the Tashkent spirit in her greetings to him on 16 January 1970—the fourth anniversary of the agreement. But that was a fugitive hope.

A disastrous cyclone that hit East Pakistan at the end of 1970 was mishandled by the authorities, adding to popular discontent. The general elections that followed gave Sheikh Mujibur Rahman's Awami League, with its platform of promised autonomy, an overall majority in the national assembly, with 160 seats in a house of 313 against 81 for Bhutto's new People's Party of Pakistan.[1] Bhutto adamantly refused to accept the logic of the poll result and insisted on co-partnership between the two wings of the country. Mujibur Rahman pushed for the implementation of his six-point programme, leading to his arrest and the declaration of martial law.

Military reinforcements were flown into the eastern wing, and there was a sudden crackdown on 26 March 1971. The Awami League responded by proclaiming Independence, leading to genocidal violence, resistance by the Mukti Bahini and a swelling exodus of refugees fleeing to safety in India. These events were widely reported contemporaneously by Anthony Mascarenhas in *The Sunday Times*, London, on 13 June 1971 and later revealed in chilling detail by Archer Blood, the US consul-general, Dhaka, in his famous *Blood Telegram* (6 April 1971). The book described his own government's complicity and utter duplicity in conniving these massacres under the Nixon-Kissinger 'policy tilt' against India.

Earlier, on 30 January 1971, a Fokker Friendship plane on a scheduled Srinagar-Delhi flight was hijacked to Lahore where, three days later, after all thirty passengers and four crew members were released, the aircraft was blown up before the police and press. The two hijackers were given asylum and lionized in public in Pakistan. The response to Indian protests was that the incident was 'the direct result of repressive measures taken by the Government of India in occupied Kashmir'![2] India retaliated by banning civil and military over-flights between West Pakistan and what it now started calling 'East Bengal', compelling all air traffic to re-route via Colombo.

Scenting trouble ahead with China and Pakistan in cahoots, India turned to the Soviet Union to procure more arms. The Sino-Soviet rift had already widened, and the Indian ambassador, D.P. Dhar, on his farewell call on the foreign affairs minister, Andrei Gromyko, was told not to worry about Pakistan but 'the unpredictable enemy from the north' (that is China)[3] which was claiming 1.5 million square kilometres of Soviet territory. Gromyko therefore proposed an Indo-Soviet treaty of mutual assistance, a draft of which he had shown to Sardar Swaran Singh three years ago. Back home, D.P. Dhar reported the conversation to the foreign secretary, also pointing to an Iranian threat to come to the aid of Pakistan, and urged a positive response.

Delhi's response was cautious. But the ensuing events in East Bengal and Chinese complicity compelled a reappraisal. The Islamic states, too, let it be known that they would not wish to see the disintegration of an Islamic country. Kosygin was blunt in urging India to build a demonstrably strong military force as a deterrent against bullying and war. The Indo-Soviet Treaty of Peace, Friendship and Cooperation was signed on 9 August 1971 for an initial duration of twenty years. The treaty provided that:

> [...] in the event of either Party being subjected to an attack or threat thereof, the [...] Parties shall immediately enter into mutual consultations in order to remove such a threat and to take effective measures to ensure peace and the security of their countries.[4]

Gromyko said China might do 'something', to which Indira Gandhi responded 'they could try to take NEFA [North-East Frontier Agency]'.[5]

Mrs Gandhi had sounded out her principal secretary, P.N. Haksar on a similar treaty with China, a proposition that the latter strongly discouraged.

Meanwhile, in July 1971, Nixon sent out Henry Kissinger, then his national security adviser, to meet Mrs Gandhi. Nixon was concerned about a possible war with the commencement of border skirmishes between Pakistan forces and the Mukti Bahini, in which the Indian military was also involved. This had resulted in the exodus by now of eight million refugees to India (soon to cross over 10 million) causing a humanitarian crisis. He also wished to explain the 'bureaucratic muddle' (as Kissinger put it) in the implementation of Washington's 25 March arms-ban policy that had resulted in the supply of military goods to Pakistan.[6]

Haksar and Swaran Singh pulled no punches in their conversations with Kissinger and rejected the notion that India was both preventing a restoration of normalcy by supporting the Mukti Bahini and hindering the return of the Bangla refugees. As Kissinger kept going round the mulberry bush—when confronted with questions about America's arms to Pakistan being consistently used against India—Haksar asked the US national security adviser if he had spent time analysing the phenomenon called Pakistan. He then gave him a brief tutorial. There are, he said, many disparities among the various regions of Pakistan (as in India), which could not be resolved by all the 'emotive power of Islam'. If, he continued, religion could provide:

> [...] a basis for creating nation-states, Europe would probably still have the Holy Roman Empire. And if national and sub-national aspirations could be made subordinate to dynastic concepts, the Austro-Hungarian Empire would not have fallen apart. And when you have a state like Pakistan defying all the laws of social and economic development and accentuating regional disparities, then you are building up an inherently unstable system. The bust-up in East Bengal and the earlier turbulence in Balochistan are all rooted in total defiance of elementary principles of social, political and economic engineering by the military in Pakistan.[7]

Kissinger feared China would react in case of a war with Pakistan. This would cause India to rely on Soviet assistance and that would in turn 'cause complications for us in America'. He went on to assure Jagjivan Ram, the defence minister, that the US would leave the Chinese in no doubt that it would take 'a very grave view [...] of any move against India.' [8]

In New York, Kissinger was later devilishly to urge the Chinese through their ambassador to the UN, Huang Hua (with whom he held a series of clandestine meetings), to move against India. He assured the ambassador that America would confront the Soviet Union should it make any response. This supreme duplicity was later exposed in considerable detail with the publication by Seymour Hersh of Kissinger's personal papers. Kissinger mumbled his protests, but his lies and double-dealing stood starkly revealed.

Months later, in February 1972, after the liberation of Bangladesh, India again turned to Moscow to replenish its depleted military arsenal. Soviet Defence Minister Marshal Andrei Grechko bluntly suggested a formal alliance against China, which he emphasized, was the real threat.

The court martial trial against Sheikh Mujib commenced in West Pakistan on 11 August 1971 in camera on the charge of 'waging war against Pakistan'[9]—this against a man whose Awami League had just won an overall majority in the Pakistan National Assembly (gaining 167 of the 169 seats in East Bengal).[10] The rules of the game were thereupon suddenly changed to stipulate that he must share power with the West wing in some kind of confederation. Pakistan and the US refused to see the obvious chicanery being practised and kept making pious, impractical suggestions and levelling dubious charges against India. Blaming the plight of the people of East Bengal on the savage cyclone that hit it the previous December was a gross simplification and cover-up of the terror that had been unleashed on the Bangla population. Pakistan's excuse was that:

> [...] those who were elected changed their mandate and instead of autonomy, for which trust had been placed in them by the electors, they sought secession. In other words, a group of self-seekers betrayed the trust of the people! [11]

The world was not taken in by such piffle, though many Islamic states were loath to see the disintegration of a Muslim country.

That Yahya Khan had completely lost his balance was further evident on 12 October when, in a national broadcast, he charged India with never having accepted Pakistan and being out to weaken and destroy it. As examples he cited 'the forcible occupation of Kashmir, the attack on Pakistan in 1965, [and] the construction of the Farakka barrage'.[12] He proposed by-elections to fill all vacant seats in the Eastern wing and the promulgation of a new Constitution on 20 December with the West wing given scarcely veiled veto powers against constitutional amendments proposed by the East wing. The proposal simply did not wash. As Indira Gandhi told the US secretary of state, William Rogers, Yahya was looking for a political solution that by-passed elected leaders.

The US and China continued to bat for Pakistan. Despite the number of Bangla refugees swelling beyond nine million (November 1971),[13] Nixon felt an Indo-Pakistan conflict could not be limited to just the two nations and 'the initiation of hostilities by India would be almost impossible to understand'.[14]

India continued to train and support the Mukti Bahini and, as the conflict intensified, Yahya opened a new front with an air attack from the West wing, undertook a major armoured thrust into the Chhamb salient in J&K and broke off diplomatic relations with India. By 4 December 1971, the nations were at war.

On 12 December, at a meeting of the Washington Special Action Group, Kissinger announced that President Nixon had called for an immediate ceasefire and added that the Seventh Fleet would sail into the Indian Ocean through the Straits of Malacca. He said that if anybody questioned the mission of the flotilla led by the nuclear-powered USS Enterprise, 'Defence could say that the purpose was to stand-by—for a possible evacuation of Americans.'[15] The tactic was obviously intended to send a strong, deterrent message to India.

Indian naval bar-room gossip (was it more?) has it that when the local Indian naval commander asked for instructions if accosted, he was advised to invite the US officers for a drink! In Moscow, the Soviet defence minister, Marshal Grechko in the presence of his general staff, was later to tell D.P. Dhar, then the chairman of the policy planning group, and General Manekshaw, the chief of army staff, in strict confidence of the 'chase by the Soviet submarine fleet' of the Seventh Fleet when it went beyond the Malacca Straits. In a note recorded by Dhar, Grechko said one of his submarines 'went 400 metres below the Enterprise; [and] that is how, General Manekshaw, the Americans wished the world to believe that they can defend their Fleet against my submarines'! [16]

The Soviet was concerned about the growing US-China entente and China's bitter hostility towards them. It now pressed for upgrading the Indo-Soviet Treaty of Peace, Friendship and Cooperation into 'an alliance'. Turning to Manekshaw, Grechko said that:

> 'India would need the Soviet Union and the Soviet Union would need India and her support to deal with the designs of China' […] It was important, therefore, to talk in terms of the realities of the situation rather than 'little phantoms like Pakistan'.[17]

For the next ten to fifteen years, China knew she was incapable to causing any harm to the Soviet Union because she would not have a nuclear arsenal ready by then. The Soviet Union had made it unequivocally clear to China that any attempt on its part to disturb the peace or encroach on Soviet territory (in Siberia) would bring about a massive retaliation in which every weapon would be used, from which it would take her long to recover.

Manekshaw repeated India's need for equipment. To this the Marshal Grechko replied, guaranteeing India's defence:

> If we have an alliance, I shall earmark 50 IBMs for your defence against China. I shall not locate them on your soil but on my own so that you do not run any risk. What else do you want for your defence?[18]

Despite Soviet anxiety to conclude something akin to a military alliance in case of a conflict with China, India steered clear of any such commitment. Dhar told Grechko that the just-signed Indo-Soviet Treaty already provided for consultation under Article IX for both sides to take stock of any threat to their security and to devise effective measures to counter the same. But what came through continually was the Soviet government's high concern of a possible military conflict with China.

We have run ahead of our story. The war in East Bengal was brought to a speedy close by India's strategy of bypassing Pakistan's fixed defences or strongpoints to close in on Dhaka, with strong and well-targetted IAF support. On 16 December, Lieutenant General Niazi, Pakistan's eastern army commander, proposed an immediate ceasefire. General Manekshaw insisted that this be accompanied by an unconditional surrender. This was taken by Lieutenant General Jagjit Singh Aurora, eastern army commander, in Dhaka despite being heavily outnumbered by an utterly demoralized Niazi and his forces numbering 90,000 men. Indira Gandhi said:

> It is a victory but a victory not only of arms but of ideals. The Mukti Bahini could not have fought so daringly but for its passionate urge for freedom and the establishment of a special identity of Bangladesh. Our own forces could not have been so fearless and relentless had they not been convinced of their cause. India has stood for breadth of vision, tolerance of the points of view of others, of being in the battle, yet above it.[19]

She announced the Indian armed forces would cease military operations in and against West Pakistan with effect from 20:00 hours on 17 December 1971.

The war over, and India turned to winning the peace. But Bhutto's obduracy and doublespeak was to thwart this endeavour. Nixon was unrepentant in blaming India, but the Soviet Union was supportive. Kosygin suggested that the situation in J&K could be normalized 'by give and take'. In his view, 'It is possible, with suitable modifications of the CFL, to convert it into an international boundary.'[20] This indeed had been India's position since the early 1960s. In thinking ahead on the line to be pursued with Pakistan post-War, D.P. Dhar advocated:

> [...] we shall have to concentrate on working on a viable, secure line of division which becomes a firm frontier and inviolate as far as possible. We should be prepared as a quid pro quo while gaining an inch here to yield an inch or two elsewhere in shaping this line.[21]

Before venturing on a peace settlement with Pakistan, however, the debris of the sundered Pak-Bangla ties had to be cleared and a new relationship established with India now necessarily involved as a third partner acting on behalf of Dhaka until the matter was settled. The canvas here covered the fate of the 93,000 Pakistani prisoners of war, and the repatriation of some 260,000 'Biharis' owning allegiance to Pakistan and desirous of repatriation there. It also included issues such as Pakistan's recognition of Bangladesh and its admission of this to the UN; Pakistan's objection to Bangladesh's plan to try 195 Pakistani prisoners of war for war crimes; Pakistan's riposte to hold back 205 Bangla civilians in the West for treason; the restoration to West Pakistan of two tehsils in Sindh and one in Punjab occupied by India; the re-establishment of communications and over-flights between India and Pakistan; and an overall Indo-Pakistan peace settlement on all matters, including J&K.

The ensuing negotiations were tortuous with Pakistan going back and forth and India having to negotiate on behalf of Bangladesh which was not at the table. Bhutto played the role of the injured party and remained as belligerent and arrogant as ever. Ultimately, the Shimla Agreement on bilateral relations between India and Pakistan was signed on 2 July 1972 by Indira Gandhi and Bhutto. This highlighted the need to respect each other's territorial integrity; refrain from the threat or use of force; prevent hostile propaganda; restore communication and trade ties; and withdraw Indian and Pakistani armed forces to their respective sides of the international border.

With respect to J&K:

> [...] the line of control resulting from the cease-fire of December 17, 1971 shall be respected by both sides without prejudice to the recognized position of either side. Neither side shall seek to alter it unilaterally, irrespective of mutual differences and legal interpretations. Both sides further undertake to refrain from the threat or use of force in violation of this Line.[22]

The phraseology, 'line of control' or 'LoC' (with territory captured by either side during the war remaining with it) implied a departure from the old CFL of 1949 and its conversion from a military to a political line as defined by the Suchetgarh Agreement reached between the military commanders of the two sides on 11 December 1972.[23]

Once again India was content to leave the northernmost end of the LoC undemarcated. The phrase 'NJ 9842', 'thence north to the glaciers'[24] was left intact without further clarification to place the intent beyond challenge. Literally, the line could run due north irrespective of the terrain or, alternatively, it could follow the ridge marking the western wall of the Siachen Glacier along the Saltoro Ridge. The failure to chisel such phraseology was to cause trouble later.

Finally, the two sides agreed to meet again to further discuss modalities for the establishment of a durable peace, the normalization of relations, the repatriation of prisoners of war and civilian internees, 'a final settlement of Jammu and Kashmir' and the resumption of diplomatic relations (now being serviced by Switzerland).[25]

The two prime ministers reached a tacit understanding that they'd make the LoC an international border in due course. Bhutto pleaded that this not be made public, else he would be torn apart back home and a hard-won democratic regime would be overturned by the military. Subsequently, in articles published in *The Times of India* in 1995, P.N. Dhar, secretary to Prime Minister Indira Gandhi in 1972, wrote: 'Bhutto agreed that the Line could be gradually endowed with the characteristic of an international border'.[26] Bhutto went some way towards implementing this understanding by making Gilgit-Baltistan a separate entity from Pakistan, but then turned his back on this understanding.

The Shimla Agreement had a mixed reception on both sides. Defending it as neither a victory nor a defeat for Pakistan, Bhutto dammed Ayub and Tashkent. Kashmir had not been surrendered but 'reactivated' and remained on the UN agenda. 'Indian hegemony' had not been accepted. In his words:

> What hegemony of India has been accepted? We said we want Indian friendship, not Indian leadership. I have said it time and again. I told Mrs Indira Gandhi, 'How do you accept your leadership to be imposed on the people of Pakistan?' Rightly or wrongly the Muslims of the subcontinent have ruled the subcontinent for 700 years. How can we now today accept their tutelage and the domination of India over us?[27]

The verbiage continued: the two-nation theory had not been compromised (with the separation of 'Muslim Bengal') and the right of the Kashmiri people to self-determination had not been put in jeopardy. Bhutto said, 'By bifurcating and delinking the international line [border] from the ceasefire line in Kashmir, we have it admitted [by India] that Kashmir is a disputed issue.'[28]

For Bhutto there was only one way to 'get' Kashmir—'neither by negotiations nor through the United Nations. If you want the people to Kashmir to secure the right of self-determination you must fight for their right of self-determination.'[29] (Incidentally, this was a right violently denied in Balochistan, PAK and the Gilgit-Baltistan area.)

Bhutto also defended his earlier remarks about a thousand-year war and confrontation with India. The language, he said, was metaphysical, though the people of Pakistan were with him in his 'concept' of confrontation as 'a nation will never surrender its rights till eternity'.[30] Such was Bhutto's demagogy, just twelve days after Shimla.

The Pakistan National Assembly adopted a resolution on 9 July 1973 recognizing Bangladesh in a 'spirit of Muslim brotherhood'. An agreement was reached on 28 August 1973 on the repatriation of all prisoners of war to Pakistan (bar the 195 wanted by Bangladesh for war trails).

Notes continued to be exchanged between India and Pakistan on hostile acts in violation of the Shimla accord. On 9 November 1973, speaking in Mirpur, Bhutto was interrupted by slogans from students calling for guerrilla warfare to liberate Kashmir. An Indian protest note stated that Bhutto's response was that he liked such 'revolutionary slogans'. He then exhorted any youth interested in guerrilla war to join Pakistan's special services guards or commandos and receive proper training. The Pakistan minister for defence and foreign affairs, Aziz Ahmed's response on 29 November 1973 was amazing. He confirmed what Bhutto had said, adding that this ended further disturbances at the meeting. He went on to assert that inviting youth to train for guerrilla warfare against India was 'the prime minister's way of handling any hecklers at public meetings'.[31]

In December 1973, India protested against Bhutto's plan to call for a hartal both in PAK and J&K to 'intensify the struggle for recognition of Kashmir's right of self-determination'.[32] It described this as a serious interference in the internal affairs of another country.

Pakistan continued to drag its feet on normalization of relations with India, but on 22 February 1974 decided to recognize Bangladesh formally after complex tripartite negotiations.[33] This decision, Bhutto stated, was spurred by the Islamic Summit Conference in Lahore. Following this, Bangladesh, as a gesture of goodwill, dropped its proposed war-crimes trial of 195 Pakistan prisoners of war, thus paving the way for their repatriation to Pakistan.

India's nuclear test in 1974 was strongly criticized by Pakistan as a threat and an unfriendly act. Islamabad went on to impugn the Indira Gandhi-Sheikh Abdullah talks in search of a rapprochement and a way forward in J&K. India retorted that Pakistan had imposed an 'interim Constitution' on PAK and set up a J&K Council for its governance chaired by the prime minister in Islamabad. Further, on 10 October 1974, the ministry of external affairs in India said that it was aware of:

> [...] the announcement by Prime Minister of Pakistan at Gilgit on September 24, bringing about the merger of Hunza and an end to its separate entity. It was also reportedly stated by the Prime Minister that the northern territories of Jammu & Kashmir under Pakistan's occupation would be given representation in Pakistan's National Assembly.[34]

While Bangladesh took its rightful place in the international community, the Shimla accord seemed to be moving grudgingly. And its key Kashmir clause was clearly going nowhere.

HANGING ISSUES

11
Siachen Follies

The origins, course, consequences and lines of resolution of the Siachen imbroglio have been misunderstood, confused and even mismanaged by Indian policy-makers over the years.

There was a flurry of interest after Pakistan's all-powerful army chief, General Ashfaq Parvez Kayani, reversing gear, suddenly declared in April 2012 that India and Pakistan must live in peaceful coexistence as defence without development was neither viable nor acceptable.[1] True!

With US aid becoming increasingly conditional on Pakistan's good conduct and delivery of prescribed outcomes, and China's reluctance to fill the breach, its economy on drip—besides the need to counter internal security threats and the spate of questions stirred by the recent Gyari avalanche disaster—Pakistan needed respite. Kayani was articulating that dawning reality.

Pakistan has long sought India's withdrawal from the glacier, a mutual pull back and demilitarization. India however insists on the authentication and demarcation of the actual ground position line (AGPL) that we hold before redeployment to mutually defined positions, to prevent the vacated area being otherwise stealthily seized. Nevertheless, the Kayani initiative was worth pursuing so that no opportunity for peace was lost.

Both Siachen 'solutions', however, beg the question: there was no AGPL prior to 1984. Where, then, did the northern extremity of the CFL or LoC lie?

The critical date is therefore not 1984, when India took control of Siachen, but 29 July 1949, when the ceasefire agreement was signed in Karachi by ranking military representatives of India and

Pakistan and the UN Military Observer Group[2] in pursuance of Part I of the key UN resolution of 8 August 1948. This was to be followed by a truce under Part II and, after full compliance, by a plebiscite under Part III.

The Karachi Agreement delineated the entire CFL, demarcating over 740 kilometres on the ground. With the ceasefire increasingly running through high mountains and glaciated areas as it traversed north, it often followed a directional path in the absence of clear landmarks—thus, 'Chalunka (on the Shyok River), Khor, thence north to the glaciers',[3] passing through grid reference NJ 9842. The segment beyond NJ 9842 was, by mutual agreement, not demarcated on the ground, being a highly elevated, glaciated, unexplored and unpopulated region that had not witnessed any fighting. A plebiscite was soon to follow and the matter, it was assumed, would be settled.

Clearly, the delineation of the northernmost segment of the CFL was unambiguous: NJ 9842, 'thence north to the glaciers'. The very next section crucially directed:

> The cease-fire line described above shall be drawn on a one inch map (where available) and then be verified mutually on the ground by local commanders on each side with the assistance of the United Nations Military Observers, so as to eliminate any no-man's land.[4]

Therefore, the line, whether delineated or demarcated, could in no way be left hanging in the air.

The CFL was ratified by both sides and deposited with the UNCIP. As mentioned in the previous chapter, it was revalidated as the LoC under the Suchetgarh Agreement of December 1972, in accordance with the clear intent of the Shimla Conference earlier that year to move from military confrontation to a political resolution in J&K. The LoC now incorporated the military gains made by either side in J&K in the 1971 war. Thus in the Kargil-Siachen sector, all territorial gains went entirely to India, which acquired the 254-square-mile Turtok salient comprising five villages just south and west of NJ 9842. This military acquisition provided India an additional territorial bulwark against hostile claims on Siachen.[5]

Earlier, in 1957-58, during the UN-designated International Geophysical Year, an Indian scientific expedition led by the Geological Survey explored the upper Nubra and Shyok valleys, mapped and measured Siachen and other glaciers, and publicly recorded its findings. No Pakistani protest followed the prolonged, internationally known and publicized presence and activity of the Indian scientists. It is simple to see why. Locate NJ 9842 on a detailed physical map of northern J&K and draw a line 'thence north' and much or most of Siachen will be found to lie on the Indian side of the CFL. Pakistani military maps, depicting Pakistan's military positions during the Kargil operations, situate the entire Siachen Glacier on the Indian side of NJ 9842 'thence north to the glaciers'.[6]

At Shimla, as we know, Mrs Gandhi demanded acceptance of the CFL/LoC as the permanent political boundary, but accepted Zulfiqar Ali Bhutto's honeyed assurances that he would take steps to promote the evolution of the LoC into a permanent boundary. But no sooner were his prisoners of war back home and his lost territories in the west restored, than he raged and reneged. Mrs Gandhi's principal secretary, P.N. Dhar put the record straight in *The Times of India* (4-5 April 1995):

> Even so, when later Pakistan sought to incorporate the Northern Areas within its territory, and still later when it announced construction of the Basha-Diamer dam, and yet again when it conferred a limited constitutional status on Gilgit-Baltistan, India protested against what it said was an infringement of its own sovereignty, betraying policy inconsistency in its stance on the contours of a final political settlement in Jammu and Kashmir.

Pakistan, the UN and global atlases depicted the CFL neutrally or correctly till around 1964-72. By the mid-1950s, China had commenced its cartographic aggression in Ladakh. In 1963, it signed a boundary agreement whereby Pakistan unilaterally ceded '2,700 sq km of Shaksgam Valley in Pakistan-occupied Kashmir to China'.[7] Thereafter, Pakistan kept extending its lines of communication eastwards and even began licensing western mountaineering expeditions to venture east of K2. It was emboldened to extend this 'eastward creep' when, between 1964 and 1972, the US Defense Mapping Agency (now the National Geospatial-Intelligence Agency), an international reference point for cartography, began depicting the CFL as extending from NJ 9842 to a point just west of the Karakoram Pass. The most charitable explanation for this totally unwarranted and unfriendly action was that it erroneously hardened what was possibly no more than an extant dotted World War II air defence information zone (ADIZ) line into a politico-military divide. World atlases followed suit, depicting the line drawn from NJ 9842 northeast to the Karakoram pass as the authentic and internationally accepted CFL/LoC, backed by international mountaineering lore that India did little to rebut or put in context.

Pakistan gladly accepted this fraudulent international endorsement and thereafter initiated moves to occupy Siachen. Reconnaissance teams were sent to the Saltoro Ridge, Siachen's western wall, in 1983. Getting wind of this stratagem, India pre-emptively occupied the glacier in March 1984.

At a US Institute for Peace conference on J&K in Washington in 1991 that I attended, delegates were delivered a map at their hotel rooms without the mandatory credit line regarding its origins. It was headed 'The Kashmir Region: Depicting the CFL/LOC, Siachen and Shaksgam'. This showed a hatched triangle NJ 9842-Karakoram Pass-K2, and Shaksgam in the north, with a legend reading, 'Indian occupied since 1983'. The conference organizers disowned what they surmised could be a Central Intelligence Agency (CIA) map and suggested it be treated as 'withdrawn'! Even so, the map not only confirmed Pakistan's claims but labelled India an aggressor. Years later, when Robert Blackwill was the US ambassador in Delhi, certain statements appeared suggesting that the US Defense Mapping Agency had got its lines wrong and that the impugned maps would be amended. Nothing ensued, and this piece of cartographic aggression remains.[8]

The fact is, if the US Defense Mapping Agency map were a product of genuine error, howsoever irresponsible, it would have been natural and simple to apologize and make amends in an appropriate manner. Nothing of the kind happened. Nor did the Indian government respond to any of these alarm bells. The American scholar, Robert G. Wirsing dwelt on this issue at some length; he wrote:

By the early 1980s, practically all the most respected atlases [...] were showing the ceasefire line/line of control extending beyond grid reference point NJ 9842 about 55 miles in a clear north-easterly direction all the way to the Karakoram Pass on the Chinese border. The extension was a distinct departure from past cartographic practice. UN maps of Kashmir produced in the early years of the dispute all terminated at the map coordinate NJ 9842. In India and Pakistan, display of the ceasefire line or line of control on publicly sold maps has been officially discouraged at least since the 1965 war; but among the scores of pre-1965 official or officially-approved maps surveyed by this author in the Library of Congress, not a single one showed any extension beyond NJ 9842.[9]

Wirsing further noted:

A nearly universal shift by mapmakers to an extended and eastward-running ceasefire line/line of control (from NJ 9842 to the Karakoram Pass) was eventually achieved. [...] One can hardly escape the conclusion that the US Defense Mapping Agency, one of the largest and probably the most influential of international mapmakers, played a far from inconsequential role in the world's cartographic award of Siachen to Pakistan.[10]

On 12 March 1987, the office of the geographer of the US state department issued guidelines to producers of official US maps that admitted past inconsistencies and specifically instructed them not to extend the line beyond NJ 9842 to the Karakoram Pass.[11] Nonetheless, the damage had been done and remains uncorrected, with no apologies by or to anybody to this date.

If innocent absentmindedness on the part of one or more official US agencies is not altogether convincing, where else might one look, howsoever tangentially, for possible explanations of the Siachen muddle? The Sino-Soviet rift was out in the open, and the US, having extricated itself from the Indo-China quagmire, had begun to review its relations with the People's Republic of China, now a nuclear power. The Sino-Pakistan rapprochement post 1963 made Pakistan a critical conduit for quiet Sino-US talks. Kissinger headed to the subcontinent to stave off the possibility of an Indo-Pakistan war on account of the Bangladesh liberation struggle, a mission famously overshadowed, as we know, by his secret dash

to Beijing from Islamabad and the ensuing announcement of a
Mao-Nixon meeting. The Indo-Soviet Friendship Pact was signed
and the notorious 'Nixon tilt' against India went into play.

Kissinger Transcripts[12] makes the extraordinary disclosure of
the secretary of state encouraging the professional regulation
commission in December 1971, through its UN ambassador, Huang
Hua in New York, with whom he was now in very close touch, to
move against India in order to divert it from severing Bangladesh
from Pakistan, a mutual ally. The US reassured Beijing that it
would counter any Soviet riposte. Nixon, if you remember, had
already ordered a US naval squadron headed by the nuclear-
powered USS Enterprise into the Indian Ocean to show the flag,
although this would have ramped up tensions with the Soviet
Union. Was it in the background of this bizarre play of events that
US map-makers started fiddling gratuitously with India's strategic
boundaries?

Look now at the implications of the options being canvassed
for a resolution of the Siachen matter. Any unqualified
redeployment from the Siachen Glacier without asserting the
correct delineation of the CFL/LoC from NJ 9842 'thence north to
the glaciers', will mean accepting the Pakistani claim and throwing
the August 1948 UN Resolution and the derivative 1949 Karachi
Agreement into the dustbin. This 'mother' resolution on J&K
implicitly found Pakistan the aggressor and intruder, required its
military personnel and tribal cohorts to leave the state forthwith,
and upheld India's de jure sovereignty over the entire state even
while preparations were made for a plebiscite. On 4 February
1948, the US representative, Senator Warren Austin, told the
Security Council that:

> The external sovereignty of Kashmir is no longer under the
> control of the Maharaja [...] With the accession of Jammu and
> Kashmir to India, this foreign [external] sovereignty [over
> Kashmir] went over to India and is exercised by India, and that
> is how India happens to be here as petitioner.[13]

The LoC is a subsequent derivative of the 8 August 1949 resolution
that drew the CFL.

The Manmohan Singh–Pervez Musharraf 2005 peace formula

would sanctify the LoC as an evolving international boundary, rendered porous as 'a mere line on a map' across which movement, investment, commerce, exchange and cooperation might be encouraged and joint institutions allowed to develop for their management.[14] Manmohan Singh had hinted that this arrangement might even include water. Such a progression could bind the peoples of J&K and of India and Pakistan together in friendship and cooperation. Indeed, this arrangement harks back to some kind of proto-confederal vision for J&K projected by Sheikh Abdullah and Jawaharlal Nehru in 1964 without prejudice to the existing twin sovereignties.

This is the only viable win-win solution for all with regard to J&K. But unless the LoC is firmly anchored to a northern terminus, it will dangle loose in no-man's land and could unravel, leaving everything up for grabs.

The AGPL is in essence a new military line. It defines post-1984 ground realities and necessarily follows a natural feature, namely, the Saltoro Ridge. Redeployment from there is a military proposition that would leave the political question untouched. If we now fiddle with the internationally-delineated LoC we will be moving from an objective to a subjective definition of that line. At the end of the day, the AGPL is an irrelevance if the aim is a political settlement.

A way out could lie in quiet authentication of the AGPL, if necessary through an annexed exchange of letters. This should be combined with agreement on the only true meaning of 'NJ 9842 thence north to the glaciers', leaving no room for any no-man's land and clearly marking a firm boundary.

Finally, there should be an understanding on converting the NJ 9842-K2-Karakoram Pass triangle into a demilitarized Third Pole International Peace Park for Glacier and World Weather Studies, hopefully with China's Shaksgam as a partner, to monitor climate change. Sovereignty within its own territory would remain with India and Pakistan, and with China, should it join. Such an arrangement would foreclose risk of any clandestine military occupation of the vacated AGPL or adjacent Pakistani positions by anybody. None need lose face. All would gain.

12

Going Nuclear

With the acquisition of nuclear capability in 1998,[1] Pakistan launched cross-border terror against India. It also exploited nuclear blackmail to get the international community to intervene—to ask India to back down, to open talks and to make concessions of one kind or another to the aggressor.[2] Following the Big Four (the USA, the UK, France, Russia), China got the bomb in 1964, and Israel thereafter.

Before Independence, in 1946, Nehru had—even while urging universal nuclear disarmament—endorsed Dr Homi Bhabha's vision of developing atomic energy for peaceful purposes through the newly established Atomic Energy Commission (AEC). Nehru had gone on to say:

> As long as the world is constituted as it is, every country will have to devise and use the latest devices for its protection. I have no doubt India will develop her scientific researches and I hope Indian scientists will use the atomic force for constructive purposes. But if India is threatened, she will inevitably try to defend herself by all means at her disposal.[3]

I had been appointed information adviser to Prime Minister Indira Gandhi in February 1966. Three months thereafter, China tested its third nuclear device on 9 May. The prime minister was called upon to make a statement in Parliament; this revealed the absence of any clear policy. It led me to suggest the need to set up a group that might spell out the political, security, technological and economic aspects of a national nuclear policy. She agreed.

Thereupon, I invited a small group, a week later, for an informal brainstorming session over lunch. But who could speak from the defence angle? Someone named a bright deputy secretary in the defence ministry, K. Subrahmanyam, or 'Subbu' as he was called. And so it was that I contacted him. Others present were Homi N. Sethna, director of Bhabha Atomic Research Centre, Bombay; Pitambar Pant of the Planning Commission; Dr. S. Gopal, the head of the historical division of the ministry of external affairs; Romesh Thapar, the founder-editor of the monthly journal *Seminar* and a contemporaneous confidant of Indira Gandhi; and myself.

Sethna talked about the wherewithal and costs, and gave a time estimate of five years at the outside for a nuclear test and for the development of a delivery system. Subbu and Gopal believed that reliance on any US nuclear guarantee to India would steadily diminish as China's capability increased. And Pitambar was concerned about the cost of an Indian nuclear programme, even after offsetting the technological gains. We dispersed after agreeing to put together a paper—with Sethna contributing to the technological parts, Subbu covering the security dimensions and Gopal providing the diplomatic implications.

I reported the discussion to Mrs Gandhi and her principal secretary, L.K. Jha. A week later, a meeting of the AEC was held in Bombay, in which Vikram Sarabhai was named the new chairman of the AEC and secretary, atomic energy. (He replaced the late Homi Bhabha who was tragically killed in an air crash.) Tentative approval was given for a study of a nuclear weapons programme and a missile system. Meanwhile, word somehow leaked of our informal luncheon group, and the prime minister informed me that she had been accosted by G.K. Reddy (eminent journalist for *The Hindu*) after a press conference, and asked when our 'committee' would submit its 'report'! By then, however, the matter had formally passed into official hands.

These events played a part in launching Subbu into what became a career path—the area of nuclear, security and strategic studies—that he soon dominated. His induction, as head of the newly-established Institute for Defence Studies and Analysis (IDSA), between 1968 and 1972, and again from 1980 to 1987, enabled him to add scholarship and depth to his in-house knowledge and experience in this field. His expertise was enriched by his stints alongside IDSA—as home secretary (Tamil Nadu), which offered him exposure to matters of internal security; as union secretary, defence production; and as chairman of the Joint Intelligence Committee. The IDSA period also allowed him to study and visit foreign countries, and to participate in Pugwash meetings, all of which sharpened his world view.

Nuclear issues were always contentious in India, and for quite some time, Subbu was rated a prime nuclear hawk. I, too, shared that view for a while, but was gradually persuaded by his logic— that the Non-Proliferation Treaty (NPT) and its affiliates made for an unequal and unfair world. He reasoned that without a credible minimum deterrent of its own, India would never be able to grow to its full stature, being subject to a variety of pressures or nuclear blackmail. That forecast was indeed borne out by subsequent events.

The Track-II Indo-Pakistan Neemrana meetings commenced in 1990. Both Subbu and I were participants. For me and many others—including the Pakistan team that comprised leading diplomats, generals and scholars—these became biannual tutorials by Subbu on nuclear-strategic affairs amid the shifting sands of the post-Cold War world. Early ideas on an Indo-Pakistan nuclear restraint regime—through concepts such as a nuclear safe zone, and a variety of other confidence-building measures—were honed at these meetings and conveyed to the two governments and military establishments for consideration. Subbu would, with great clarity, place these discussions within the framework of the fast-changing international scene, keeping a wary eye on what was happening in, and between, China, Korea, Iran and Pakistan, as well as in NATO (North Atlantic Treaty Organization), Russia and Israel.

No surprise, then, that Subbu was named convenor of the first National Security Advisory Board (NSAB) in 1998, which he steered with distinction, establishing guidelines and conventions—always through consensus. The first NSAB will be remembered for two things above all. It wrote the draft Nuclear Doctrine,[4] which the government subsequently adopted, virtually in toto. It also submitted to the government a Strategic Defence Review, looking at all aspects of security in a holistic manner. This was perhaps the first time that such a document had ever been prepared.

The draft report of the National Security Advisory Board on the Indian Nuclear Doctrine was released in August 1999. It argued that:

> [...] In the absence of global nuclear disarmament, India's strategic interests require effective, credible nuclear deterrence and adequate retaliatory capability, should deterrence fail. This would be consistent with the UN Charter, which sanctions the right of self-defence.

> [...] India shall pursue a doctrine of credible minimum nuclear deterrence. In this policy of 'retaliation only', the survivability of our arsenal is critical. This is a dynamic concept related to the strategic environment, technological imperatives and the needs of national security. The actual size components, deployment and employment of nuclear forces will be decided in the light of these factors. India's peacetime posture aims at convincing any potential aggressor that:

> (a) any threat of use of nuclear weapons against India shall invoke measures to counter the threat: and (b) any nuclear attack on India and its forces shall result in punitive retaliation with nuclear weapons to inflict damage unacceptable to the aggressor.

> [...] The fundamental purpose of Indian nuclear weapons is to deter the use and threat of use of nuclear weapons by any State or entity against India and its forces. India will not be the first to initiate a nuclear strike, but will respond with punitive retaliation should deterrence fail [...][5]

The draft was refined and adopted, and a command and control set-up was established firmly under civil auspices.

A more challenging task came Subbu's way when he was asked to head the Kargil Review Committee (KRC), on which K.K. Hazari, Satish Chandra and I also served. The press and Parliament were baying for blood, wanting to see heads roll, and for that reason, completely missed the purpose and potency of the KRC. The committee was viewed as a toothless body in relation to commissions of inquiry or a Joint Parliamentary Committee (JPC), and was thought to have vague terms of reference that could only result in a whitewash. Nothing could have been more erroneous.

The KRC was not an inquisitorial body charged with fixing responsibility, but was asked to review the circumstances leading up to the event that was Kargil, and to recommend measures to prevent such armed incursions in the future. This gave the committee a broad remit and great flexibility. Further, it freed it from the narrowly interpreted confines and lumbering gait of commissions of inquiry, many of which have proved ineffective. Indeed, the pious notion that judges epitomize ultimate wisdom in all circumstances has invariably led to a failure to distinguish between the judicious and the judicial while considering complex political and social issues. JPCs, too, have often failed to deliver, on account of the play of partisan politics.

In the space of time that it takes most commissions of inquiry to begin their task, the KRC not only completed its work, but also put out its report in the form of a commercial issuance through Sage Publications.[6] The procedure adopted was novel. The KRC had the cabinet secretary send out a letter, calling on all departments of the government (including the military, paramilitary and intelligence services) to share full information with the committee.

This opened all doors, with the committee having access to all echelons in the field, down to the lowest level. Current and former prime ministers; defence, foreign and home ministers; service and intelligence chiefs; defence, science, nuclear and space research heads; the media; and a range of other persons all met with the committee. The ensuing transcripts were sent back to them for any necessary additions or amendments, and returned endorsed with their signatures. No commission or JPC, since Independence, has enjoyed the degree of access and trust vouchsafed to the KRC.

*

Pakistan's nuclear trajectory, upon Independence, was very different from India's. It was based on countering and even overawing India, did not eschew a first strike or the tactical use of these weapons, and was under military control and command. The fiasco of Operation Gibraltar and the 1965 war proved a bitter pill for the ambitious Zulfiqar Ali Bhutto, who was now on the path of political ascendancy. He ranted and vowed to keep the nuclear equation equal, even if Pakistanis had to 'eat grass to ensure nuclear parity with India'. Meanwhile, using the Indian test as a rallying point for showing his patriotism with regard to Kashmir, he promised to 'wage a war for a thousand years' but not give up the vale.[7]

Bhutto had been urging a full-blooded nuclear programme since becoming foreign minister in 1963. The actual decision to go nuclear was, however, taken only when he became prime minister in 1973. It was soon thereafter that the notorious Dr Abdul Qadeer Khan volunteered to assist Bhutto in what, for both, had become a sacred mission.

A.Q. Khan was a nuclear metallurgist who, after studying in various countries of Europe, was absorbed in URENCO—a highly secret enrichment facility established in 1970 by the governments of Britain, West Germany and the Netherlands. Its mission was to manufacture top-quality centrifuges, and to produce highly-enriched uranium for use in power plants and nuclear weapons, rather than to follow what was until then the traditional plutonium route.

Khan's knowledge of English, French and German became an asset in translating documents into English. This task enabled him to gain access to highly privileged information whose importance he was quick to realize. He thereupon started copying select documents which he then took to Pakistan, and together with other stolen material, accumulated a priceless archive of advanced knowledge for use in his home country that enabled him to assert with confidence to Bhutto, that Pakistan should follow the uranium route in making fissile material.

Following India's test explosion in 1974, Khan visited Pakistan and won over Bhutto, asserting that Pakistan should follow the uranium route in making fissile material. Bhutto readily engaged him to develop nuclear capability, in parallel with Pakistan's official nuclear establishment.

Soon, the BVD, a Dutch intelligence service, started investigating A.Q. Khan over suspicions that he was stealing highly classified documents and suppliers' lists from URENCO. Certain clandestine links were uncovered and the Dutch planned to arrest Khan. Learning of this, the CIA—according to Ruud Lubbers, former Dutch minister for economic affairs—advised the Dutch government to let Khan continue with his activities.[8] 'The Americans wished to follow and watch Khan to get more information,' Lubbers told Dutch radio three decades later.[9] While Lubbers claims he questioned this line, the CIA told him to block Khan's access to the secrets, which the Dutch did, by promoting him to a job where he no longer had access to sensitive data. Lubbers later suggested that the real reason the US did not want Khan arrested was because it wished to help Pakistan, an enemy of Soviet-leaning India. Authors David Armstrong and Joe Trento would later comment:

> What no one yet realized was that Khan had already absconded with the plans for almost every centrifuge on URENCO's drawing board, including the all-important G-2 [centrifuge]. It would prove to be one of the greatest nuclear heists of all time.[10]

Khan, now, alert to the fact that he was under surveillance, fled to Pakistan in December 1975. On his return home, A.Q. Khan was formally hired by Bhutto to assist with Pakistan's programme to build nuclear weapons. He was appointed director of Pakistan's uranium-enrichment project, which was separated from the Pakistan Atomic Energy Commission (PAEC). Khan was instructed to report directly to the prime minister.

In 1975, Pakistan's President Bhutto approved the construction of a centrifuge-enrichment facility in Kahuta, then named Engineering Research Laboratories (ERL). A.Q. Khan consequently sowed the dragon's teeth from Kahuta, with the full support of the Pakistan state and a protective US cover.

Burgeoning activity at Kahuta and Khan's frenzied efforts to get parts and equipment from around the world through shell companies and devious routes had attracted attention. Fearing time may be short, A.Q. Khan launched 'Project 706', aiming to establish self-sufficiency in manufacturing nuclear components and acquire capability through reverse engineering. This was followed by 'Project AB' (atom bomb) to realize Bhutto's dream of an 'Islamic Bomb'. This needed independent funding which was soon achieved by an increasingly boastful and arrogant Khan through the sales of nuclear fuel, parts and components to Libya, Iran and possibly even to al Qaeda agents.

The Americans (and Israelis) were by now sufficiently alarmed to consider bombing Kahuta. They also confronted the Pakistanis and urged them to desist from proliferation, but to no avail. The genie was out of the bottle.

Undaunted, in 1981, the new Pakistani president, General Muhammad Zia ul-Haq asked Khan to initiate a second programme to design a nuclear warhead at his research centre in Kahuta. What saved Pakistan from international ire was the overthrow of the Shah of Iran. With the US hostage crisis, or 'Irangate', Pakistan was called upon to mediate in getting the Americans off the hook. Simultaneously, news arrived of the Soviet invasion of Afghanistan. All was forgiven, and Pakistan was once more a favoured frontline state. It was propped up with aid, through a Faustian bargain.

In the meanwhile, A.Q. Khan's past had begun catching up. At the end of March 1979, after a German television programme revealed that Pakistan, through Khan, had access to URENCO UC technology, the Dutch launched an investigation into the matter. With new reports in early June of that year revealing that centrifuges identical to the Dutch ones were already working in Pakistan, the authorities intensified their investigation.[11] The world was alerted. Finally, in 1983, A.Q. Khan was sentenced in absentia by a Dutch court to four years of imprisonment for nuclear espionage.

Yet, soon after, in 1985, Khan's conviction was overturned based on an appeal that he had not received a proper summons. The Dutch prosecution did not renew charges.

Full of misplaced bravado, Khan, in 1984, admitted to a nuclear weapons programme and slammed the West:

> Western countries had never imagined that a poor and backward country like Pakistan would end their [nuclear] monopoly in such a short time [...] As soon as they realized that Pakistan had dashed their dreams to the ground, they pounced at Pakistan and me like hungry jackals and began attacking us with all kinds of accusations and falsehood [...] How could they tolerate a Muslim country becoming their equal in this field [...] All Western countries including Israel are not only the enemies of Pakistan but in fact of Islam [....] All these activities are part of the crusade which Christians and Jews have been carrying on against Muslims for about one thousand years.[12]

Further, in 1987 A.Q. Khan told Indian journalist Kuldip Nayyar that Pakistan had the bomb.[13] According to investigative journalist, Seymour Hersh, the purpose of the interview was to 'convey a not very subtle message to the Indians: that any attempt to dismember Pakistan would be countered with the bomb.'[14] This was an embarrassment to the US government, which had aided Pakistan during the Soviet-Afghan War while shutting its eyes to Pakistan's clandestine nuclear programme with Chinese and, later, North Korean assistance.

In the meanwhile, A.Q. Khan, with the full support of the Pakistan establishment and the ISI (Inter-services Intelligence), was now like a man possessed. A two-way collaboration between China and A.Q. Khan flourished. China, it has been documented:

> [...] had transferred a complete nuclear weapon design to Pakistan, along with enough weapons-grade uranium for two nuclear weapons. In 1986, China concluded a comprehensive nuclear cooperation agreement with Pakistan. That same year, Chinese scientists had begun assisting Pakistan with the enrichment of weapons-grade uranium, and China also reportedly transferred enough tritium gas to Pakistan for 10 nuclear weapons. Since then, China has supplied Pakistan with a variety of nuclear products and services, ranging from uranium enrichment technology to research and power reactors. China allegedly involved Pakistani scientists in a nuclear test at its Lop Nur test site in 1989.[15]

The Pakistan-China honeymoon had commenced in 1963 and was cemented by 1971, when Pakistan, as a staunch American ally,[16] facilitated the US-China rapprochement, and lobbied to secure Taiwan's seat in the Security Council for mainland China. Benazir Bhutto, as prime minister, visited North Korea in 1993, and as the military's cat's paw, sought No-dong missile blueprints from President Kim Il-Sung to strengthen Pakistan's nuclear-delivery system. The deal was struck.

Regime followed regime in both Pakistan and the US, but A.Q. Khan seemed to grow larger than life, one step ahead of those out to get him, at home and abroad. He moved from nuclear acquisition to nuclear proliferation, having built a nuclear arsenal and delivery system (the North Korean-modelled Ghauri and F-16s, converted to carry nuclear bombs) and a stockpile of enriched uranium and equipment to trade with (what the Americans called) the Axis of Evil.

Whenever A.Q. Khan's dirty tricks were exposed, and he or his agents were caught red-handed around the world stealing and smuggling nuclear material, various governments, notably the US, but also the British, Dutch, German and the Canadians, were prevailed upon to desist from pursuing the matter and to allow the trail to run cold. The Americans led the pack, and orchestrated the obfuscation surrounding A.Q. Khan's activities. Men like Richard Barlow, a CIA expert on Pakistan's clandestine nuclear activities, and later, Joseph Wilson, a US diplomat, were side-tracked and destroyed. Congressional committees were misled and stymied. Successive US presidents lied to Congress so as to grant Pakistan annual certification that it was not violating nuclear norms. A completely bogus case was construed against Iraq without credible evidence, but despite clear proof of Pakistan's dangerous waywardness, it was let off the hook. Instead, Britain slapped a case against a customs agent who probed A.Q. Khan for violating the Official Secrets Act![17]

Realizing that his Dubai base for orchestrating global undercover transactions, procurement and distributive sources elsewhere was increasingly exposed, A.Q. Khan helped set up a nuclear-component-manufacturing plant in Malaysia, followed by offices in Sudan and Timbuktu, in Mali. He and his agents travelled incessantly to Pyongyang, Tripoli, Afghanistan, Tehran and Timbuktu, freely using the Pakistan military and other official facilities.[18] And, all the while, US aid to Pakistan mounted. Journalists Adrian Levy and Catherine Scott-Clarke estimate that maybe up to US$1 billion of American aid to Islamabad was funnelled into Pakistan's nuclear programme.[19]

At the turn of the millennium, the Pakistan army went so far as to stage 'IDEAS 2000', an international munitions fair in Karachi— the centrepiece of which was Khan Research Laboratories' exhibit, with glossy brochures promoting the sales of centrifuges, replete with after-sales consultancy services that included installation, repair and maintenance, all officially cleared for export. It was brazen.

Indo-Pakistan relations, in the meanwhile, were far from robust. They had plummeted with the launch of Pakistan's proxy-jihadi war in J&K in 1989, and had not recovered. The US was tireless in describing Kashmir as a global danger and nuclear flashpoint, and sent out a mission under the US secretary of defence Robert Gates to avert a nuclear exchange. It remained unmindful, as earlier and since, that the source of that danger—whether in Kashmir, Iraq, Iran or North Korea—was its own reckless and flagrant patronage of Pakistan's nuclear proliferation. The latter had even extended to talks with al Qaeda agents, with concurrent plans to help them develop a dirty bomb with which to blackmail America too!

When US intelligence got into Kabul in November 2001, along with the victorious Northern Alliance, it discovered evidence that pointed to Pakistan's WMD (weapons of mass destruction) flirtation with the al Qaeda.[20] Earlier, word was out regarding Pakistan's plans to offer Saddam Hussein blueprints to set up a uranium enrichment plant, as also recycled nuclear bomb designs.[21] International Atomic Energy Agency (IAEA) inspectors in Iraq were later able to collect more direct evidence of this, but failed to excite any American interest in the matter. In any event, Iraq was bombed into submission, and Pakistan continued to be mollycoddled.

Soon, 9/11 unfolded, which alarmed the US, and Pervez Musharraf once again became America's foremost partner in the war against terror. Again, all was forgiven. A fleeing Taliban was given safe haven in Pakistan.

However, with the declaration of 'Mission Accomplished' in Iraq, President George Bush turned the heat on Musharraf. A.Q. Khan was 'retired', and in 2003, the Americans confronted Musharraf in New York. Musharraf records in his autobiography, that at the UN summit he was attending:

> [President Bush] drew me aside and asked me if I could spare some time the next morning for the CIA director, George Tenet. [...] I agreed. Tenet arrived at my hotel suite the next morning, drew out some papers and placed them before me. I immediately recognized them as detailed drawings of Pakistan's P-1 centrifuges [...] I did not know what to say. I have seldom found myself at a loss for words.[22]

But Musharraf quickly found his tongue to distance the Pakistani government and himself from A.Q. Khan, who was denounced as a braggart and a dangerous megalomaniac. This pretence convinced nobody. The Pakistan government and Musharraf, personally, were closely involved. The one reason A.Q. Khan, though questioned, was not brought to trial, is because he had prepared a brief on Pakistan's clandestine nuclear adventures, and sent it off to London with his younger daughter for publication, if he came to any harm.[23] The blackmail worked.

In 2005, after a powerful earthquake laid to waste areas along the LoC in PAK, and part of the Kahuta nuclear complex, causing something of a 'nuclear accident', Musharraf called on A.Q. Khan for help. Khan refused. However, the restoration has proceeded, even as more evidence has come to light—this time through German intelligence—that Pakistan continues to trade in nuclear weapons technology, buying and selling, as before, to Iran and Saudi Arabia. New clients include Syria, Egypt, and others unnamed and unknown, leading to apprehensions of a widening circle of proliferation.[24]

*

Prior to America's direct confrontation with Musharraf in 2003, the breathless American telephonic workings with Islamabad, and the to-ing and fro-ing of emissaries from Washington to Musharraf had been to little avail. Now, the US saw that its pet had become a monster that the master did not quite know how to tame. In seeking to trade every kind of aid and political comfort so as to keep 'fighting terror', successive US regimes (with other western members of the 'coalition of the willing') had built Pakistan into a fount of terror itself. It seemed all right (though at terrible cost to the hapless people of Pakistan) as long as others were victims. India, too, paid a huge unacknowledged price for such 'collateral damage' that made America's own 'terror' casualties puny by comparison.

Despite talk on restoring 'democracy' in Pakistan, the US joined Musharraf's game of dumb charades, which even Benazir Bhutto— a handy façade, and no great democratic icon herself—had discovered to her cost. Musharraf's promises, timetables and democratic vision entailed grandstanding, and if he moved from supporting jihad to 'fighting terror' in stages, the move was first tactical, then strategic, and totally amoral and opportunistic.

To rattle his American interlocutors, Musharraf averred that Pakistan's nuclear armoury was safe in the hands of the military, but that elections held in a 'disturbed (read: democratic) environment' could result in control over nuclear weapons falling into the hands of 'dangerous elements'.[25] Such blackmail was a timely reminder to Washington that it had, over the years, condoned or even assisted the garnering of nuclear-weapons capability by Pakistan, and even negotiated for its sale by the latter to rogue states and non-state actors, in exchange for short-term gains—some of them cosmetic, but entirely self-serving—in the War on Terror.

Much of this was no secret and had been revealed, from time to time in credible media disclosures, only to be met with thundering silence. In this regard, the grim catalogue of American guilt, treachery and practiced deceit was chillingly recited by Adrian Levy and Catherine Scott-Clarke. Successive US presidents stoically lied to Congress, the American people and the world, to 'conjure a grand deception', which, the authors write, 'served further to destabilize it and to empower those bent on global jihad'.[26]

Back in 1979-80, following the Soviet invasion of Afghanistan, General K.M. Arif—Zia ul-Haq's close aide—and Agha Shahi, former foreign minister, visited the US. The US was eager to use Pakistan as a strategic gateway to access Afghanistan, and as an ally in the war on terror. The Pakistani delegates said that everything was possible, provided US arms were channelled through the ISI for delivery to the Afghan freedom fighters, and no questions were asked of Pakistan's nuclear programme.[27] The US readily agreed, only drawing the line at Islamabad exploding a nuclear device! Maybe up to 30 per cent, or more, of US aid was diverted by the ISI for its cross-border terror strikes in India, while Taliban terrorists were offered a happy hunting ground for jihad in J&K and beyond.[28] The US looked away, and directly or indirectly, endorsed Pakistan's tutelage of the Taliban and other forms of Islamic radicalism to rear 'good Muslims' who would confront the Soviet atheists. It also encouraged proliferation of small arms that were to wreak havoc on human rights in South Asia, and of narcotics to keep Afghan warlords happy and in funds. The born-again Ugly American played Jekyll and Hyde with consummate skill.

The US bombed Iraq in 2003 in search of non-existent weapons of mass destruction, even as it rewarded Pakistan—despite knowing its dirty games. The demonization of Islam by the US, in the wake of Afghanistan, was matched by the Islamic radicalization of Pakistan as state policy. All these chickens later come home to roost.

Despite all its homilies and alarms about controlling proliferation, the US has clearly been part of the epidemic, and it is not yet certain whether it has turned over a new leaf. The US is afraid to turn the screws on its ally, Pakistan, as it fears that any consequent regime instability there could result in nuclear technology and materials falling into the hands of rogue elements. The story is far from over.

13

The Indus: Waters of Unity

The dispute between India and Pakistan over the Indus waters has been a great bane. But, handled right—in a broader perspective of enlightened self-interest—it could prove to be an even greater boon for both nations, and also bind them in friendship and cooperation. That day may not be far—with contemporary opinion in Pakistan wearying of self-inflicted jihadi tyranny and an endless confrontation with India as a permanent enemy in order to wrest Kashmir, as well as democratic roots establishing themselves in the wake of a weakening army. India should not merely watch this development, but assist it with positive responses.

Possibly no water dispute has been on the global agenda for as long as this one, triggering periodic fears of this stubborn conflict spilling over into yet another Indo-Pakistan war, with a nuclear overhang. Yet the Indus Waters Treaty must rank among the more tangible achievements of the United Nations system since it was signed in 1960. Despite several alarms from time to time, it has upheld a delicately poised peace, with the onus of performance largely falling on the upper-riparian India. Nevertheless, the dispute festers for obvious, but less perceived, reasons.

The Indus dispute is not merely about sharing and managing the waters of a common river basin. It is seen by Pakistan as an existential threat, entailing denial of its territorial claim—even *right*—to the princely state of J&K.[1] This extends itself to its Islamic identity, and very existence, by virtue of India's control over its singular water lifeline, or jugular. By constant iteration, as a clear and present danger to its being, the Indus waters question has been made into a deeply emotional and political issue for Pakistan.

It has, in some ways, become an inextricable extension of the 'Kashmir Question' and what is termed as the 'ideology of Pakistan', whatever that represents.

Indeed, this water wrangle became apparent not merely during the prolonged Indus Treaty negotiations, but even earlier, during the debates on Kashmir in the UN Security Council. The Pakistani foreign minister, Zafrullah Khan, made a pointed reference to India's 1948 spring offensive[2], threatening to cut off the old Mangla Headworks on the Jhelum (in the Pakistan-controlled part of J&K), and subsequently the site of the Mangla Dam. The Indus rivers again figured in the Swaran Singh-Bhutto talks in 1963,[3] with Pakistan insisting that its border in J&K must, at the very least, lie on the Chenab to safeguard its water interests.

Therefore, to define the Indus waters imbroglio as no more than a classic water dispute would be a gross simplification. Unfortunately, this nuanced understanding is lacking among international scholars and interlocutors, and possibly even within the contours of subcontinental discourse. Jihadi elements in Pakistan—like the Lashkar-e-Taiba (LeT), reborn as the Jamaat-ud-Dawa (JuD), and led by the UN-declared terrorist, Hafiz Saeed—keep singing the refrain on public thoroughfares in Muzaffarbad, Lahore, and other major cities, that the Indus dispute is no more than a water imbroglio.

In the world inherited post 9/11, Pakistan found itself on the back foot, following exposure of its involvement with the Taliban in Afghanistan—despite joining the War on Terror. It also stood exposed for fostering cross-border terror on the Indian side of the LoC in J&K. Aware of the parlous position he was in, President Musharraf made a 180-degree turn on the ideological or territorial aspect of the J&K question, the so-called 'unfinished business of Partition'. He put forward a formulation for resolving the Kashmir Question—without invoking the 1948-49 UN resolutions that had called for a plebiscite, and to which Pakistan had so tenaciously clung despite grievous and deliberate default on its own part. Yet, wanting to signal that it had not relented on the 'core' issue of Kashmir, Pakistan returned to the charge that India was threatening its lifeline. That it was not merely misappropriating Indus waters in violation of its treaty obligations, but in so doing, was—by building (run-of-the-river) dams—developing strategic capability to hurt Pakistan, by drying up these rivers or causing floods![4]

*

The complex network of Indus basin barrages, sub-basin transfer links, and irrigation canals, had been developed over the previous century as a single, integrated irrigation system, spread over 26 million acres of land,[5] with canal colonies established to settle farmers on hitherto arid lands. The major part of the development took place in what became West Punjab, with its vast revenue-yielding crown lands. What became East Punjab was considerably smaller in area, and less favoured, as it fell within the territory of the princely states of Patiala, Kapurthala, Faridkot, Jind and Malerkotla—to which the Raj felt no special obligation, as the revenues generated would enrich these princely exchequers, but not its own.

On 15 August 1947, 21 million acres of the Indus irrigation system fell into Pakistan, and only 5 million acres in India.[6] The canals in Pakistan used 64.4 maf (million acre-feet) of water as against 8.3 maf flowing through the Indian canals. The rest escaped to the sea. This bias in distribution was in conformity with an all-India pattern of 'imperial preference'—with the princely states receiving step-motherly treatment in matters such as irrigation and railway development—except when geography dictated otherwise.

The 'lifeline' issue was first raised when East Punjab withdrew supplies to the Central Bari Doab and Dipalpur Canals in West Punjab, on 1 April 1948—a day after the expiry of the Standstill Agreement[7] on canal waters. Pakistan had been alerted by East Punjab, two days before the deadline, that the interim agreement was due to expire in a couple of days, but the West Punjab administration failed to respond.

The supplies cut-off amounted to 6 per cent of the total canal flow to Pakistan, and did not affect the large flows serving dozens of its other canals. In any case, talks resumed on 30 April 1948, and a new agreement was ratified by India and Pakistan on 4 May, according to which India was required to release sufficient waters to the Pakistani basin areas in return for annual payments from the government of Pakistan. In the meantime, Nehru upbraided East Punjab for acting unilaterally and cutting off supplies. But the state government argued that had it allowed canal flows to continue, without any bilateral understanding, Pakistan may have claimed this to be an inherent right. Chaudhury Mohammad Ali, Pakistan's secretary general, was later to write that while East Punjab showed 'Machiavellian duplicity', West Punjab displayed 'neglect of duty, complacency and lack of common prudence' in failing to renew the original Standstill Agreement in time.[8]

The 1948 canal-water dispute triggered complex negotiations culminating in the Indus Waters Treaty between India and Pakistan. Brokered by the World Bank, the 168.5 to 170 maf average annual flow of the Indus was divided approximately 80:20,[9] with Pakistan getting the lion's share in the form of the entire flows of the three western rivers—the Indus, Jhelum and Chenab—save for some limited Indian uses in J&K. The Indus discharge as given, also incorporated the River Kabul's then considerable flow of some 27 maf of water (now somewhat lower), possibly on account of limited Afghan uses. India was, in turn, allocated the entire waters of the three smaller eastern rivers—the Ravi, Beas and Sutlej—barring some minor uses for Pakistan, from the Ravi.

India had to struggle to get western Rajasthan included as an integral part of the Indus basin, and so get a fair share of water. It finally allocated 8 maf for Rajasthan out of its entitlement from the eastern rivers.

Pakistan, on its part, received generous assistance from a Bank-led consortium, on top of India being called upon to pay 62 million pounds sterling to Pakistan[10] towards replacement works to be built by it, within a transitional period of ten years, ending in 1970. With this settlement, Pakistan was able to develop a completely independent irrigation system, with storages at Tarbela (Indus) and Mangla (Jhelum). On the other side, India was able to carry forward and complete Bhakra-Nangal, and go on to build the Pong and Thein dams (on the Beas and Ravi), as well as other storages. Assurance of the Indus waters was an important factor, making way for the Green Revolution that followed in India.

There was added reason for India's sense of urgency in concluding the Indus Treaty. The predominantly farming families streaming into India—seeking refuge from West Punjab on account of Partition—needed to be viably resettled. While the refugees who went from East to West Punjab could move into flourishing canal colonies, there was no comparable comfort on the Indian side. Both surface and tubewell irrigation were limited, and needed to be rapidly expanded. The Bhakra-Nangal system was speeded up to provide the required water and energy; delay would have proved costly. Few realize or remember the vital role played by Bhakra-Nangal in helping mitigate—if not overcome—the refugee problem in rural Punjab and Haryana, which could otherwise have led to massive political and social unrest.

*

The Indus Waters Treaty was signed on 19 September 1960, in Karachi, by Jawaharlal Nehru—the prime minister of India, and Field Marshal Mohammad Ayub Khan—the president of Pakistan. Subsequently, despite wars, proxy wars, cross-border terror, and alarms and excursions of every kind—when everything else failed—the Indus commissioners (as dictated by the treaty) have met, and the Indus Treaty has worked. For a while, the 'lifeline' problem, it seemed, was demonstrably laid to rest. Recent events, however, have sadly sought to fan those embers.

India's rights on the three western rivers are clearly and specifically set out in the treaty. All pre-1947 irrigation and hydro-electric systems, flood moderation and navigational uses in J&K were protected. Over and beyond that, India was permitted to develop additional irrigation of 1.34 million acres in J&K, against which only 6,42, 477 acres has been achieved, leaving a balance of some half a million acres that can still be irrigated. Further, India is allowed 3.60 maf of storage (0.40 maf on the Indus, 1.50 maf on the Jhelum and 1.70 maf on the Chenab). This, in turn, has been categorized sector-wise: 2.85 maf for conservation storage (divided into 1.25 maf for 'general storage' and 1.60 maf for 'power storage'), and an additional 0.75 maf for 'flood storage'.[11] These have been further defined in location-specific terms, as being on 'main rivers' and 'tributaries'.

The fact is that until today, India is yet to attain these permissible limits in any sector and category of usage, and has built practically no 'storage' capacity as opposed to run-of-the-river 'pondages'.

The treaty binds India to inform or consult Pakistan on planned withdrawals and works on the western rivers, and to ensure no harm or derogation of its water rights. There had, at last count, been at least twenty-seven occasions when such information had been passed, or consultations arranged. The record shows that Pakistan raised objections in virtually all cases—even with regard to mini/micro hydro-electric plants with miniscule pondages—in respect of which adverse comments were passed and the matter dropped, only if below 1 megawatt (Mw) capacity. The objections were generally qualitative (treaty violations) without quantification and substantiation. In other words, though dressed up as design or engineering objections or queries, the objective was political, and the motivation apparently intended to delay—if not deny— progress that would have primarily benefitted J&K.

The treaty draws a clear distinction between storage dams and run-of-the-river projects. The latter only generate power, and return the waters to the river, after passing through the turbines, precluding any diversion. Hence run-of-the-river schemes are non-consumptive, unlike irrigation projects that divert water. A sharp distinction is also to be made between 'storages' and 'pondages'. Both run-of-the-river and storage schemes have, of necessity, a 'dead storage'—which is essentially a silt trap that gradually fills, over the life of the dam, without affecting power output, as there is no loss of 'live storage' that is drawn down and refilled diurnally.

These categories, their definition and purpose, are meticulously spelt out in Annexure D of the treaty, leaving no scope for ambiguity. It is necessary to spell out these details, as many critics and so-called experts who write and speak on the water issue have not read the treaty, or wilfully misrepresent it. Thus, the annexure states:

(a) 'Dead Storage' means that portion of the storage which is not used for operational purposes and 'Dead Storage Level' means the level corresponding to Dead Storage.
(b) 'Live Storage' means all storage above Dead Storage.
(c) 'Pondage' means Live Storage of only sufficient magnitude to meet fluctuations in the discharge of the turbines arising from variations in the daily and the weekly loads of the plant.

(d) 'Full Pondage Level' means the level corresponding to the maximum Pondage provided in the design in accordance with Paragraph 8(c).

(e) 'Surcharge Storage' means uncontrollable storage occupying space above the Full Pondage Level.

(f) 'Operating Pool' means the storage capacity between Dead Storage Level and Full Pondage Level.

(g) 'Run-of-the-River Plant' means a hydro-electric plant that develops power without Live Storage as an integral part of the plant, except for Pondage and Surcharge Storage.

(h) 'Regulating Basin' means the basin whose only purpose is to even out fluctuations in the discharge from the turbines arising from variations in the daily and the weekly loads of the plant.

(i) 'Firm Power' means the hydro-electric power corresponding to the minimum mean discharge at the site of a plant [...]

(j) 'Secondary Power' means the power, other than Firm Power, available only during certain periods of the year.[12]

Since run-of-the-river plants require diurnal storage to generate peak power during given morning and evening hours, the volume of water ponded during any seven-day period 'shall be delivered into the river below the Plant during the same seven-day period'.[13]
Further:

> [...] in any one period of 24 hours within that seven-day period, the volume delivered into the river below the Plant shall be not less than 30%, and not more than 130%, of the volume received in the river above the Plant during the same 24-hour period [...][14]

This would normally preclude 'flooding' or 'drying up' of the river downstream, as feared by Pakistan.

India has complete entitlement to the entire waters of the Sutlej, Beas and Ravi, leaving Pakistan with no rights on them— excepting for no more than 100 acres of irrigation from the Basantar, a tributary of the Ravi. Despite this, India released as much as 4.85 maf on an average (mostly flood waters), down the Sutlej and Ravi, into Pakistan, between 1990 and 2002 . This has since declined to about 3 maf[15] following completion of the Thein dam on the Ravi, with the balance still escaping, on account of the dispute between East Punjab and Haryana over the Sutlej-Yamuna Link.

Additionally, the full irrigation potential of the Indira Gandhi (Rajasthan) Canal is still to be attained. This is due to the problems of canal colonization, and the inevitably slow process of creating a new breed of non-traditional farmers in desert settlements, entailing sand-dune reclamation, new cropping patterns and acclimatization.

Nevertheless, critics in J&K feel that the state has had to bear the burden of the Indus Treaty—with the benefits flowing into Punjab, Haryana, Rajasthan, Delhi, and other parts of the country. Abrogation of the treaty has sometimes been advocated. This is a mistaken view, as J&K and India as a whole, have yet to utilize their full entitlement. Moreover, talk of abrogating the treaty would gratuitously revive and justify Pakistan's 'lifeline' argument.

*

India moved towards the Green Revolution in the 1970s. Pakistan was, however, for long, losing land on account of over-irrigation, a lack of vertical and horizontal drainage and poor water management. Alarm over mounting seepage from unlined canals resulted in growing waterlogging and salinity. A call for assistance from the World Bank and America resulted in a massive SCARP (Salinity Control and Reclamation Programme) that entailed the construction of horizontal and vertical drainage—the latter through public tubewells. This has helped improve matters, but much remains to be done.

A few years ago, this writer was a participant in a leading Indo-Pakistan Track-II Dialogue in Bhurban, near Murree, to which agricultural experts had been invited from both countries, to discuss the agricultural situation and possible agricultural cooperation. Representing the two sides were vice-chancellors of the (West) Punjab Agricultural University in Lyallpur (now Faisalabad) and the (East) Punjab Agricultural University, Ludhiana. What was said presented a striking contrast. The Pakistani expert lamented the decline in agricultural research and extension in his country, and spoke of indifferent yields other than for cotton and kinnoo. The Indian scientist, in turn, spoke of the Green Revolution in (East) Punjab,[16] the introduction of new seed varieties (that were being smuggled to Pakistan), and so forth.

Both sides expressed keen interest in cooperation and exchange of researchers at various levels but, at the end of the day, the upshot was that Pakistan was constrained to maintain a standoff until the 'core issue', Kashmir, was settled. This was the refrain time and again, on other issues too—such as exchanges in the field of technological education and IT, and trade and investment. Ideology, as we have seen, has invaded every field in Pakistan. It has been Kashmir or nothing.

The discourse on water, in Pakistan, is full of alleged Indian malafides which, they claim, has been the root cause of every problem or shortcoming in Pakistan. Unbridled charges of 'theft' of water have been levelled against India, combined with dire warnings that it must stop 'water terror', and 'water must flow or else blood will flow'. This campaign peaked, but did not end, with the filling of the Baglihar pond in August 2008, when India—under certain compulsions—overstepped the stipulated treaty time-limit for filling operations. It resulted in a shortfall of the specified 55,000 cusec minimum flow, downstream of Marala, for one or two days. Pakistan controverted these figures, both in terms of time and quantum of flows, but the matter was amicably settled thereafter, and mutually treated as closed.

Sensing that matters were liable to get out of hand, the then foreign minister of Pakistan, Shah Mohammad Qureshi, had stated in a widely broadcast statement that India was not stealing water, but Pakistan was wasting a third of the supplies delivered to it. Qureshi remarked:

> We tend to exaggerate our differences with India and pass the buck. India supplies 104 maf of water but the water that is consumed in Pakistan is 70 million acre feet. Where are the 34 million acre feet of water going? Is India stealing that water from you? No, it is not. Please do not fool yourselves and do not misguide the nation. We are mismanaging that water.[17]

The Pakistan Indus waters commissioner, Jamaat Ali Shah, also denied that India was stealing water. However, he added, India was not providing the information required under the 1960 pact, to prove that it was not violating the treaty. India, he continued, denied any intention to cut off water to Pakistan, and maintained that it had complied with the treaty. But 'as with other issues between the two countries, mistrust runs high'. The remark caused many unkind critics to mock Jamaat Ali Shah's alleged partiality towards India. He was later served with an 'exit control order' (which only reached him after he had left for Canada for personal reasons) and subjected to an inquiry for alleged negligence in not blocking India's 45 Mw Nimoo Bazgo project that was said to have brought comfort to Indian troops in Siachen! Shah was, however, exonerated some years later.

*

Baglihar is a run-of-the-river peaking project on the Chenab, above the Salal Dam, and over 110 kilometres from the Pakistan border. It has an installed capacity of 450 Mw, and a live pondage of 37.5 million cubic metres of water, the balance of the gross 39.6 million cubic metres pondage being dead storage. Its commissioning was delayed by a Pakistani challenge placed before a Swiss neutral expert, Raymond Lafitte, under the Indus Waters Treaty dispute resolution provisions.

With the addition of more turbines and some other minor works, Baglihar-II can generate another 450 Mw of secondary power for three or four monsoon months. Pakistan was informed as far back as 1992 that India planned to go ahead with Baglihar. Work commenced in 2000, on the basis of a twenty-five-year flow data that had been communicated to—and never challenged by—Islamabad. The minimum average flow of the Chenab at Baglihar, in January, is 125 cubic metres per second (cumecs), and the dam is designed to pass a maximum flood of 12,600 cumecs. It was only later, in January 2005, that objections were pressed, and actually specified. The six objections raised variously related to pondage, gated spillways, under sluices and the level of the intake channel. But the punch line was this—that the dam would be able to store/ release a sufficient quantum of water to flood Pakistan, or dry up the river for several days.

These fears are fanciful, as all the parameters conform to the treaty, and flooding or drying up of the river (and Pakistan's anti-tank ditches) is simply not possible. The fallacy lies in the adding of dead storage to live pondage, and assuming malafide intent that would, in fact, primarily and adversely affect the Indian villages and infrastructure along the Chenab Valley and the Salal Dam. Indeed, Pakistan is so far away that any flood waters would dissipate before they reached the border. The quantum of pondage that can be released, juxtaposed against the geometry of the river downstream of the dam, should remove fears of flooding.

The same argument of flooding or drying up the river has been used to stymie other Indian proposals too—be it Salal, Uri or Dulhasti. In short, Pakistan's argument appears to be that every dam can be used as a strategic weapon of war. This is perverse reasoning and would defy every provision of the Indus Treaty.

Indian experts were of the view that, if another couple of rounds of talks had been held, after Pakistan quantified its objections, maybe convergence would have followed. Unfortunately, Pakistan insisted on resorting to the difference-dispute settlement mechanism under the treaty.

*

The Jhelum was traditionally used for navigation, and for floating timber down to Sopore and Baramulla, before the river silted in more recent times. The Tulbul project was accordingly designed to retard the Jhelum flood within the natural confines of the Wular lake, through which the river passes. Instead of emptying swiftly with the receding flood, a control structure at the lake's exit would have permitted steady releases of this natural pondage—of some 0.3 maf of water—through the lean months from October to May. This would have reduced silt flows downstream, to the benefit of both the Uri and Mangla projects in India and Pakistan, respectively, and augmented their power output. However, Pakistan argues that Tulbul would be a storage dam, and is therefore barred by the Indus Treaty. India looks on it as no more than a flood-retardation device. Thanks to Pakistan, Tulbul remains in limbo.

Turn to Kishanganga, or the Neelum—as this tributary of the Jhelum is known in Pakistan. Rising near Gurez, the river flows through J&K and then crosses the LoC to enter PAK, before falling into the Jhelum near Muzaffarabad. The original Indian project envisaged a 75-metre-high concrete dam on the Kishanganga at Gurez, at an altitude of about 8,000 feet. This would have stored 0.14 maf of water, and diverted flows southwards—through a

22-kilometre tunnel—into a Jhelum tributary, the Madmati Nala, that flows into the Wulur Lake. The water diversion proposed was modest; but, given a height of about 600 metres, an installed capacity of 330 Mw was planned.

The quantum of displacement and the environmental impact within India's Gurez Valley, however, raised sensitive issues. Local objections resulted in scrapping the high dam and its replacement by a smaller run-of-the-river project. (An incidental advantage of the originally conceptualized Kishanganga storage and diversion would have been to flush the Wulur Lake and help rejuvenate this important waterbody.)

India communicated its intention of going ahead with the Kishanganga project in June 1992, and Pakistan responded soon after, listing three objections. The first was that inter-tributary diversions are barred, and that water drawn from a given river must be returned to that same river. The second was that existing Pakistani uses must be protected, and India's Kishanganga project would deprive it of 27 per cent of the river's natural flows. This would inflict injury to its existing 1,33,000 hectares of irrigation in the Neelum Valley, as also to a 969-Mw Neelum-Jhelum hydro station on which construction had commenced at Nowshera. The third objection related to certain design features of the dam.[18]

The Indian response was that the treaty is unambiguously in its favour:

> Where a plant is located on a tributary of the Jhelum on which Pakistan has an agricultural use or hydro-electric use, the water released below the plant may be delivered, if necessary, into another Tributary but only to the extent that the then existing agricultural use or hydro-electric use by Pakistan on the former Tributary would not be adversely affected.[19]

A plain reading of this would suggest that inter-tributary diversions in the Jhelum basin are permitted, and that only the 'then existing' agricultural and hydro-electric uses shall be protected.

The next question was what 'then existing' uses implied? Pakistan had to substantiate, and not merely assert, 1,33,000 hectares of irrigation. Hard evidence on this was not forthcoming. Also, what was the stage of construction or operation of the

Nowshera hydro-electric plant, and what were its specifications? A planned use would be a future use, not an existing one. In any event, the Neelum catchment below the Kishanganga dam river receives several influent flows that make the discharge at Nowshera larger than the mean flows at Gurez.

Both sides were to visit the other's Kishanganga/Neelum site prior to the deadline Pakistan set, before it formally called for reference of this 'difference' to a neutral expert. It was willing to consider an extension of time only if India agreed to halt construction on the Kishanganga project. India declined to entertain the proposition, knowing from past experience—as at Tulbul—that delay means denial. Pakistan, thereupon, took the matter to a court of arbitration.

The arbitral award, delivered in two instalments in 2013, permitted India to go ahead with the project—subject to guaranteeing Pakistan a minimum discharge of nine cumecs for its Neelum-Jhelum hydro-electric project and ecological needs further downstream. But it reversed the neutral expert's ruling on Baglihar, subject to review after seven years. Both sides are now going ahead on the basis of the arbitral award.[20]

However, Pakistan has other grievances too. Its foreign secretary, Salman Bashir, served India a non-paper when he met with his Indian counterpart in Delhi on 25 February 2010. He listed five complaints: Indus Treaty violations, an unwillingness to resolve issues, ongoing project concerns, deforestation in the upper watersheds and glacial melt because of human (presumably military) activity. Most of these objections have been discussed in this chapter, and lack credible evidence of malafides.

As for the impact of human intervention on Siachen by Indian armed forces: today, it is minimal, on account of a number of technological innovations introduced to minimize ecological damage. Precise areas of soil erosion on account of deforestation have been indicated; joint water-discharge measurements have been advocated; and a telemetry system to convey real time information has been proposed, but remains to be costed and implemented. This is not a treaty violation; rather it could be a confidence-building measure.

It has also been argued that allocating the entre flows of the eastern rivers to India could potentially leave these three rivers high and dry, as they cross the border into Pakistan. This may be so in theory, but the treaty mandated replacement works in Pakistan, to which India made a substantial financial contribution. The expectation, then, was that Pakistan would replace a minimal ecological flow downstream of its border through these replacement works. It would, in any event, guarantee a minimum ecological flow below the Kotri Barrage in Sindh, to maintain the health of the Indus delta, mangrove and coastal ecology. The default lies within Pakistan itself. Indeed, Sindh has bitterly complained of consistent violations by (West) Punjab of minimal ecological flows as nationally agreed.

*

India will need to build storages to utilize the additional irrigation permitted under the Indus Treaty. J&K also has considerable hydro potential that should be exploited for the benefit of the state, and for the country as a whole. Projects on a Chenab tributary such as Sewa (120 Mw), Sawalkote (600 Mw), Bursar (1200 Mw), Pakal Dul (1000 Mw) and Kirthai I and II (600 Mw); Parnai (37.5 Mw) on the Poonch river; Ujh (96 Mw) on a Ravi tributary; and several smaller, and mini/micro schemes are on the anvil, in the state and central sectors. These, if sanctioned and initiated, will stimulate development and employment in J&K, and help open up remote areas by providing connectivity.

A 1987 river resource reassessment, by the Central Electricity Authority, placed J&K's identified and unutilized hydro potential at 14,146 Mw (installed capacity)[21]—17 per cent of this on the Indus spread over a number of small schemes, 19 per cent on the Jhelum and over 63 per cent on the Chenab (some of this in Himachal).

The Indus Commission is required to submit an annual report to the two governments before 1 June each year, and may, at the request of either commissioner, undertake a tour of inspection of such works or sites, as may be considered necessary, for ascertaining the facts. This is in addition to the duty enjoined on the commission to undertake 'a general tour of inspection' every five years, to ascertain facts pertaining to the rivers and works thereon.[22] It would be in the fitness of things that this right is exercised, as developments are taking place, or planned, or under discussion—in the Northern Areas, in PAK, and in Pakistan proper—as these may also require closer understanding and public airing.

Pakistan has an entitlement to 140 maf of the total 170 maf discharge of the Indus system. Inter-provincial discords and planning delays have come in the way of their fuller utilization through further storages. The Kalabagh dam (gross storage of 7.9 maf) has been stalled for years by NWFP and Sindh, which see Punjab benefitting at their cost. A run-of-the-river Ghazi Barotha hydro-electric project came on-stream in 2004, but the huge US$8.5 billion 4500 Mw Diamer-Basha storage dam on the Chitral-Gilgit-Baltistan border ran into interstate hassles at the feasibility stage. Though that matter has been more or less resolved, construction requires lifting the Karakoram Highway to a higher elevation to avoid flooding. This is a considerable and complex project in itself, since aggravated by a massive lake created by a glacial-debris dam formation at Attabad on the Hunza River that has blocked the watercourse since May 2010. A dam-break has been averted but the situation remains perilous despite construction of an artificial spillway. Funding the Bhasha dam has been a problem, though the project is said to be moving forward slowly.

The Bunji dam (7100 Mw), 83 kilometres from Gilgit, is meanwhile undergoing feasibility studies by an international consortium.

The Mangla dam, on the Jhelum, was completed as part of the transition works under the Indus Treaty. It had a gross storage of 4.5 maf, but suffered heavy siltation that reduced its effective capacity. Pakistan, accordingly, contracted the China International Water and Electric Corporation in June 2004, to raise the height of the dam by 30 feet to store an additional 2.88 maf of water, and yield some 12 per cent more energy. The project was calculated to displace 44, 000 persons, and 15, 780 acres of land was acquired for a new resettlement colony. A bridge across the Jhelum and an 18-kilometre Mirpur by-pass are also part of the compensation package. These were important adjuncts, as failure to pay adequate compensation and provide alternative connectivity for villages displaced and divided by the Mangla lake in the 1960s, had led to a mass exodus of marginalized Mirpuris to the UK.

What triggered far greater anxiety for a time was the investigation being pursued by Pakistan's WAPDA (Water and Power Development Authority), amidst much controversy, of a giant Skardu dam on the Indus, at Katzarah, downstream of Skardu. The 35 maf Skardu Dam reservoir is believed to have huge hydro potential, and its driving force—Fatehullah Khan, former chairman of the Indus River System Authority and chair of WAPDA's Technical Committee on Water Resources—reportedly believed that the Skardu project could be more than a substitute for the Kalabagh and Bhasha dams, and an answer to Pakistan's long-term water requirements.

However, this mega-dam, if ever built, is likely to submerge the entire Skardu bowl and Shigar Valley leading up to K2, displacing a population of around 300,000,[23] and possibly half the Balti population in Gilgit-Baltistan (which might then seek refuge in Ladakh). It will all but drown and obliterate the finest in Balti culture and heritage. Consequently, when the project was announced, Balawaristan nationalists and Pakistani conservationists were predictably up in arms, while the military objected as the proposed project would submerge Pakistan's strategic roads, airfields and military supply lines in the region. The Skardu dam may never move beyond the drawing board.

But India should want to know more about this, and about other Pakistani projects across the LoC in J&K. It should seek site visits, if necessary, to ascertain the facts, and assess the situation. There has already been much demographic change in politically-closed Gilgit-Baltistan (or the former Northern Areas) to the detriment of the local Shia, Ismaili and Sufi communities.

*

Following Partition and the canal-waters dispute, men of goodwill and experience like David Lilienthal—former chairman of the much-admired Tennessee Valley Authority, and Eugene Black—former president of the World Bank, pleaded that even if India had been partitioned, the Indus should not suffer the same fate. They urged that the Indus irrigation network should be preserved and further developed, as a unified and integrated system, under joint management. This would have been an ideal and optimal solution. But bitterness and strife had so engulfed the region that this was politically infeasible.

The Indus Waters Treaty that was negotiated was admittedly sub-optimal, despite the two governments '[…] being equally desirous of attaining the most complete and satisfactory utilization of the waters of the Indus system of rivers […]', as stated in its Preamble. However, after spelling out the details of the settlement, Article VII of the treaty addressed the issue of 'Future Cooperation'. The article proposed another and more rational way for the two sides to seek water security. It points to a 'common interest in the optimum development of the Rivers', and calls upon both sides 'to cooperate, by mutual agreement, to the fullest possible extent. […] in undertaking engineering works in the Rivers'.[24]

The 1960 treaty was a crisis-management, conflict-resolution arrangement that divided the waters so that immediate problems could be set aside, and development plans could move forward. It has served that purpose well enough, but leaves behind a large untapped potential in the three western rivers—these are allocated to Pakistan (barring certain uses to India), but the upper catchments are under Indian control. This potential needs to be thoroughly surveyed, and could thereafter be harnessed through joint investment, construction, management and control.

Pakistan cannot continue to deny India its limited entitlement in the western rivers, and also freeze all further development, if it wants to grasp what could be a far larger prize—by way of additional storage, flood moderation and hydro power—which both could share. India, too, could benefit from cooperative drainage arrangements in the middle and lower Indus basins. Were this to happen, Pakistan would not even have to think of grotesque schemes such as the Skardu dam that would spell doom to a proud civilization.

Article XII of the treaty states that its provisions '[…] may from time to time be modified by a duly ratified Treaty concluded for that purpose between the two Governments'.[25] Thus an Indus-II could be constructed on the foundations of Indus-I.

When the original treaty was being negotiated, India suggested a 2.5-maf storage on the Chenab at Dhiangarh,[26] with a tunnel at Mahru to divert waters to the Ravi and Beas for delivery to Pakistan below Ferozepur, in lieu of some other replacement works. That was totally unacceptable to Pakistan at the time. Would it be acceptable to Pakistan today, if feasible, and were it to offer promise of adding to net water availability on both sides? The Chenab could perhaps store more water in its upper reaches— the Indus has not really been surveyed from the point of view of storage. There may be little or nothing there. Do we know? That both sides could benefit from Indus-II is certain. What is not known for sure is the quantum of those benefits, and the costs involved.

*

With climate change, we have entered an uncertain hydrological era. Frontiers and borders have been rendered irrelevant in the new calculus. Glaciers are in retreat both in the Karakoram—one of the most glaciated regions in the world, with the largest glaciers outside Antarctica—as well as in Tibet, which is where the Indus and Sutlej rise. The Tibetan Plateau is underlain by 'tjale', or permafrost, that shows signs of thawing—partly on account of mistaken Chinese efforts in using the northwest Tibetan range lands to produce more grain, meat and milk, in order to feed its military and other immigrant settlers from the Han region. This effort was abandoned once its damaging consequences were noted and it became obvious that the delicate balance of complex weather and moisture patterns was getting affected, leading to enhanced glacier melt and thawing permafrost. This, in turn, could increase flows in the Indus basin for some decades, before declining sharply over the ensuing years, as the body of ice shrinks. These developments are also believed to have triggered subtle shifts in rainfall patterns, giving rise to the possibility of episodic bursts of aberrant precipitation in some areas.

The consequent uncertainties underline the need for maximizing conservation storage within the limits of prudence and sustainability. Climate change will not respect boundaries. Both Pakistan and northwest India, as wards of the Indus, therefore have a common interest—making a concerted effort to study glacial behaviour, and insuring against future hazards from diminished glacial melt and stream flows, and from larger sedimentation and debris/glacial lake hazards.

*

Dr Manmohan Singh had stated in 2005 that J&K's boundaries could not be redrawn, but soft borders could render them increasingly irrelevant. At a meeting with the Editors' Guild of India in Delhi, on 18 April 2005, President Musharraf went along with this proposition, with the rider that the LoC as a permanent boundary could not be a final and lasting solution by itself.[27] He said that the challenge therefore was to find a solution within these three parameters. The president was asked if he would be ready to explore Indus-II as part of the answer to his conundrum. He replied in the affirmative, provided confidence was first assured on Indus-I.

Soft borders, trade, tourism and the management of Indus-II could, with other blossoming relationships, create cross-border mechanisms in J&K that foster interlocking jurisdictions on both sides of the LoC, without derogation of the existing twin sovereignties. Indus-II could therefore be fed into the current peace process as a means of both defusing current political strains over Indus-I, and insuring against climate change. Moreover, it could reinforce the basis for a lasting solution to the J&K question— by helping transform relationships across the LoC, and reinventing it as a bridge, from its present avatar as a prickly and dangerous divide. Dr Manmohan Singh hinted at his willingness to explore this line of resolution as the basis of a new era of cooperation in all fields.

Speaking on the occasion of the inauguration of an Amritsar-Nankana Sahib bus service, in 2006, here is an excerpt of what Dr Manmohahn Singh said:

> […] A step-by-step approach has to be adopted given the inherent difficulties involved in finding practical solutions. I suggest that both sides should begin a dialogue with the people in their areas of control to improve the quality of governance so as to give the people on both sides a greater chance of leading a life of dignity and self-respect.

I have often said that borders cannot be redrawn but we can work towards making them irrelevant—towards making them just lines on a map. People on both sides of the LoC should be able to move more freely and trade with one another.

I also envisage a situation where the two parts of Jammu & Kashmir can, with the active encouragement of the governments of India and Pakistan, work out cooperative, consultative mechanisms so as to maximize the gains of cooperation, in solving problems of social and economic development of the region.

The vision that guides us is that the destinies of our peoples are interlinked. That our two countries must therefore devise effective cooperative strategies to give concrete shape and meaning to this shared vision. India sincerely believes that a strong, stable, prosperous and moderate Pakistan is in the interest of India and entire South Asia. We are sincerely committed to the prosperity, unity, development and well-being of Pakistan. We want good neighbourly relations. We want all the people of South Asia to live a life of dignity and self-respect. When our neighbours live in peace, we live in peace.

[...] We must move forward. We want to move forward. We need to do much more to create the environment in which we can move forward. It is possible for us to come to a meaningful agreement on issues like Siachen, Sir Creek, Baglihar. We can move forward if all concerned are willing to accept the ground realities; if all concerned take a long view of history and of our destiny. The time has come to leave behind the animosities and the misgivings of the past and to think the unthinkable, of moving together in pursuit of our common objective, of getting rid of chronic poverty, ignorance and disease that still afflict millions of our citizens. India and Pakistan must work together to open up new opportunities of economic cooperation, not only with South Asia, but also with West Asia and Central Asia. Cities like Lahore and Amritsar should once again become throbbing international commercial centres serving the entire region.

Instead of looking at each other as adversaries, we must have the courage to see each other as supporting the other for the realization of a better tomorrow, for all the people of India and Pakistan. I have a vision that the peace-making process must ultimately culminate in our two countries entering into a

Treaty of Peace, Security and Friendship to give meaning and
substance to our quest for shared goals. I make this offer to the
people of Pakistan on this historic occasion. I am sure the
leadership of Pakistan will reciprocate.[28]

That was most sincerely and eloquently spoken. Unfortunately,
even as an agreement appeared in sight, President Musharraf ran
into difficulties at home, stalling further forward movement. He
was subsequently removed, and the successor government, under
Asif Ali Zardari (the late Benazir Bhutto's husband), virtually
disowned the understanding. Nawaz Sharif, the new prime
minister of Pakistan, has again spoken of fostering friendly relations
with India. However, he has to battle fundamentalist, jihadi, Taliban
elements still intent on cross-border terror, and an army afraid of
losing its salience in Pakistan should the 'permanent enemy',
India, be no longer seen as an ever-present threat.

There are hardliners in India, too, and one has to see what
policy framework the current government in Delhi will take.
Cooperation in mapping and combating climate change should be
on the agenda, as also carrying forward the constructive discussions
that have continued through official back channels.

It would be a boon were the Siachen imbroglio to be resolved
by converting the entire region under dispute—between the
Karakoram Pass, K2 and the last demarcated grid reference on the
LoC, NJ 9842—into an international peace park and a site for
scientific research. If the land immediately to the north, in
Shaksgam—illegally ceded by Pakistan to China in 1963—were
added to the peace park, this would be a major step towards a
three-way settlement of an area that has become the focus of a new
Great Game.

*

Activating Article VII ('Future Cooperation') of the treaty could be
the first step in ending what has now become a zero-sum game.
Pakistan, as I've pointed out, has thwarted India's efforts to
maximize its entitlements on the three western rivers; Pakistan, in
turn, is unable to access the full potential of the these rivers
allocated to it by the treaty, since their upper reaches, especially of
the Chenab, lie within India. Under Article VII, both sides could

agree jointly to survey the problems and possibilities of soil conservation, disaster-warning systems and possible storages on both sides of the LoC.

Under the treaty, the Chenab in J&K has almost five times the storage potential allowed to India. The heights of some of the existing Indian dams could perhaps be raised, if technically feasible, to augment power and storage capacity. The costs and benefits could be duly apportioned to the two sides to mutual benefit. If jointly surveyed, investigated, built, managed and overseen by engineers of both sides, there would be no room for mistrust.

Impossible, some would say. But India, Bangaldesh and Bhutan have already tentatively agreed to such a proposition regarding joint investigation and management of projects on the Teesta and the Tipaimukh dam in Manipur within the Ganga-Brahmaputra basin.[29] A start has yet to be made, but the ice has hopefully been broken.

Cooperation need not be confined to the upper catchments, but could be explored and, where feasible, executed all along the line down to the sea, including joint climate-change monitoring, data exchange, interlocking disaster-management systems, joint telemetry readings, discharge and silt observations, soil conservation, mutually reinforcing drainage systems, and so forth. In short, the original hope of optimization could be restored and the Indus basin—from source to sea—be treated as an integrated unit.

Impossible, again, many would exclaim! Imagination and will are needed. Wars begin in the minds of men. So do great ideas that ensure peace has its victories, no less renowned than those of war. In keeping with this grand vision, one must work backwards to see what it is that must or must not be done, here and now, so as not to forfeit the future. Then, armed with this roadmap, we must move forward along the road less travelled.

Given access to the Chenab through joint development, under Article VII, Pakistan will have achieved emotionally—through water cooperation—what it has been unable to achieve through war and terror, with no loss to India. Open borders, cooperation and joint management between the two halves of J&K (on either side of the LoC), and under regimes of greater autonomy, could also give quietus to the stubborn Kashmir question that has defied solution until now.

No one really wished Partition in 1947. Bluff and folly pushed both sides inexorably towards a parting. Even so, it was hoped that, though two siblings might part, once tempers cooled and the dust settled, they would get together again to live—as sovereign nations—but in peace and cooperation. This dream can still be achieved, and nothing would make borders more irrelevant, yet safe and secure, than the fulfilment of the vision of Article VII. Fundamentalism and terror will not disappear overnight. However, a grander vision may overcome that menace, for, walking together, we will discover that the suspect 'other' whom we kept at a distance as a stranger—even an enemy—is but a friend we had not met before.

[Adapted from the paper for 'The Chaophraya Dialogue: The Indus Dispute'. Sponsored by RSIS-APU, Singapore, May 2014]

DECONSTRUCTING PAKISTAN

14

What is Pakistan?
An Inconvenient Truth

For Pakistan, Kashmir is only a mask for the 'core' issue. Haksar was blunt in his discussions with Aziz Ahmed and Bhutto who kept going around the mulberry bush. On not taking back Pakistani nationals of Bangladesh who had declared themselves Pakistanis and opted for repatriation to the West, Haksar averred that Pakistan *had* to accept them, and could not hedge the issue by talking about 'Islamic nationality'. 'What is this concept of nationality without territory?' he asked. 'The days of the Holy Roman Empire are gone long ago'.[1] Again, he asked Aziz Ahmed:

> One hears so much of thousands of years of confrontation. We simply do not understand what is meant by this confrontation and what is the purpose to be served by these pronouncements? Do you speak of it as a matter of history or a projection of the future? [...] Can you produce any speech by our political leaders between 1947 and 1973 ever referring to any confrontation between us? I hope you don't think of yourselves in terms of descendants or inheritors of some political ambitions of thousands of years [...] In Shimla, your President had said confrontation was a matter of the past [...] and he was the author of confrontation which he wanted to bury. But yesterday in a press conference, he referred to a thousand years of confrontation. There is a credibility gap. This must be bridged by you.[2]

Yet again, at a meeting with Bhutto at his residence in Islamabad on 27 July 1973, Haksar pointed to a picture of the Buddha on the wall, and asked the president what he felt about that picture. Bhutto replied he respected the Buddha. Haksar responded:

> Then why do you talk of conflict of a thousand years? Are you in conflict with your own history? Is Pakistan in conflict with its own personality? To talk of confrontation has an impact on the minds and hearts of people in India and Pakistan. It will be picked up by the wrong people in India. Is that a contribution to durable peace in the sub-continent? [...] In Iran, is there a conflict between the period of Cyrus the Great and the post-Islam period? You said the Sindhi language is 5,000 years old. Is there a confrontation in Sindh between the last 1,000 years and the previous 4,000 years?[3]

Bhutto muttered, 'I will say less of it in future,' was embarrassed and confused, then said, 'It was for internal [...]',[4] but did not complete the sentence.

This is the inconvenient truth, as I have mentioned in my preface. Pakistan has cut itself off from its past history and culture, and has sought to reinvent its geography by medieval concepts of Islamic or 'ideological' frontiers—the ummah perhaps? It has remained a rootless entity that Bhutto himself described in his *Myth of Independence* as a 'moth-eaten Pakistan'[5]—not territorially, but conceptually—and morally crippled until it was able to discover its soul. He discarded the myths, distortions, omissions and plain lies that are contained in its state-sponsored textbooks to this day.

Liberal Pakistanis and objective historians are ashamed and horrified by such myth-making. Indeed, the official textbooks of Pakistan that glorify hate against a permanent enemy—'India'—based on a mythical history, geography and sheer lies, constitute a Faustian bargain; Pakistan has created a false identity of itself that is essentially a sorry caricature of what it actually is.

School textbooks follow strict directives issued by the Federal Directorate of Education, and are produced accordingly by the provinces in Urdu, and until lately, not in the provincial languages of Punjabi, Sindhi, Balochi and Pushto. The Kashmir issue and the Indus waters question are largely products of that problematic outlook. In the India-Pakistan Track-II dialogues, our Pakistan colleagues have no answer to this travesty. They are shame-faced and can only plead that amendments are being made to the texts.

There is a very outspoken and courageous critique of these textbooks entitled *The Subtle Subversion*, under the auspices of the Sustainable Development Policy Centre, Islamabad, and edited by A.H. Nayyar and Ahmed Salim, together with such respected historians as Rubina Saigol, Ayesha Jalal, and others. According to A.H. Nayyar, four themes emerge most strongly, as constituting the bulk of the curricula and textbooks of the three compulsory subjects: that Pakistan is for Muslims alone; that Islamic teachings—including compulsory reading and memorization of the Quran—are to be included in every subject, hence to be forcibly taught to all students whatever their faith; that the ideology of Pakistan be internalized as faith, and hate be stoked against Hindus and India; and that students be urged to take the path of jihad and shahadat (martyrdom).

A decade after the publication of *The Subtle Subversion* there has been some—but not too much—of the change Musharraf had once promised.

*

Many scholars forcefully contend with textual evidence that the concept of the 'ideology of Pakistan' did not exist when Pakistan was created. Justice Munir has identified the first time the phrase was coined: in his monograph *From Jinnah to Zia*, he writes:

> The Quaid-i-Azam never used the words 'Ideology of Pakistan'… For fifteen years after the establishment of Pakistan, the Ideology of Pakistan was not known to anybody until in 1962 a solitary member of the Jama'at-I-Islami used the words for the first time when the Political Parties Bill was being discussed. On this, Chaudhry Fazal Elahi, who has recently retired as President of Pakistan, rose from his seat and objected that the 'Ideology of Pakistan' shall have to be defined. The member who had proposed the original amendment replied that the 'Ideology of Pakistan was Islam'.[6]

Thus it is clear that the phrase 'ideology of Pakistan' had no historical basis in the Pakistan movement.[7] For upholders of the 'Ideology of Pakistan', the existence of Pakistan was defined only in relation to Hindus, and hence the Hindus had to be painted as negatively as possible. Textbooks used in schools prior to the

1970s did not contain this hatred, and included objective references to the Buddha, the Mauryas, Gandhi, etc.

After the 1970s, Indo-Pakistan history and geography were replaced with 'Pakistan studies', and Pakistan was defined as an Islamic state. The history of Pakistan became equivalent to the history of Muslims in the subcontinent, starting with the Arab conquest of Sindh and swiftly jumping to the Muslim conquerors from Central Asia. Simultaneously, the so-called 'ideology of Pakistan' created an ideological straitjacket in which the history of Pakistan, especially that of the 'Pakistan movement' was rewritten.

Pakistan was said to have been created to establish a truly Islamic state in accordance with the tenets of the Quran and Sunnah. The result of defining Pakistan in terms of religion alone is unprecedented in historical narration. A textbook of 'Pakistan studies' states:

> [...] as a matter of fact, Pakistan came to be established for the first time when the Arabs, led by Muhammad-bin-Qasim, occupied Sindh and Multan in the early years of the eighth century, and established Muslim rule in this part of the South-Asian sub-continent. Pakistan under the Arabs comprised the Lower Indus Valley.[8]

The flight of imagination of the author is extraordinary:

> [...] during the 11th century, the Ghaznavid Empire comprised what is now Pakistan and Afghanistan. During the 12th century the Ghaznavids lost Afghanistan, and their rule came to be confined to Pakistan. [...] By the 13th century, Pakistan had spread to include the whole of Northern India and Bengal [...] Under the Khiljis, Pakistan moved further Southward to include a greater part of Central India and the Deccan [...] Many Mongols accepted Islam. As such, Pakistan remained safe for Islam [...] During the 16th century, 'Hindustan' disappeared and was completely absorbed in 'Pakistan' [...] Under Aurangzeb, the Pakistan spirit gathered in strength. This evoked the opposition of the Hindus... After the death of Aurangzeb in 1707, the process of the disintegration of Mughal Rule set in, and weakened the Pakistan spirit [...] The shape of Pakistan in the 18th Century was thus more or less the same as it was under the Ghaznavids in the 11th century.[9]

This is not all. The author continues:

> Shah Waliullah accordingly appealed to Ahmad Shah Durrani, the ruler of Afghanistan and Pakistan to come to the rescue of the Muslims of Mughal India, and save them from the tyrannies of the Marhattas [...] Ahmad Shah Durrani died in 1773, and with his death things became dark for the Muslims, both in 'Pakistan' and Mughal India. In the 'Pakistan' territories the Sikhs raised their head in the Punjab and became a great headache for the successors of Ahmad Shah Durrani [...] In the 'Pakistan' territories, where a Sikh state had come to be established, the Muslims were denied the freedom of religion. The Mujahideen set up an Islamic state in the North-West Frontier Province (NWFP) which was a manifestation of the Pakistan spirit [...] Thus by the middle [of] the 19th century both Pakistan and Hindustan had ceased to exist; instead British India had come into existence. Although Pakistan was created in August 1947, yet except for its name, the present-day Pakistan has existed, as a more or less single entity, for centuries.[10]

The separation of East Pakistan is narrated in a similarly distorted manner in another textbook:

> After the 1965 war, India, with the help of the Hindus living in East Pakistan, instigated the people living there against the people of West Pakistan, and at last in December 1971, herself invaded East Pakistan. The conspiracy resulted in the separation of East Pakistan from us. All of us should receive military training and be prepared to fight the enemy.[11]

The Jinnah Institute, Islamabad, in a policy brief, writes about Pakistan's 'curriculum of hatred'. It points out that these books not only ground nationhood in religion but also 'serve to entrench denominational thinking' that has led to religious bigotry. It goes on to find empirical evidence that links the mindset created in schools to extremism and religious militancy that threaten Pakistan's internal and external security—with 'non-Muslims [being...] depicted as enemies of Islam'; '*Nazariya Pakistan* (the ideology of Pakistan) [dominating] the tone of text'; women being marginalized; and no words being minced in attributing all the ills that ever befell Pakistan on 'Hindus' and India.[12]

The Jinnah Institute notes the irony that, during the Afghan war in the 1980s, the US contributed significantly to this bias by eulogizing the 'good' (read extremist) Muslim as the best fighter against Soviet atheism. The American contribution towards building, financing and supporting the Taliban through Pakistan is a saga of perfidy and folly that has caused huge collateral damage—not least to India— through cross-border terrorism and incidents such as the terror attack on Mumbai. 'Today's extremists are yesterday's children that were raised on a diet of these textbooks'.[13] Elite Pakistanis have access to better books, magazines, TV programmes and travel. But the ordinary Pakistani goes to a local school or madrassa, where he is taught by those already prejudiced by the system, and then goes on to become someone who preaches hatred.

Latterly, a new phrase has crept into the discourse, namely, the concept of the 'ideological frontiers of Pakistan', a non-territorial claim to rights over—or an interest in—other lands peopled by Muslims. In 2002, Rubina Saigol, the well-known historian, had written perceptively on this. In her view:

> History, as taught in the middle and high schools in Pakistan, is the tool of official remembering. It determines how we remember, whom we choose to forget, how we choose to forget and what we must, for our survival in Otherness, remember. [...] History is the official censor that tells the story of the nation by screening out the unacceptable and inventing the digestible... National identity in Pakistan is formed and reformed (in Pakistan Studies) within the interlocking discourses of time (history), space (geography) and power (civics)'. [...] One of the formative aspects of national remembering is the renewal of national enmity. Without enemies surrounding the nation, lurking on its borders, and residing within its core, there is no self either. The self can exist [only] in opposition to its detractors.[14]

This is chilling. However, let India not preen. The 'saffronization' of education became a major issue a decade and more back, and there are continuing dangers that what the then BJP education minister, Murli Manohar Joshi called 'a second war for the country's cultural freedom' might be revived.[15] The matter was documented in '"Communalisation of Education: The History Textbooks Controversy'," published by the Delhi Historians Group in

December 2001. The group noted that textbooks issued by the RSS (Rashtriya Swayamsevak Sangh) for its Saraswati Shishu Mandirs and Vidya Bharati schools treated non-Hindus as 'foreigners', described the 'Muslim period' as one of oppression and decline, and treated mythological figures as real historical characters. These books claimed that the Qutab Minar was built by Samudragupta and that Ashoka's ahimsa spread 'cowardice'. The National Steering Committee on Textbook Evaluation, set up by the National Council for Educational Research and Training (NCERT), concluded that 'the main purpose which these books would serve is gradually to transform the young children into [...] bigoted morons in the garb of instilling in them patriotism'.[16] That tide of intolerance was stemmed, but the evil—including virulent regional chauvinism—persists. Our cultural freedoms in literature, art and other forms of expression remain under threat. But liberal opinion has remained strong and so has it, increasingly, in Pakistan too—a trend that merits applause.

A new phase of Hindu chauvinism is apparent in Narendra Modi's India. Hindutva is being sold as India's true identity by the RSS chief, Mohan Bhagwat. Hate campaigns based on alleged forcible conversions, 'love jihad' and cow slaughter, are being fanned. Modi has lauded Akhand Bharat, and supported the right-wing activist, Dinanath Batra by projecting the view that all science and invention stems from Vedic times.[17]

The action-reaction dynamic between the two fundamentalist forces, and the narrow bigoted cultural nationalism they profess, spells danger. Fortunately, the civilizational roots of India are too deep to be easily shaken by fanatics.

15
Flawed at Birth

Pakistan was flawed at birth by the two-nation theory (with its inherent contradictions) that Jinnah, its grand preceptor, was to discover. India and Pakistan became independent in August 1947. 'India, that is Bharat'[1]—a hoary civilizational entity and concept—was indeed truncated but nevertheless remained forever 'India'.

But whatever happened to Pakistan? It is neither a state nor nation but has chosen to remain a non-state actor. Many, even within that country, worry that it is perhaps a failed state. Hopefully not, for that would cause many problems. It is not in India's interest that Pakistan fails or disintegrates.

Bangladesh was a different matter, a strange add-on to Pakistan. Indeed, as Indian scholar and diplomat Sisir Gupta would tellingly remark, there was no way of drawing a map of (what was then) Pakistan without drawing India,[2] which separated the two wings by 1,800 kilometres. This unique compulsion must have been psychologically embarrassing for some, infuriating for others.

The new Pakistan needed to establish something more than a mere territorial identity. This, it singularly failed to do, and even its given territorial expression suffered amputation when Bangladesh decided to take its destiny into its own hands. With Bangladesh gone, Pakistan became partly whole as a more integrated entity. But, other than the new territorial definition of the residual state, what was 'Pakistan'? It still lacked a real identity, and is yet to discover its soul and come to terms with itself.

The 26/11 Mumbai attack provided vivid proof of its hand in that dastardly crime[3]—as in previous terror strikes—but Islamabad initially remained in denial, moving from one fallback position to another. Unmindful of gathering contradictions, it brazened it out to maintain innocence as a comparable victim of terrorist violence: as a US partner in the War on Terror in Afghanistan, and in its own FATA[4] region.

*

The story of Partition is interwoven with many complex strands, dyed in blood and knitted in emotion. The purpose here is not to delve into that chapter of history, or apportion blame. Suffice it to say that the Muslim League, under Jinnah, propounded the two-nation theory in the run-up to Independence on the premise that the Muslims would remain a permanently persecuted minority within a united 'Hindu India'. Therefore, to Jinnah's mind, reason and equity demanded that an independent Muslim homeland be separately carved out of the Muslim-majority areas of northwestern and eastern India, to constitute Pakistan.

The Congress did not accept the strange logic of the two-nation theory but nonetheless accepted Partition as a lesser evil than delayed independence and prolonged and bitter communal strife. The hope was that once the two countries gained independence they would come together as good neighbours and live side by side in a spirit of peace, amity and cooperation. That hope was regrettably belied, though it remains a cherished goal.

The fallacy in the two-nation theory was that in a highly plural society, the homeland of the erstwhile dominant minority—once elevated to the status of 'ruling majority'—would inevitably spawn a new dominant minority within its bounds. The new state would then confront the same two-nation theory on a lesser scale, with a revision of roles on the basis of nationality, language and/or culture. This is what happened in respect of Bangladesh, and which is now manifest in the demands for privileging the Pakhtun, Baloch or Sindhi identity, on the theory of majority dominance and minority sufferance.

The very proposition is destabilizing and undermines nation building. An analysis of Pakistan school textbooks, *The Subtle Subversion*, discovered that the stereotyped Pakistani was a macho, Muslim, Sunni, Punjabi male. This depiction relegated Ahmadiyyas, Shias, Agha Khans, Nurbakshis and other minority

Muslim denominations, the non-Punjabi nationalities, and women to beyond the pale.[5]

A glaring contradiction inherent in the Partition saga, was that the battle for Pakistan was fought and won in what is today India—in the Muslim-minority provinces of the Raj—that is Delhi, Lucknow, Mumbai, Bhopal, Hyderabad, Patna and elsewhere. It was not fought in the territories that now constitute Pakistan— where the Muslim League was a minority everywhere—namely, Punjab (West), the Frontier, Balochistan and Sindh. Interestingly, even though Muslims were in a majority in these areas, with no reason to fear 'Hindu-Sikh' domination, they kept the Muslim League at bay through a succession of unionist ministries in Punjab, Congress regimes in the Frontier and Balochistan, and for the most part, non-League regimes in Sindh.

Even elsewhere, Muslim fears of Hindu competition and domination were largely urban middle-class concerns. The rural masses—irrespective of faith—by and large shared each other's joys and sorrows whether these were fairs and festivals, famines and floods, or the feudal oppression of Hindu and Muslim zamindars and moneylenders. (Riots were a latter-day phenomenon, politically induced rather than socially motivated.)

So when Partition came, many among the Muslim elite migrated to Pakistan, followed by millions of hapless refugees tragically driven out of their ancestral homes by manufactured hatred, violence and fear. The refugees that came to India were absorbed in the communities within which they settled. Three generations later, those who went to Pakistan are still classified as mohajirs (refugees).

Jinnah, a Westernized, cosmopolitan, liberal statesman who loved the good things in life, and was no more than a nominal Muslim, recognized the danger. For him the two-nation theory, and Islam, had been little more than tactical ploys to garner support for a community that was reluctant to modernize, and was thereby left behind by history, in the despair, shock and grief of political and cultural dethronement in the aftermath of 1857.

Jinnah's very first address to the Pakistan constituent assembly in Karachi on 11 August 1947, delivered just three days before the birth of the homeland he had created, went straight to the point.

Now that Pakistan has been won, Jinnah told his people, they must forget the past. His words bear repetition and should find an echo in India as well:

[…] Any idea of a united India would never have worked, and in my judgement it would have led us to terrific disaster. May be that view is correct; may be it is not; that remains to be seen.

[…] Now, if we want to make this great state of Pakistan happy and prosperous, we should wholly and solely concentrate on the well-being of the people, and especially of the masses and the poor. If you work in cooperation, forgetting the past, burying the hatchet, you are bound to succeed. If you change your past and work together in a spirit that every one of you, no matter to what community he belongs, no matter what relations he had with you in the past, no matter what his colour, caste or creed, is first, second and last a citizen of this State with equal rights, privileges and obligations, there will be no end to the progress you will make.

[…] I cannot emphasise it too much. We should begin to work in that spirit, and in course of time all these angularities of the majority and minority communities, the Hindu community and the Muslim community—because even regards Muslims you have Pathans, Punjabis, Shias, Sunnis and so on, and among the Hindus you have Brahmins, Vaishnavas, Khatris, also Bengalees, Madrasis and so on—will vanish.

Jinnah goes on to say:

You are free, you are free to go to your temples, you are free to go to your mosques, or to any other place of worship in this State of Pakistan. You may belong to any religion, caste, or creed—that has nothing to do with the business of the State. […] We are starting in the days when there is no discrimination, no distinction between one community and the other, no distinction between one caste or creed and another. We are starting with this fundamental principle: that we are all citizens, and equal citizens, of one State.

[…] Now I think we should keep that in front of us as our ideal and you will find, in course of time, Hindus would cease to be Hindus and Muslims would cease to be Muslims, not in the religious sense, because that is the personal faith of each individual, but in the political sense as citizens of the state.[6]

That was a noble speech (delivered too late), and emphasized inclusiveness and equality among people, which is what Islam preaches. From espousing the two-nation theory to emphasizing the idea of equal citizenship, was a historic leap that Jinnah knew was absolutely essential for the very being and survival of Pakistan. Unfortunately, he was isolated. His address was virtually blacked out by the state apparatus[7] and, within months, he himself helplessly repudiated it, returning to the theme that Pakistan's Constitution should be founded on Islam and the Shariat.

Jinnah was by now a sick man, and died in September 1948. His 11 August speech was buried with him and forgotten by a State that feared the wisdom of its founder. The text did not appear in the *Selected Writings of Jinnah*, published in 1967. Liaqat Ali Khan might have trodden his master's path, but he was soon assassinated, and the slide to Islamism began, gathering momentum over time.

In 1953, Pakistan was rocked by anti-Ahmadiyya riots aimed at declaring this Islamic sect a minority community. An inquiry commission was appointed under two justices of the Lahore High Court, Muhammad Munir and M.R. Kayani. In the course of the inquiry, the commission sought the assistance of learned ulema (religious scholars), including leaders of the Jamaat-e-Islami, and was pained to find that the ideal of Pakistani nationhood—set out by the Quaid-e Azam—was unanimously rejected by them as un-Islamic. When the ulema were further asked to explain what Islam is, and who a momin or a Muslim is, Justices Munir and Kayani noted:

> [...] it was a matter of infinite regret to us that the ulema whose first duty should be to have settled views on this subject, were hopelessly disagreed among themselves [...The net result of all of this is that] neither Shias nor Sunnis nor Deobandis nor Ahl-i-Hadith nor Barelvis are Muslims [...][8]

Five Thousand Years of Pakistan by Feroz Khan Noon (the seventh prime minister of Pakistan), which spoke of Mohenjodaro and Taxila, was similarly mothballed for decades—as were those actual, wonderful excavation sites—because Pakistan had to have an Islamic lineage with no non-Muslim foundations or associations. Hence, as *The Subtle Subversion* notes, Muhammad bin Qasim was named the first proto-Pakistani,[9] but the true prototype was Mohammad Ghori![10] This startling denial of history and common sense left Pakistan bereft of historical and cultural moorings. Later still, Ayub Khan was to try and turn Pakistan's back on South Asia, and don a Middle Eastern identity by joining Iran and Turkey in the Regional Cooperation for Development (RCD) association.[11]

More recently, Aitzaz Ahsan, the well-known lawyer and politician, in his book, *The Indus Saga and the Making of Pakistan*[12], sought to theorize a unique racial and cultural personality for Pakistan, asserting that the northwest of the subcontinent, comprising the valley of the Indus and its major tributaries, has always been distinct from India.

Essentially, all of India's history pre-1947 is intrinsically Pakistan's very own history, too, and a proud one at that. But the laboured efforts to repudiate or reinterpret its history, geography and culture have conceptually orphaned the very idea of Pakistan, gratuitously leaving it with no more than a precarious post-AD 1000, and highly selective regional Islamic history at best. This has lent substance to the very real and continuing contemporary query as to 'where and how and why and what' is Pakistan that has taken refuge in a nonsense world of its own making.

*

Given this self-proclaimed lack of anchorage or rootedness, it is no surprise then that Pakistan has found it so difficult to frame and uphold a Constitution, or to build a cohesive federalism.

To counter East Pakistan, the four provinces of West Pakistan were, for a time, unceremoniously herded into what was termed 'One Unit'.[13] The FATA areas in the far northwest, bordering Afghanistan, are still something of a no-man's land where many constitutional provisions do not apply; nor have they been integrated into Pakistan. Likewise, while the Muzaffarabad region is described as 'Azad Kashmir', the Northern Areas are neither part of it nor of Pakistan, and are not an autonomous region either.

This huge expanse, with 1.5 million or more people, is in limbo and remains one of the last 'pure' colonies in the world, with pathetically few democratic rights.

The quip goes that while states have armies, the Pakistan army has a state. This goes back to the negativism of the two-nation theory. When Pakistan was achieved, the 'ideology of Pakistan' was (and has long remained) little more than being 'the other' to 'Hindu' India. This early Islamist posture centred on winning J&K in order to complete the unfinished business of Partition, and perhaps establishing a new ideological frontier for Pakistan.

Consequently, a very recent critique of Pakistan offers an acute analysis of the country's pathology. According to the scholar C. Christine Fair, no amount of militarization and preparedness can address 'Pakistan's neuralgic existential fear of India, and its resistance to the prospect of Indian hegemony'. She concludes:

> Pakistan may have legitimate security concerns, but at the root of its revisionism is not security, but rather, deep ideological commitments that predate the independence of the state.[14]

If the role of Pakistan was to defend Islam (from whom?) and win Kashmir, the instrument for this purpose was its army and a horde of jihadis—or non-state actors—operating under its umbrella. It is from these beginnings that Pakistan has steadily become a militarized state wherein the army is called upon to win Kashmir, ward off India's alleged hegemonistic designs and save Pakistan from its own people. Thus, for about half its existence, Pakistan has been under direct military rule, and indirectly for an even longer period—with the GHQ[15] and IS1[16] a brooding presence.

The failure of the feudal political class in Pakistan to provide good and stable governance has, time and again, given a handle for military intervention. Even otherwise, matters pertaining to national security, Kashmir, nuclear development and strategic foreign-policy issues have been the preserve of the military. The political leadership is often kept out of the loop, as Benazir Bhutto plaintively lamented.[17] The military budget is a secret, with the National Assembly vouchsafing for not much more than the global figure of the proposed annual outlay, now perhaps marginally more.[18]

Despite being perceived a long-time US ally and frontline state with substantial foreign military funding and purchase of military equipment at concessional prices—and despite receiving assistance from China and sundry Arab sources—Pakistan's defence spending has accounted for a disproportionately large part of the national budget, with the squeeze being on development. In addition, Pakistani re-armament and defence spending have been hugely sustained by the US since the early 1950s.

Over and beyond that, the army has spawned the ISI—a dirty-tricks department— that has operated as a state within the state, and is involved in a variety of extracurricular activities that has included upholding jihadi terror.

The military has also built an enormous economic empire and landed zamindari— in terms of the large number of major corporate entities they own and operate— through the Fauji (Army), Shaheen (Air Force) and Bahria (Navy) foundations, the Army Welfare Trust, and their several subsidiaries. These activities include banking, insurance, transport, toll roads, shipping, airlines, communications, construction, contracting, IT services, hotels, wheat-storage facilities, heavy manufactures, cement, fertilizer, power, oil terminals, food products, sugar, fisheries, poultry, bakeries, cinemas, gas stations, commercial plazas and more. The Fauji Foundation alone employs 6,000-7,000 retired military personnel, but is headed by a board comprising senior serving army officers.[19]

Substantial land grants to serving personnel of all ranks makes the military one of the largest landowners in the country. The system has permitted significant military penetration of the economy and created a strong vested interest in the growth and protection of this military-industrial complex.[20]

During periods of martial law, many key departments of government have been headed by military officers. Otherwise, too, the Pakistan Constitution has been treated with scant respect, and amended and manipulated by military dictators. The courts have tried to stand up from time to time, but have ultimately bowed to military power in critical rulings, by recourse to a so-called 'doctrine of necessity'.[21] This is, hopefully, now changing.

The projected 'core issue' to wrest Kashmir, or assure 'self-determination' for J&K, has increasingly found a faltering state seeking support and justification by nailing its flag to the Islamic mast. The 'Islamic Republic of Pakistan' went beyond tokenism with the introduction of sharia courts and abolition of interest on financial transactions under Zia ul-Haq's proclamation of the goal of 'Nizam-e- Mustafa' ('Order of the Prophet' or 'Muhammad's Islam').[22]

The Soviet intervention in Afghanistan (1979-89) was a turning point. Pakistan was refurbished as a frontline state and there was a trumpet call by the US to rally 'good Muslims' to fight the atheist 'evil empire'. A CIA-ISI compact sealed by the US and Pakistan was the conduit that delivered huge volumes of American military and monetary assistance to the Afghan resistance via Pakistan.

It is now well documented that anything up to 30 per cent of this assistance was siphoned off by the ISI, to train and fund global jihadis to fight the good fight in Kashmir, and to establish an Eastern Caliphate. Pakistan also trained and helped officer the Taliban in Afghanistan, with indirect US funding. A Pakistan component of the Taliban was repatriated to the Frontier when, first Kunduz and then Tora Bora, fell. Levels of violence went up exponentially, and the alarming spread of small arms and drugs, Talibanization, and nuclear proliferation (through the aegis of Dr A. Q. Khan who ran a nuclear Wal-Mart) were to take an enormous toll in collateral damage.

Osama bin Laden found a new mission. Al Qaeda was born; 9/11 followed. India paid a very heavy price.

16

A Warrior State

While India has been invaded from the northeast and the coast, it is the northwest passage that has historically been the main strategic gateway through which conquerors and caravans have entered—Alexander being an early visitor. It is perhaps easy to see why this was so. India was long a source of pepper, spices and fine calicoes for Greek, Roman and Arab traders, and regarded as a fabled land of wealth and wisdom lying athwart both the Silk and Spice Routes. Hsuan Tsang, Marco Polo, Ibn Battuta and other travellers wrote of its wonders. To those living in the arid or cold deserts of West and Central Asia, the well-watered plains of India seemed most inviting.

While the British conquered India from the sea, and fought off the Portuguese, Dutch and French for supremacy, it was Russian penetration from the northwest that it most feared. The Great Game[1] was played out along the wild, tribal marches of the Northwest Frontier and the High Karakoram. The nature of the Game changed after the Second World War, when containing communism became the prime Western agenda.

As the Second World War wound down, Britain wondered how it might dispose of India should irrevocable differences between the Muslim League and Congress force Partition. The British 'breakdown plan' favoured the creation of two Muslim-dominated Anglo-US allies—in the northwest and northeast of the subcontinent—to halt the march of communism.

Both the UK and the US would have preferred to partner with the larger and more resourceful India, but Nehru's non-alignment principle and seeming Soviet-Chinese tilt were suspect. Pakistan, staunchly Islamic and in need of support against what it saw as a larger permanent and ideological Indian enemy, readily fit the bill. It was also strategically placed, especially as guardian of the passes to Afghanistan and beyond.

No surprise then that Pakistan soon became a staunch ally, a 'frontline state', a strategic partner and a base of operations for the West in containing communism and controlling the emerging oil wealth of Iran and the Arab lands beyond. Pakistan's ideology, rooted in faith and geography, endowed her with strategic value on which her leaders traded.

South Asia scholar T.V. Paul sums up this geopolitical asset as a 'strategic curse'.[2] A feudal, emigre-led people—divorced from its historical, geographical and cultural roots to embrace a wholly negative non-Indian, non-Hindu identity—became a rentier state, trading its strategic utility for military and economic assistance.

*

As noted earlier, Jinnah's very first address to the new Pakistan constituent assembly totally repudiated the two-nation theory as false and untenable. But the twist in the tale is that it was Jinnah who was repudiated by his people, and who died espousing the two-nation ideological curse.

Indians, however, would do well to remember that it was Veer (or Vinayak Damodar) Savarkar, the Hindutva leader, who in 1937 spoke of Hindus and Muslims as 'two nations'. In his presidential address of that year—to the 19th session of the Hindu Mahasabha in Ahmedabad—Savarkar stated: 'India cannot be assumed today to be a unitarian and homogeneous nation, but on the contrary there are two nations in the main, the Hindus and the Moslems, in India.'[3]

He sought to explain away the reference, but M.S. Golwalkar—who succeeded Hedgewar as head of the RSS in 1940—reaffirmed that sentiment in other words. Golwalkar was vehemently opposed to the concept of a secular Indian state. He stated that:

> [...] the non-Hindu people of Hindustan must either adopt Hindu culture and language, must learn and respect and hold in reverence the Hindu religion, must entertain no idea but of those of glorification of the Hindu race and culture [...] or may

stay in the country, wholly subordinated to the Hindu nation, claiming nothing, deserving no privileges, far less any preferential treatment—not even citizens' rights.[4]

The Sangh Parivar, and hardcore Hindutva elements within it, still harbour the idea of Hindu Rashtra, and go back to Vedic learning and legend for inspiration. Yet, these pernicious theories have been consistently fought off in India, and stand rejected by law and the Constitution, unlike in Pakistan where state patronage clearly persists.

Pakistan, an 'Islamic State', was born to defend Islam and the ideological frontiers of Islam. Yet it is, even today, unable to define the true Muslim. The true Muslim has been reduced to a Wahabi, Deobandi, jihadi, the Taliban, and such medieval fanatics, whose goal it is to establish a new Caliphate. This protection of Islam, its borders, and its integrity—against a malign India—has reduced Pakistan to a garrison state where the military-mullah nexus has assumed control, as described in the previous chapter.

In the meantime, the US has given Pakistan US$33 billion in bilateral economic aid since 1947, and US$73 billion in economic and military aid from 1960-2002. Since 2002, Pakistan has received about US$20 billion from the US, mostly again in military aid.[5] Even so, such an over-militarized garrison state can find itself developmentally debilitated. In a population fast approaching 200 million, only 2.5 million are registered tax payers.[6] Defence appropriates the largest slice of the budget, with additional unaccounted amounts going into developing and augmenting nuclear arms, including tactical weapons.

T.V. Paul notes that the people's critical faculties have been dulled by tendentious and poisonous textbooks and ideologically oriented madrasas, whose products preach from pulpits. Jinnah, Bhutto and Zia led Pakistan down the slippery slope of Islamization and militarization. They were unabashedly aided by the US, which remained totally unmindful of the tremendous collateral damage to world peace and stability caused by its devious policies and its War on Terror—a vicious saga of arrogance, violence and intrigue in itself. Paul estimates that around 35,000 jihadis from forty-five countries trained in Pakistan to unleash mayhem prior to 9/11.[7] It is today a country at war with itself, and a menace to others.

Paul's conclusion: Pakistan's transformation will only take place if both its strategic circumstances and the ideas and assumptions that the leading elite hold change fundamentally.[8] His is only one of a whole series of refreshingly critical books on Pakistan, published by domestic and foreign authors, about what they describe—but do not quite name—as a failed state.[9] Similarly, few are sparing of Jinnah who, as we know, spoke of Pakistan as a Sharia state, as far back as November 1945.[10]

Writer Ishtiaq Ahmed, on his part, dispels the myth that Lord Louis Mountbatten conspired with Sir Cyril Radcliffe to gift India some Muslim-majority tehsils of Gurdaspur, primarily to justify the fact that Lahore was handed over to Pakistan. In fact, Ahmed notes that such a division of territories was part of the Wavell Breakdown Plan[11] so as to ensure that Amritsar at least, though not Nankana Sahib—both Sikh holy places—remained with India.

With equal astuteness, Ahmed describes the sharing of the Indus Waters as a geo-political issue linked to Kashmir. And, like others, he cites Major General Akbar Khan and Air Chief Marshal Nur Khan for affirming that the 1947 and 1965 invasions of J&K were staged by Pakistan. In addition, he refers to Brigadier S.K. Malik's *The Quranic Concept of War* (which carries an approving preface by Zia ul-Haq). According to Malik:

> The Quranic military strategy thus enjoins us to prepare ourselves for war to the utmost in order to strike terror into the heart of the enemy [...This] is not only a means, it is the end in itself. It is the point where the means and the end meet and merge.[12]

No surprise then that fundamentalist terrorist cells have sprouted in Pakistan, and have been sponsored by the state when required. They have carried out attacks on its general headquarters in Rawalpindi, the Mehran naval base, and on other similar targets. Pakistan has been reduced to a non-state actor itself, as no one quite knows who is or what is the locus of the Pakistani state at any given time.

Islamic radicalism, born of despair over lost glory and current-day injustices, has grown exponentially since the War on Terror that has spawned a new Caliphate, steeped in fundamentalist doctrine. The clash of rival fundamentalisms could, however, spell even greater danger. Inner rot could preclude India from providing reassurance and friendship to those in Pakistan—and there are many who are fighting to salvage the subcontinent's true Islamic heritage of tolerance and fraternity.

*

Every religion is a step towards reforming society, and reflects the social and cultural realities of the time. Thus Judaism was 'carried forward' by Christianity through the New Testament. Similarly, Islam was followed by the syncretic trends manifest in Sufism. Orthodoxy was challenged by the Reformation—as in Europe—leading to the Renaissance with advances in science and inquiry. Protestantism challenged doctrinaire Catholicism. In India, Jainism, Buddhism and later, Sikhism sought to reform certain aspects of the Brahmanical tradition, with movements such as the Brahmo Samaj and Arya Samaj to follow.

The fundamental tenets of Islam are set out in the Shariah, representing the words of the Prophet, as recoded in the eighth and ninth centuries. Almost as revered are the 'Hadith', or sayings of the Prophet, as documented by his contemporaries and closest companions.

But, as journalist Hasan Suroor said:

> The Koranic text is a minefield of ambiguity, allowing people to cherry-pick its equivocal and often contradictory verses to back their argument. Similarly, it is easy to manipulate the Hadith […] another major source of legitimacy for Islamic acts. This is because they are too numerous, were pronounced in vastly different situations and compiled many years after his death with the result that the precise meaning was frequently lost in translation.[13]

Further, Hasan Suroor mentioned:

> […] while other religious movements, particularly Christianity, got over their early violent origins, it [Islam] failed to move on and update its theological precepts […] The Islamic mindset remains awkwardly out of step with historical progress and therefore with modern times.[14]

Aware of the dynamism of society, the Prophet himself had provided for 'Ijtehad', or an innovative interpretation of the scripture to suit the requirements of changing times. It was the creative use of Ijtehad that led to the flowering of Islamic civilization and science in the centuries that followed. This liberalism was, in time, challenged by fundamentalists and traditionalists. They circumscribed any potential resort to Ijtehad—resulting in the current crisis in Islam, and in the rise of jihadists, some of whom read the Quran as Zia ul-Haq did—to glorify war and justify the existence of Pakistan as a warrior state.

As a result, Pakistan has resiled from the rich tradition of humanistic Islam—as still practised in the Indian subcontinent—through which the winds of the world have always blown. Hasan Suroor pleads for 'an Islamic equivalent of the New Testament', put together by 'learned Islamic scholars,' and, 'declared as the authorised version of Islamic beliefs.'[15]

Such a call is of vital significance. Together, South Asian Islam constitutes more than 40 per cent of the global Islamic population. Given its economic potential and rich cultural roots, a united and revivified South Asian Islam could help redeem world Islam, and steer it to a new era of hope and greatness. Men like Nehru and Patel hoped that—once the madness and bitterness of Partition had passed and the wounds healed—the estranged siblings would come together, not to undo Partition, but to live together as good neighbours in friendship and cooperation. That time has come. Jinnah too had hoped that, once a Muslim homeland was achieved, Pakistan would become a secular, liberal, democratic state. Alas, he aborted his own dream. We must assist its realization.

*

If we analyse modern-day Pakistan, we see that instead of moving forward with the times, the country has moved backwards deeper and deeper into the medieval ages. Its jihadist proclivities have shifted beyond 'struggle' with the enemy to governance by violence and deceit. Recall the fairy tale spun by Islamabad around Osama bin Laden's long and cosy sojourn in Pakistan. Much as in Alice's Wonderland, things in Pakistan seem to get increasingly curious as we begin investigating the story, to the point that unfolding events and explanations strain credulity.

A bewildering twist in the tale was the report of the official

Inquiry Committee, set up by the previous government in Islamabad, to look into the saga of the fugitive Osama bin Laden's mysterious killing—by US Navy SEALs in Abbottabad—after nine years of hiding in Pakistan. The commission, headed by Justice Javed Iqbal of the Supreme Court, and with three other members— a retired police officer, a retired diplomat and a retired army general—specifically sought early publication of the report. This was withheld, and finally leaked to Al Jazeera in July 2013.[16]

Even at the time of the US raid to get Osama, the world wondered how his presence in the high-security garrison town of Abbottabad—near Pakistan's prestigious Pakistan Army Command and Staff College—went unnoticed and unchallenged. For, his abode there stood out like a sore thumb! His newly constructed, illegally built and hermetically sealed 'fortress', with high walls and barbed wire, was officially registered as 'uninhabited'—despite harbouring Osama, his wives, children and aides, numbering twenty-seven residents in all, since 2005. The native curiosity of neighbourhood residents, and the prying eyes of Pakistan's police and intelligence services, were astonishingly never attracted to this unusual mansion.

The 337-page report is scathing in denouncing the absolute incompetence, lack of vigilance, criminal negligence, lack of coordination and follow-up by the civil and military authorities at all levels. The ISI chief, Lieutenant General Shuja Pasha, is quoted as describing what happened, as the 'collective systemic failure' of a 'failing state' suffering from a 'government implosion syndrome'.[17] The army is indicted for the 'exercise of authority and influence in policy and administrative areas, for which it has neither constitutional nor legal authority, nor the necessary expertise and competence'.

The findings are damning but the blame generic. Nobody is specifically charged for utter dereliction of duty although the commission was required to assign responsibility. The report concludes that it is unnecessary to name those responsible 'as it is obvious who they are'! No action is recommended against anybody but it is piously pleaded that 'the honourable thing' must be done through a 'formal apology' to the nation.[18] When everybody is declared guilty, nobody is held guilty, let alone accountable. The thieves come out smelling of roses!

As for the US raid that killed Osama, this is described as an 'act of war' on the part of the Americans, and a Pakistani 'intelligence-security failure'.[19] The Pakistan army and air force reacted only after the commotion—a helicopter crash, gunfire and the escape. The commission attributes this to the Pakistan military's blinding obsession with India, resulting in a mistaken focus on its eastern border, when the larger threat came from US drone and jihadi attacks from the west.

The next, and not least important, aspect of the commission's report is its finding of the manner in which Osama bin Laden was killed. He did not die in combat. He was unarmed and did not seek to take shelter behind his wives. He did not resist, and was executed in cold blood. The Americans will protest that Osama was the brain behind 9/11 and was killed in battle. None knew that he was unarmed, and had no armed support at hand. That may be true, but the US must be held to the same standards it demands of others. Thirty bullets were pumped into the man. He was not asked to surrender. He was assassinated and buried somewhere at sea. End of story.

At the culmination of the report, the Pakistani establishment emerged as fools or liars, and the American role also seemed dubious.[20] The US and Pakistan may denounce such speculation. But they have lied over much, and could be protesting too much. Pakistan has classically been in denial since 1947. It may be beginning to turn over a new leaf, but the jury is still out on these conjectures.

As for the report itself, it provides a convenient exit for all the dramatis personae: civil, military, intelligence and the US. Had Osama been taken alive he would have had to be tried, and some of his revelations could have proved extremely embarrassing— many skeletons might have come alive in the US-NATO cupboard; much duplicity, deceit and double-dealing.

For Pakistan, a mysterious 'they' were guilty, but 'we' are okay; Pakistan milked its strategic importance for the US (vis-à-vis the War on Terror) in every way. It used it as a cover to cosy up to the Taliban—furthering A.Q. Khan's nuclear gamesmanship, cultivating jihadis for cross-border terrorism in India and blackmailing the US to pay more, and yet more, for its perfidy.

It is also perfectly possible that the commission's findings are in order, and that singular ineptitude, all down the line, was indeed blameable for the incredible farce enacted—as the report conveyed, Pakistan's military and political leaders 'collectively displayed a degree of incompetence and irresponsibility which was truly breathtaking'.[21] Yet, can a more diabolical hypothesis be altogether discounted without deeper scrutiny? That the Pakistanis knew, or got to know, where Osama bin Laden was hiding, but played along with him as a possible lever against the US? Did it finally connive with the US—which was by now ready to have him eliminated in a manner that might suit all concerned, with no questions asked? In other words, Abbottabad could have been an extravaganza—carefully contrived, executed and televised as high drama—to lay to rest what remains an untold story. Everybody benefits.

*

The story repeats itself in the case of the UN inquiry into the assassination of Benazir Bhutto—as told by its chair, the Chilean diplomat Heraldo Munoz.[22] Munoz details how the UN Commission of Inquiry's work was thwarted and obfuscated by the Pakistani authorities at every stage. Indeed, the military and ISI have been virtually accused of preventing an autopsy of Benazir Bhutto and hosing down the assassination site, thus removing vital evidence and obstructing the commission's own inquiries.

Pakistan remains steadfastly in denial. It further argues that its government alone, is in a position to release the commission's report. The commission's seventy-page findings were finally presented to the media in New York by Munoz on 15 April 2010.[23] The Pakistan ambassador boycotted the function.

According to a columnist of *Dawn*, the Pakistani authorities wished the 'establishment' to see the report before they shared its contents with the general public. Why it might have been thought prudent to provide the 'establishment' with prior information becomes apparent from the report. It severely indicts the Musharraf regime of wilful negligence and cover-up. Also indicted was the Pakistan Peoples Party interior minister from 2008–13, Rehman Malik, who was travelling in the stand-by bulletproof Mercedes that was found missing from the scene—when it could have rushed Benazir Bhutto to hospital.[24]

Consequently, the report calls on Pakistan to set up a 'truth commission' to get to the bottom of the crime. The unfolding in Islamabad will now be watched with interest. Of special concern to India are the commission's findings that a probable reason for removing Benazir Bhutto was her 'independent position on the urgent need to improve relations with India, and its implications for the Kashmir dispute, which the military regarded as its policy domain.' Additionally, the commission found evidence that the army and ISI used terrorist groups to further their strategic objectives, and that 'the bulk of the anti-Indian activity was, and still remains, the work of groups such as the Lashkar-e-Taiba, which has close links with the ISI.'[25]

*

Musharraf quite clearly lied about Kargil, about the nuclear proliferator A.Q. Khan (who was no lone wolf) and the use of jihadi terror against India. Asif Ali Zardari of the Pakistan Peoples Party, on his part, declared that his government would not allow the soil of Pakistan to be used for cross-border terror against India. That commitment has not been honoured.[26]

Amidst the shrill voices of hate, bigotry, pettiness, greed and trivia we hear all around us, there was a poignant moment on 12 July 2013, when a sixteen-year old Pakistani girl, Malala Yousafzai, addressed the world through the United Nations Youth Assembly in New York. A victim of a Taliban assault in Swat in 2012, she spoke with a rare conviction and grace that went straight to the heart. She said:

> I am not against anyone. Neither am I here to speak in terms of personal revenge against the Taliban, or any other terrorist group. I am here to speak up for the right of education of every child. I want education for the sons and the daughters of all the extremists, especially the Taliban.
>
> [...] So let us wage a global struggle against illiteracy, poverty and terrorism and let us pick up our books and pens. They are our most powerful weapons. One child, one teacher, one pen and one book can change the world.[27]

What a powerful message of tolerance, forgiveness and fraternity! Malala represents Pakistan more than the many of those who strut the stage and claim attention.

17

Pakistan@In-denial.com

Contradictions within Pakistan led to Kargil and the Pervez Musharraf takeover in 2001. There was also a backlash as Talibanization took root in parts of the NWFP and Balochistan. The many madrasas, preaching radical Islam and churning out perfervid jihadis, turned their attention to whatever benefitted them within Pakistan. There was the sorry spectacle of the leaders of Pakistan's three main parties—the Pakistan Peoples Party (PPP), the Pakistan Muslim League (ML) and Muttahida Qaumi Movement (MQM)—then led by Benazir Bhutto, Nawaz Sharif and Altaf Hussain respectively—seeking to fight for the restoration of Pakistan's democracy from their places of exile in London, Saudi Arabia and the UK.

Overtures from India—for normalizing relations and promoting trade, investments and cultural exchange—long floundered on account of the 'core issue'. Musharraf partly broke loose from the tyranny of Kashmir, but was ultimately trapped in the coils of his own intrigues and double talk, and by the very jihadi monsters he and his predecessors had themselves created. All this, despite the fact that the peace process with India was poised to roll on.

The arrogance of power, growing disillusionment about the direction Pakistan was headed in and mounting anger at the military's conduct gave impetus to incipient democratic forces which triumphed at the 2007 polls. It did, though, cost Benazir Bhutto her life. The democratic coalition in Pakistan unfortunately did not hold, but nonetheless, Asif Ali Zardari took office supported by Nawaz Sharif from outside. This was a tightrope walk for them, and the dastardly Mumbai 26/11 attack and events in its wake suggested that behind the façade of civilian rule, the military still called the shots.

It was in this fraught situation that India had to determine its response to Mumbai. Public anger was palpable—but to give way to raw emotion, and to blindly hit back would be misplaced. Consequently, a credible rather than crudely muscular response followed, in order to endeavour to win not merely the battle, but also the war for peace.

Pakistan, however, remained defiant and in denial. There is today a clear divide in Pakistan between the military and the mullahs on the one hand, and incipient democratic forces on the other. The people of Pakistan are by and large liberal, secular Muslims—and not fundamentalists—desiring peace and amity with India. They have begun to see through the Kashmir charade— that far from being the 'core issue', it has led to the militarization and Islamization of a state, and brought an ideologically rudderless Pakistan to the brink of becoming a failed state that might fragment.

There is a mood of disillusionment, cynicism, deep disappointment and resentment in Pakistan over ever so many wasted years. A significant and growingly assertive democratic tendency is discernible; the nation is anxious to build liberal democratic institutions, and live as a good neighbour with India. These are the forces we must support and partner, against the machinations of the military and the mullahs who hold the country in thrall.

When Musharraf, as Pakistan's last overt military dictator, stated, soon after taking over, that if the Kashmir question were ever resolved, Pakistan would have to invent another 'Kashmir', he was not alone. Farzana Shaikh, a specialist on Pakistan and the regional politics of South Asia, explains why.[1] In brief, the argument is that the battle for Pakistan was almost entirely fought by the Muslim League in what is now India. That, upon Independence, Jinnah and his cohorts arrived in the new Muslim homeland as 'migrants' to take over a country whose people had never truly sought Pakistan, and did not fully understand what it was all about. Pakistan therefore started with what Shaikh calls a 'negative identity' of being assertively 'not-Indian', reluctant to accept—or even repudiating—its Indo-Islamic history, culture and ethos. This hothouse plant obviously had difficulty taking root, with mohajirs lording over proud Sindhi, Pathan and Baloch ethnic identities with established traditions, languages and histories of their own.

The binding element came from a clear resort to 'Islam', which became the 'ideology of Pakistan'. By the territorial logic of the two-nation theory, J&K—being majority Muslim and contiguous—was by definition an integral part of Pakistan (though this would confound the issues of Hyderabad, Junagadh, et al). Even so, the two-nation theory was not easily validated in the new homeland, which started out with a 12 per cent minority population, and soon had Bengali linguistic nationalism trump the religious Islamic one. There were other contradictions too. Was Pakistan to be an ideologically Islamic state based on the Sharia, or a Muslim homeland with a minority population that was to be held hostage to India's fair treatment of its residual Muslim population?

Shaikh traces the further development of Islamization. Zulfikar Ali Bhutto was determined to create an 'Islamic bomb' that would re-establish parity with India, and put Pakistan in a position to claim a certain Islamic leadership. Then Zia ul-Haq forged a military-mullah alliance to stave off the 'Movement for the Restoration of Democracy'. Harkat-ul-Jihad-e-Islami's (HUJI's) Binori madrasa in Karachi, the LeT's Mudrike seminary, the Lal Masjid, and associated Quranic Schools in Islamabad, were products of this time. Benazir Bhutto and Nawaz Sharif thereafter variously sought to curry favour with the Islamists in their competition against one another and the military.

Pakistan had by now become a pan-Islamic hub of jihadi terror, spreading its tentacles as far as Chechnya, the Philippines, Bosnia, Xinjiang, the Arab lands and, of course, Kashmir/India. The Soviet invasion of Afghanistan brought everything together in favour of the Islamists. The US, once again, adopted Pakistan as a 'frontline state' and shut its eyes to proliferation, drug trafficking, the Kalashnikov culture (which it indirectly bankrolled) and Talibanization by Islamabad's Talibs—the first of the jihadis—who swarmed J&K. There was also the 'good Muslim' who would fight atheist communism in Afghanistan.

Pakistan handed this enterprise to the ISI, under men like Hamid Gul and Javed Nasir. Pushtun Afghans were favoured by it—against the Tajik-led Northern Alliance—so that Pakistan would gain 'strategic depth' against India, and inherit Afghanistan's Taliban protégés once the Russians and Americans left. Even as Pakistan searched for territorial identity—in the guise of an Islamic 'state' and an Islamic 'nation'—it sought 'parity' with India in international councils, and as a nuclear power and protector. This played out in the new Great Game to keep India out of Afghanistan where, it was feared, its presence spelt danger to the idea and security of Pakistan. Both its nuclear and Afghanistan policies are designed as Indian equalizers.

Once unleashed, Talibanization spread back into Pakistan. Musharraf was forced to change tack after 9/11, and was more surely brought to heel in 2002. But despite US pressure, he limited his fight first to the al Qaeda, and then to the Afghan Taliban. Mounting opposition to him at home saw him cosying up to the Islamists. He was instrumental, through the military, in building up the Muttahida Majlis-e-Amal (MMA), a coalition of the religious right, which took office in the NWFP and Balochistan after the 2002 elections. Paving the way for the Talibanization of Pakistan, it is the monster that is now devouring the state.

The army has not been free of Islamist tendencies, as recent conspiracies have shown. Both have fed on one another. The West fears that a failed or Talibanized Pakistan state could enable non-state actors to acquire nuclear wherewithal. Hence, Shaikh believes, the international community is engaged in propping up a failing state, putting a brake on needed political reforms—and thereby buttressing the military for fear of the consequences of letting go.

This unfolds at a time when a new civil society in Pakistan—the media, artists, writers, historians, the legal community and human rights activists—sees the need to move away from a perennial confrontation with India, and over Kashmir. They wish to return to the country's real roots, which lie in its cultural heritage of a syncretic Indian Islam. Sections of Indian opinion, too, are veering around to a similar view, that would reorient Delhi's policies towards Pakistan. This calls for a paradigm shift that should be fostered, not repelled.

The notion that the Kashmir question is a regional cancer, and a 'Muslim' problem, in respect of which Pakistan is somehow entitled to seek relief, is a gross falsification of fact. Pakistan covets J&K, but has no legal or moral basis for its claim to it. Its primary association with J&K comes from its initial aggression in 1947 that put it in wrongful occupation of PAK and the Northern Areas. Ever since, it has resorted to continuous machinations to wrest the rest of the state, and particularly the Valley, from India.

The Partition settlement and Britain's India Independence Act[2] did not allocate the princely states to one side or the other, and specifically did not touch on the disposition of J&K.[3] The argument that J&K is majority Muslim, and contiguous with Pakistan, is specious since the future of the NWFP—a Muslim-majority province—was determined by a referendum in 1947. No UN document or resolution has ever challenged J&K's accession to India.

Pakistan has been in denial over J&K from 1947, since the initial Standstill Agreement, through its repeated invasions—overt and covert—in 1948, 1965, 1971, Siachen, Kargil, to date, and the jihadi war that has targetted all of India.[4] Yet India has persevered with the peace process.

The Manmohan-Musharraf roadmap is based on the proposition that J&K's boundaries (read: LOC) should be made irrelevant without impairing the existing twin sovereignties.

This formulation offers the possibility of fashioning a variety of trans-border mechanisms for trade, tourism, investments, cultural exchange, and even for the cooperative management of the upper Indus system in keeping with the Indus Waters Treaty to contend with the looming threat of climate change. All this could, over time, result in the establishment of an informal, or even formal, joint consultative body, imbuing a Greater J&K with the characteristics of a confederation—a concept blessed by Nehru and Sheikh Abdullah in 1963. This entity would be cocooned within a South Asian Community to which the SAARC (South Asian Association for Regional Cooperation) members are already, in principle, committed.

Meanwhile, every effort should be made to seek a just and honourable resolution of the internal J&K question on the Indian side of the LoC. This can be addressed by conferring greater autonomy on, and within, J&K. The degree of regional autonomy can be adjusted on a differentiated basis to suit varying local aspirations within Ladakh and J&K. The constitutional mandate for this exists under Articles 258 and 258A of the Indian Constitution. They provide for various degrees of 'entrustment', both up and down (federally, and among regions within states), as has been demonstrated in India's northeast region.

Other elements could include: looking into residual human rights grievances and 'disappearances' by means of a healing touch; a thinning out of the security forces; and selective cancellations of declarations notifying certain regions as 'disturbed areas'. These form a pre-condition to the application of the Armed Forces (Special Powers) Act (AFSPA, which could be repealed or incorporated in other civil legislation, as recommended by a Commission in 2004 that reported on the matter under Justice Jeevan Reddy).

Further steps must include measures to facilitate the safe and honourable return of the Pandits, and an imaginative development package around improved rail, road, air and broadband connectivity, and power supply. Movement in this direction would allay local discontent and regional tensions. It would offset the calls for azadi—exemplified already by the repeatedly high turnouts at successive J&K polls, in the face of the dire calls for boycott by separatists. Such action in J&K would probably arouse similar demands for the long overdue democratization of PAK and the Northern Areas, too.

What would Pakistan get out of such an unfolding? It would gain legitimacy for its presence in PAK and the Northern Areas, and would informally secure peaceful 'access' to the other part of J&K that it has coveted, and sought to seize through violent means. More than that, such a resolution would erode the dominating raison d'être for a highly militarized and Islamized state, and liberate it from the crippling inferiority and futility of playing the Indian 'other' that has dwarfed and distorted its national personality.

By turning its back on both—the military and the mullahs— Pakistan would rediscover its soul, and find fulfilment in embracing Jinnah's initial concept of a liberal, democratic, secular, inclusive state. It will become a pillar of SAARC (including Afghanistan and perhaps, even Iran), and a much more powerful and prosperous member of a vibrant South Asian community, at peace with itself and its neighbours.

The same formulation of a soft border between the two parts of J&K could, with modification, apply to the Pakhtun marches along both sides of the Durand Line, and bring quietus to the troubled relationship between Pakistan and Afghanistan. By these means, Pakistan would be able to reclaim its geography, history, culture and strategic depth, standing tall as the northwestern bastion of South Asia.

What would India gain? An end to the Kashmir dispute that has been a wounding distraction, and 'access' to PAK and the Northern Areas that it claims as its own. It would, in due course, be able to thin down its forces in J&K, withdraw many divisions from its western border, and make do with a leaner and meaner army. Its diplomacy would no longer be inhibited by the Pakistan/ Kashmir factor, and it would have access to Afghanistan, Iran and Central Asia through Pakistan.

A settlement with Pakistan would change the internal dynamics of South Asia, and breathe new life into SAARC, making it a powerful force for peace and stability in the larger Asian neighbourhood and the Indian Ocean region. With its 500 million Muslims, or over 40 per cent of global Islam, India, Pakistan and Bangladesh could make a notable contribution towards a new Islamic renaissance.

At home, the Hindu-Muslim divide would steadily dissolve, and a new relationship based on fraternity, inclusiveness and the constitutional ideal of a common and equal citizenship would begin to emerge and gain ascendancy. Gradually relegating all brands of religious and 'cultural' fundamentalism and divisive revivalism to the back-burner, it would restore the innate tolerance of Indian society—which has been a civilizational hallmark, despite some warts.

For almost seventy years, India and Pakistan have suffered the lingering tragedy of Partition. The kind of resolution envisaged herein is by no means impossible, and is perhaps nearer than many believe. It could see a transition and transformation from tragedy to triumph, as two estranged siblings come together to build a better future, and enable South Asia to truly come into its own.

SEEKING SOLUTIONS

18

Autonomy, Restructuring and Peaceful Resolution

Once upon a time, long, long ago—so long ago as to have been mostly forgotten—

Hence the need for retelling the Kashmir story.

A Conglomerate

The civilizational and political basis of India's connection with J&K may be better understood in the historical context. The temples of Ganpatyar in Srinagar and Kheer Bhawani, near Ganderbal, are associated with the Mahabharata. Ashoka's conquest of Kashmir introduced Buddhism into the Valley. The Kushans swept across the Karakoram in AD 2, and took possession of Kashmir and a vast swathe of upper India. The third Buddhist Council was held in the Valley during the reign of Kanishka. The so-called Gilgit Manuscript, found at Naupur in 1931, is one of the oldest Buddhist Pali texts extant, and dates back to that period. The Shaivite influence of Shankaracharya is commemorated in the temple atop the hill, bearing his name, that dominates Srinagar. Lalitaditya's reign (AD 724-760) was witness to a great Kashmiri empire that spread to Bengal and Gujarat, and a flourish of art of which the Sun Temple at Martand was a supreme example.

Islam came to Kashmir from Persia and Central Asia, steeped in the Sufi tradition. It was adopted by the then Buddhist ruler, Rinchen, as a faith already embraced by many of his subjects. This was to have a profound effect on the further evolution of social and religious traditions in the Valley, which saw a synthesis rather than any discontinuity or antagonism, between rival faiths. The names, dress, language, food and culture remained the same. The sufi-rishi tradition took firm root in this soil. The great sage Sheikh Nooruddin, whose dargah (destroyed by fire in 1995, but now restored) attracts hundreds of thousands of devotees of all faiths, was powerfully influenced by the venerated mystic, Lalleshwari or Lal Ded. This deeply rooted tradition was to lay the foundation of Kashmiriyat, a bond transcending faith.

The Amarnath yatra that brings vast numbers of Hindu pilgrims from the far corners of India each year to ascend the perilous path to the ice cave, is again unique. The cave was said to have been discovered by a Muslim family whose descendants remain its keepers, informally.

Likewise, Buddhism and Islam co-mingled without strife or stress in Ladakh, with different members of the same family professing the two religions. It is only recently that discords have intruded into this happy inter-faith communion that has been characteristic of J&K.

*

Jammu and Kashmir, as the very name suggests, is not a single, homogenous entity, but a very plural political conglomerate. Its many constituent units, including those in the Northern Areas (now with Pakistan), have their own political and social history, ethnic and linguistic particularities, cultural traditions, agro-climatic practices and varied trade links. As separate principalities, they have retained these characteristics over the centuries, even when they have occasionally been incorporated in one or other empires: Asokan, Kushan, Mughal, British.

In-between these imperial episodes, Kashmir, Janm lll and the other entities were separate, or tossed between different suzerainties. Kashmir enjoyed a long spell of independence, except latterly—when for some 350 years—it came under Afghan, Mughal, Sikh and then Dogra rule. Its more recent history starts with the detachment of Kashmir from the Sikh empire after the Anglo-Sikh wars, and its sale by the British to Gulab Singh, the Dogra governor of Jammu, for aiding the British against Ranjit Singh. That was the beginning of Dogra rule. The Dogra general, Zorawar Singh, conquered Ladakh. The British later encouraged and assisted Gulab Singh and his successors to take possession of Baltistan and the Northern Areas, as part of the Great Game, designed to hold the Russian bear beyond the Pamirs.

The four broad constituent units of J&K on the eve of independence were Jammu, Kashmir, Ladakh, Gilgit and the Frontier Illaqas. Parts of Jammu and Ladakh provinces now lie beyond the LoC, in 'Azad' J&K (AJK), and the Northern Areas. The former, with its capital at Muzaffarabad, is a thin slice of territory encompassing part of the Jhelum and Kishanganga (Neelam) valleys. The latter incorporates Gilgit, Skardu tehsil (Western Baltistan) and the Frontier ilaquas of Hunza, Nagar, Punial, Yasin, Kuh, Ghizar, Ishkoman and Chilas—all petty chieftainships in feudatory relationships with the maharaja of J&K.

Pakistan reorganized the Northern Areas, and gave away the Shaksgam Valley to China in a border deal in 1963. China also appropriated the unpopulated Aksai Chin plateau, and adjacent areas in Ladakh, between 1959 and 1962.

Of an estimated population of around twelve million in all of J&K, over eight million live on the Indian side and the rest across the LoC. The population of Ladakh is about 1,25,000, more or less evenly divided between the Leh and Kargil tehsils. The population ratio, as between Kashmir and Jammu, would be about 60:40. AJK has about 2.5 million inhabitants and the Northern Areas between 0.8 and 1.3 million.

Ethno-cultural Mosaic

The ethno-geographical and geo-political breakdown of J&K is distinctive. The LoC, partly by accident but perhaps not altogether without design, marks a broad ethno-cultural divide. What is called Kashmir is confined to the Valley and the hills girding it. There are few, if any, Kashmiris or Kashmiri-speaking people in AJK, though some do spill east into Doda. Within the Valley itself, while the Kashmiri Muslims are dominant, the Pandits had a significant presence until 1990-91, while the Gujjars and Bakarwals continue to do so.

The Jammu province has a strong Hindu (Dogra) presence in

the Jammu-Kathua-Udhampur and Kishtwar-Bhaderwah regions. But Rajouri and Poonch are peopled by Muslims, Punjabis, Paharis and Gujjars. Zanskar is Buddhist. There are also some Sikhs in the J&K province. Ladakh is divided—with the Leh tehsil being Buddhist; and Kargil, Shia Muslim.

Linguistically, the language of Kashmir and parts of Doda is Kashmiri. Dogri, Pahari, Punjabi and Gojri are spoken in Jammu (and the Kashmir hills); Ladakhi (akin to Tibetan) in Leh; and Baltic and Dardic dialects in Kargil.

The position across the LoC is different. The people of AJK are mostly Sunni Muslims, and speak a mix of Punjabi, Pahari and Pushto. The Northern Areas' main ethnic groups are Balti, Shin, Yashkun, Pathan, Ladakhi and Turk; the languages they speak are Balti, Shina, Burushaski, Khawar, Wakhi, Tibeti, Pushto, Urdu and Persian. The principal Muslim denominations are Shia (55 per cent—including the Sufi-Shia Nurbakshis), Sunni (15 per cent), and Ismaili (30 per cent).

This thumbnail sketch overlooks many nuances, but is broadly indicative of the ethno-diversity of J&K, on either side of the LoC. This has a bearing on the 'self' and on the nature of the 'determination' inherent in any discussion of autonomy, self-determination and azadi.

Geo-political Influences

The geo-political influences impinging on J&K are equally varied. Jammu's cultural and commercial ties with the Indian plains are close. The Buddhist population, too, has a strong attachment to India, though some Ladakhis say they would rather identify with Tibet were this link ever severed. Leh was on an ancient trade route—an arm of the Silk Road—from Khotan and Yarkand to India. Caravans would meet here to exchange goods brought from China, Sinkiang, Tibet and Central Asia, with the produce of Kashmir and other parts of Hindustan.

The vocal 'Kashmiri' community in the UK is essentially Mirpuri. Depression in the 1930s led to the first recruitment of Mirpuri stevedores by P&O. Others followed, including many displaced without compensation by the Mangla reservoir in the 1960s. The rest of AJK has strong ties with Punjab and the Frontier

Province. The Northern Areas' ties are with Central Asia, though the British discouraged any great contact in that direction beyond a point.

All these many local identities loosely coalesced in certain regions, but remained distinctive and aloof in others because of physical and ethno-linguistic barriers. They generally had little in common, other than involuntarily sharing a common administrative dispensation under the J&K durbar. Given half a chance, some of them were possibly in competition or, in some cases—as between Jammu, Kashmir and Ladakh—in strong rivalry. These identities, in turn, spawned regional and local sub-nationalisms that continue to be in play.

Any political restructuring of J&K on either side of the LoC, or across it, must take this reality into account. Talking of J&K as a single entity is totally misplaced. Alongside these several identities is also the shadow of an Indian identity in the state, on account of the ancient cultural Hindu-Buddhist, and sufi-rishi links, which long pre-date accession.

Kashmiri Nationalism

Prior to the division of the state, Jammu was only a little less populous than Kashmir, but more influential on account of Dogra rule and a certain Hindu weightage in the administration. The drawing of a CFL and the loss of the Muslim-dominant areas of AJK and the Northern Areas to Pakistan created new jurisdictions and a new political demography. The ending of the monarchy, the abolition of large landed estates without compensation and the primacy of the National Conference resulted in an internal 'transfer of power' from Jammu to Srinagar.

Ever since the Afghan conquest, the Kashmir Valley had sought to reassert its independence. The rise of Kashmiri nationalism in the 1930s led to the formation of the Muslim Conference, which Sheikh Abdullah shortly thereafter converted into the secular and progressive National Conference. The Sheikh's logic was that the struggle was not one of Muslims against Hindus but of the common people, whatever their faith, against the feudal tyranny of Dogra rule.

The National Conference was largely confined to the Valley,

and the cry of 'Quit Kashmir' in 1946 was addressed to the maharaja. Kashmiri nationalism thus exclusively targetted Dogra rule. It was Jawaharlal Nehru's friendship with and influence over the Sheikh that made Abdullah see the larger dimension of the Indian freedom struggle to which he was soon attracted. The National Conference joined the States Peoples Conference in 1941, making Kashmir's nationalist struggle part of the wider Indian independence movement.

The National Conference's Naya Kashmir manifesto of 1944 [1] also drew inspiration from the progressive economic thinking of the Congress. Abdullah was later to say that Kashmiris could be good Muslims in India, and yet be partners in its democratic, secular and modernizing economic development enterprise. In endorsing the maharaja's decision to accede to India—when the tribal raiders were at the ramparts of Srinagar—and in subsequently negotiating Article 370 and the Delhi Agreement, the Sheikh opted for autonomy or self-determination within India. He subsequently wavered on sensing certain negative trends, but returned to his original moorings after 1975.

The Dispute

This, then, is a brief history of Kashmir.

Yet, today, time and again, the chorus is the same. Hardline Hurriyat leader, Syed Ali Shah Geelani has outlined a pre-dialogue 'agenda' for Kashmir: India must acknowledge an 'international dispute', commence demilitarization under UN supervision, rein in the security forces, unconditionally release all youth and political prisoners—including (back then) Afzal Guru—and initiate proceedings against all those responsible for 'war crimes' in the state.[2] Mirwaiz Umar Farooq, another Kashmiri separatist leader, challenges accession, asserts Kashmiris are not Indians, and seeks demilitarization, the repeal of 'black laws, and a referendum.[3] Masarat Alam Bhat, yet another Kashmiri separatist leader, avers Kashmir is the unfinished business of Partition and demands complete azadi. Delusive agenda items must be firmly put aside.

Shah Mahmood Qureshi, Pakistan's ex-foreign minister, crisply insists on a 'result-oriented dialogue'.[4] He rewinds from Musharraf's promising 'out-of-the-box' solutions to hark back to the UN resolutions, envisaging an evolving confederal entity over time, without prejudice to existing sovereignties. No one talks of the pathetic colonial situation in PAK and the Gilgit-Baltistan area, where Pakistan firmly determines who is the 'self' in question, and what is to be determined.

Some basic clarifications are in order if there is to be any progress. The problem is not about the fact, but the nature of the dispute. India went to the UN on a question of aggression by Pakistan. Cutting through all the cant, this was upheld by the UN representative, Owen Dixon, and endorsed by the UN Security Council in its defining resolution of 13 August 1948. This called for the immediate withdrawal of the tribal raiders and Pakistani military personnel from J&K and the disbandment of all 'Azad' Kashmir forces, as the first order of business prior to a plebiscite. Pakistan's deliberate default, its subsequent invasions and cross-border terror ploys through mercenaries and jihadis is what the current problem is all about.

The UN resolutions died long back. If one asks, 'Why not a plebiscite today?', the chief reason is that it is too late, with major demographic changes—natural and engineered—across the LoC, and the ethnic cleansing in the Valley. There is a totally different political context three generations down the road, and a wholly new international geo-strategic environment. Further, Pakistan, sections of the separatists, and the jihadis make a case for the visisection of lands based on dominant religious beliefs—thus reopening the still-healing wounds of Partition, and reviving the fatuity of the two-nation theory, that, as we know, Jinnah himself eloquently repudiated. To sustain its sadly negative ideological identity as India's 'other', Pakistan has projected Kashmir as unfinished business and sought 'strategic depth' to realize the warped dream of a Talibanized caliphate. This perverse goal feeds the self-aggrandizing paranoia of the military-mullah cabal that holds the Pakistani people in thrall. India is simply not prepared to revive the madness of 1947, and self-destruct.

What, then, is the road ahead in J&K? The external aspect is not the most critical. We must certainly talk to Pakistan, but forward movement depends on Islamabad's willingness to end terror as an instrument of policy. Casting the blame on 'non-state actors' will not wash. This was brazenly pleaded in 1947, 1948, 1965, 1989, 1999, in between and thereafter, and reveals a warped mindset that explains Pakistan's irrational behaviour—one based on a cultivated Indophobia—that ordinary Pakistanis do not share.

We should be wary but not alarmist about Chinese PLA units reportedly safeguarding Chinese workers, engaged in road and other development projects along the damaged Karakoram Highway, from jihadi attacks in Gilgit-Baltistan. A small Indo-Tibet Border Police force in Afghanistan plays a similar role.

An internal dialogue in, and over J&K, could lead the way to a just resolution that addresses local, regional and centre-state-level grievances and aspirations, and thereby make it increasingly difficult for external actors to fish in troubled waters. The dialogue could cover Geelani's five points, minus the rhetorical flourishes. It could also cover the variant azadi-autonomy, 'sky is the limit',[5] self-rule formulations of the National Conference, Congress, People's Democratic Party, Sajjad Lone, Mirwaiz Umar Farooq, and others. Indeed, the Indian Constitution permits extraordinary flexibility in accommodating diversity, to match regional and sectoral needs, through such instruments of entrustment provided under Articles 258[6] and 258A.[7]

The reports of ex-prime minister, Manmohan Singh's task forces on development, border management, security and reconciliation could provide the basis for progress along multiple tracks, and help build confidence and trust. Simultaneously, there must be a parallel dialogue with national parties and stakeholders in New Delhi, so that there is a matching consensus about directions and content.

Besides, any dialogue about J&K should weigh the possibility of repatriation of the Pandits and Muslim families who fled the Valley, and those trapped in PAK. This is best done by creating new employment opportunities in the Valley, where other internally displaced and unemployed youth can be relocated with due training; encouraging matching progammes for Jammu, Rajouri, Poonch, Doda, Ladakh and Kargil; and repairing the social infrastructure over the next five years, assisted by a youth peace corps.

Additionally, an empowered panchayati raj would give real

meaning to azadi, self-determination and inclusive growth. None need fear that greater 'autonomy', or 'self-rule' within the terms of the 1952 Delhi Agreement,[8] or the restoration of nomenclatures like Wazir-e-Azam and Sadr-i-Riyasat, spell secession. The J&K and Indian Constitutions are joined by an umbilical cord. What is removed from one can be incorporated in the other, so that common values and principles remain. Too much time has been wasted by little men on little things. Opportunity beckons.

Shaping International Opinion

International opinion needs to be enlightened and re-educated on the facts underlying the Kashmir imbroglio, as also India's relationship with Pakistan. The former US secretary of state, Condoleezza Rice advised Delhi to be generous in its statements on, and interpretations of, Pakistan so as to help stabilize its fledgling civilian government.[9] There was also a suggestion that India should note that the US had pressured Islamabad to move forward on its bounden duty and solemn commitments.

These propositions bear examination, as we have heard them before and could hear more of them in the future. The fact is that the government of India has consistently differentiated between the people of Pakistan, its fledgling civil government and emerging democracy on the one hand—and the still-powerful and unaccountable military, jihadi hardliners and religious right, on the other. The latter have to be brought to heel, and subordinated to the elected government. Further massive military aid to Pakistan is therefore not the answer.

The former British foreign secretary, David Miliband, on his part, brashly and erroneously linked the 26/11 Mumbai attack to 'root causes' in Kashmir. There was a further hint to keep in mind the impact of counter-terrorism strategies on Muslim Indians. Miliband found Islamabad's insistence on bringing the Mumbai terror culprits to trial in Pakistan justified, on grounds of the absence of an extradition treaty with India, and confidence in Pakistan's justice system. All this earned him a well-deserved snub from the Indian government.[10]

The Mumbai-terror 'root cause' link is pernicious nonsense, and suggestively upholds the 'right' of a country or organization exporting terror to do so. It extenuates its criminality in killing total innocents at random, on the plea—howsoever tenuous or false—that it is part of a 'liberation struggle'. There can be no 'Kashmir link' to terrorism, whether in J&K itself or elsewhere in India. This is where the reported LeT offer, of ending jihadi terror if the world 'liberates' Kashmir for Pakistan, is a thundering misjoinder.

Further, Pakistan has no extradition treaty with India, but it has obligations under the SAARC convention and commitments to the UN—particularly because Ajmal Kasab, a confirmed Pakistani, who was part of the 26/11 terror attack on Mumbai, admitted to committing the crime. He was the only terrorist to be caught alive and tried, and subsequently executed. Would the UK agree to a trial in a terror accused's homeland in similar circumstances, especially when that country had been prevaricating for years about its role in exporting terror? Indeed, Britain has been insistent on the extradition of a Russian businessman, Andrei Lugovoi, for his alleged connection with the death, in London, of a former KGB agent, Alexander Litvinenko, despite there being no bilateral UK-Russian extradition agreement.

While, undoubtedly, there is admiration in India for the manner in which some judges in Pakistan refused to bow before Musharraf, the Pakistan judiciary has been known to plead the 'doctrine of necessity' out of sheer helplessness. Who is prepared to award high marks to Pakistan for its investigation and 'house arrest' of the notorious nuclear wheeler-dealer, A.Q. Khan? Consequently—and specifically because he was not sure of a fair investigation at home—Asif Zardari wanted his wife, Benazir Bhutto's assassination to be probed by the UN.

The Indian case is, however, not improved by the misconceived campaign by a section of the bar, and extreme political groups, threatening any lawyer who defends a terror suspect. However, if any trial is to be held in Pakistan, then India could seek to be legally represented as part of the prosecution, or even as a court observer.

*

An LeT spokesman has stated, that Britain 'did not implement the agreed upon agenda of Partition',[11] namely, that J&K should go to

Pakistan. This is totally unhistorical and part of a long-time myth that many in the West have bought, thereby linking J&K to a so-called 'Muslim question' rooted in the two-nation theory. This has no foundation in fact whatsoever, whether in the pre-Independence negotiations, the Indian Independence Act, Pakistan's counter-complaint to the UN or the UN resolutions. This Pakistani myth was accepted and internationalized by the US and Britain as a justification of their adoption of Pakistan as a frontline state and ally from 1949 onwards. Furthermore, the collateral damage to India from the West's default has been enormous and cannot be self-servingly brushed aside.

Unfortunately, the Indian government has been remiss in informing the Indian people, and the world, of the facts and merits of the Kashmir question and the sequence of events. Documenting this data from official non-Indian records and from subsequent Pakistani revelations of home truths that have unravelled previous solemn and sworn denials would be extremely useful for wide national and international circulation.

The Kashmir question has been one of India's major security and diplomatic concerns since Independence. Maharaja Hari Singh's accession of J&K to India in October 1947 followed the tribal invasion of the state with Pakistan's full support, thus legitimizing India's military intervention. The ensuing war ended in the first days of January 1949, virtually partitioning the state along a CFL that left a third of the population and territory under the control of Pakistan.

India's acceptance of the Instrument of Accession was complete in every respect. Yet, in his letter to the maharaja, Governor General Lord Mountbatten said:

> It is my Government's wish that as soon as law and order have been restored in Jammu and Kashmir and her soil cleared of the invader the question of the State's accession should be settled by a reference to the people.[12]

However, the governing resolution of the United Nations of 13 August 1948—calling for a ceasefire, and followed by a truce, as essential conditions for a plebiscite—were not implemented by Pakistan, and were, in fact, openly flouted by it. The armed raiders were not disbanded, nor were Pakistan's regular forces withdrawn. Indeed, they were augmented.

Ten years later, as we know, the UN representative, Gunnar Jarring opined that the passage of time and changing circumstances had rendered the UN resolutions obsolete. This had precisely been the Indian view. Several wars, proxy wars and cross-border terror strikes later, the situation remains unchanged. Pakistan has failed to annex the state, which remains divided and bruised. While a secessionist group continues to seek 'self-determination' by union with Pakistan, even while opposing elections, the Jammu Kashmir Liberation Front on both sides seeks independence for all of J&K. Neither is feasible. J&K is now an integral part of India, and there will be no second Partition. Several fair and free elections have been held at the national, state and local levels, with very large turnouts despite threats and boycotts. The people have spoken.

Yes, there has undeniably been discontent and alienation at certain levels, because of maladroit political management of the state—between 1952 and 1975, in 1983, from 1984 to 1987, and sporadically thereafter. Some 3,00,000 Pandits were forced to flee the Valley from 1989 as Muslim militancy peaked, as well as over 50,000 Muslim families, whose daughters were cruelly preyed upon by muhajideen, and houses forcibly used as shelters and arms dumps. Armed insurgency was born in the later 1980s, much of it fuelled by cross-border elements and separatists. This has only brought more grief. However, the use of arms and senseless killings have not yielded the results that terrorists would hope for. Nationalist forces have rallied, while those alienated from the Indian state have come to adopt a more realisable and practical objective—of seeking greater autonomy, self-determination and azadi within India.

The government of India has stated its willingness to consider greater internal autonomy for J&K. After Narasimha Rao spoke of granting Kashmir 'anything short of independence' in 1995, the Deve Gowda government referred to 'maximum autonomy'.[13] The National Conference government subsequently set up two committees—one to outline a framework of autonomy, and the other to report on regional autonomy among the regions of the state.

The term 'autonomy' , so widely used, essentially implies an adjustment in centre-state relations. The use of symbols like a state flag and nomenclatures such as Sadr-i-Riyasat and Wazir-e-Azam for governor and chief minister, respectively, are really subsidiary issues. Yet symbols are important when dealing with a people's psyches.

It would be useful to lay to rest a popular muddle that has entrapped highly placed minds—this is that more autonomy means less 'integration' with India, and vice versa, and that 'full integration' will only be achieved by abrogation of Article 370 of the Constitution that regulates centre-state relations in regard to J&K. The fact is that integration is governed by Article 1 of the Constitution, which posits that 'India, that is Bharat, shall be a Union of States. The States and the territories thereof shall be as specified in the First Schedule'—which in turn places J&K alongside Andhra Pradesh, Bihar, and several other states, in alphabetical order.

The maharaja of Kashmir acceded to India under the standard Instrument of Accession adapted from the 1935 Government of India Act. This was applicable to all princely states alike. There was no special or separate dispensation for J&K. The Instrument of Accession transferred responsibility for three items to the union, namely defence, foreign affairs and communications. In short, Article 370 was to regulate centre-state relations with regard to J&K.

Article 370 provides:

(1) Notwithstanding anything contained in this Constitution,
   (a) the provisions of Article 238 shall not apply now in relation to the state of Jammu and Kashmir;
   (b) the power of Parliament to make laws for the said state shall be limited to:
       (i) those matters in the Union List and the Concurrent List which, in consultation with the Government of the State, are declared by the President to correspond to matters specified in the Instrument of Accession governing the accession of the State to the Dominion of India as the matters with respect to which the Dominion Legislature may make laws for that State; and
       (ii) such other matters in the said Lists as, with the concurrence

of the Government of the State, the President may by order specify.

(c) the provisions of Article 1 and of this article shall apply in relation to that State;

(d) such of the other provisions of this Constitution shall apply in relation to that State subject to such exceptions and modifications as the President may by order specify:

Provided that no such order which relates to the matters specified in the Instrument of Accession of the State referred to in paragraph (i) of sub-clause (b) shall be issued except in consultation with that Government.

(2) If the concurrence of the Government of the State referred to in paragraph (ii) of sub-clause (b) of clause (1) or in the second proviso to sub-clause (d) of that clause be given before the constituent assembly for the purpose of framing the Constitution of the State is convened, it shall be placed before such Assembly for such decision as it may take thereon.

(3) Notwithstanding anything in the foregoing provisions of this article, the President may, by public notification, declare that this article shall cease to be operative or shall be operative only with such exceptions and modifications and from such date as he may specify:

Provided that the recommendation of the constituent assembly of the State referred to in clause (2) shall be necessary before the President issues such a notification

The meaning is quite clear. The terms of Article 370 shall not be varied in the direction either of enlarging or diminishing the centre's jurisdiction in J&K, or abrogating the article altogether without the concurrence of the state. Some critics have argued that since specific mention is made of the J&K constituent assembly, which ceased to exist after 1956, no change could have been effected subsequently as the validating mechanism had ceased to exist. This is a mistaken view, as the constituent assembly was succeeded by the state legislature which has continuing constituent powers.

Before examining the extent of the original ambit of Article 370, and its subsequent modifications in relation to centre-J&K relations, it would be useful to note certain other relevant issues.

J&K Constitution

J&K is the only state in India which has a Constitution of its own. All other princely states first acceded to and then merged with the Indian union; sent representatives to the Indian constituent assembly; and/or freely accepted the Indian Constitution as finally adopted.

There is, however, an organic nexus between the J&K and Indian Constitutions. The preamble to the J&K Constitution, drawn up 'in pursuance of the accession of this State to India', and more specifically Article 3 in Part II asserts that 'the State of Jammu and Kashmir is and shall be an integral part of the Union of India'.[14] Section 5 provides that the executive and legislative power of the State extends to all matters 'with respect to which Parliament of India has power to make laws for the State under the provisions of the Constitution of India'.[15]

Section 147, pertaining to amendment of the Constitution, clearly stipulates that:

[...] no bill or amendment seeking to make any change in
(a) this Section; or
(b) the provisions of Sections 3 and 5; or
(c) the provisions of the Constitution of India as applicable in relation to the State; shall be introduced or moved in either house of the legislature.

Kashmir is not uniquely special. There are some who ask how J&K can be treated differently from any other state. The fact that J&K is different—by virtue of the terms of accession—has been categorically upheld by the Supreme Court. In Khazan Chand vs the State of J&K, 1984, the Court held that the state 'holds a special position in the constitutional setup of our country'. It went on to explain the ambit and meaning of Article 370, and the Constitution (Application to Jammu and Kashmir) Order, promulgated on 26 January 1950, in accordance with the provisions of Article 370. It was thus that 'the basis for a constitutional relationship between the Union and the State was defined'.[16]

Furthermore, J&K is not the only state that enjoys a distinctive constitutional position. The Indian Constitution is extremely flexible and pragmatic and has carved out a number of territorial and non-territorial exceptions. The scheduled castes and tribes, other backward classes and minorities enjoy certain preferences.

Territorially, Article 371 and Articles 371(A) to 371 (I) list special provisions pertaining to the states of Maharashtra and Gujarat, Nagaland, Assam, Manipur, Andhra Pradesh, Sikkim, Mizoram, Arunachal Pradesh and Goa. Article 290A contains special provisions pertaining to Kerala and Tamil Nadu. The Fifth and Sixth Schedules also prescribe a special dispensation for certain tribal areas. The Constitution preserves unity with diversity in many ways.

Scope of the Original Accession

Article 246[17] read with the Seventh Schedule[18] specifies the heads of 'Union' (List I), 'State' (List II) and 'Concurrent' (List III) legislation with 97, 61 and 47 entries respectively. Let's understand this more clearly.

The original heads covered by J&K's Instrument of Accession were, nominally, only three—defence, foreign affairs and communication. The Sarkaria Commission on Centre-State Relations, 1988, examined this, and concluded that there were several other sub-heads under defence (the armed forces, cantonments, military works, arms, defence industries, war and peace, etc); foreign affairs (conferences, treaties and agreements with foreign countries, foreign jurisdiction, extradition, citizenship, passports and visas, piracy, port quarantine, foreign loans, international trade and fishing beyond territorial waters); and communications (railways, national highways, shipping and navigation, ports, airways, posts and telegraph, wireless broadcasting and telecommunications).

Altogether, these account for 37 out of 97 entries in List I. The Sarkaria Commission, adopting American jurisprudence on 'the doctrine of incidental and ancillary powers', further opined that certain other powers had to be added in. Among these, the commission enumerated currency and banking (six entries); matters vital for the functioning of the union (properties of the union, industrial disputes concerning union employees, the UPSC, union pensions); parliamentary, presidential and vice-presidential elections; the salaries of MPs and the emoluments of the president and governors; privileges of Parliament; audit of union and state accounts; and inquiries, surveys and statistics with regard to any of these (15 entries).

The commission spelt out certain other matters which it felt had 'national dimensions'. These covered inter-state trade and commerce; incorporation and regulation of manufacturing, trading and other institutions which have inter-state jurisdiction, inter-state migration, census, insurance, the survey of India; the botanical, zoological and geological surveys of India; establishing standards for weights and measures; and patents (12 entries).

Finally, the commission referred to certain taxes like customs, excise, corporation and income, which require uniform principles and which, by their very nature, are best administered centrally (13 entries). The proceeds of some of these taxes are, however, transferred by the union to the states by way of tax sharing or grants as determined also by the finance commission.

On such a reading, as many as 83 of the 97 entries in List I may be seen as legitimately within the province of the union. The State List or List II is in any case under the exclusive jurisdiction of the states.

The real bone of contention, then, is the Concurrent List. This sets out matters of common interest to both the union and states, and requires uniformity of principles in their application, throughout the country. Here—while it is open to any state to legislate on any of the subjects listed—union legislation enjoys supremacy.

This, then, is the theoretical position.

1950 Presidential Order

The coming into force of the Indian Constitution on 26 January 1950 made it both possible and necessary to forge a nexus between the union and J&K on the basis of Article 370. Accordingly, the president promulgated the Constitution (Application to Jammu and Kashmir) Order, 1950, in consultation with the state government, specifying the heads under which Parliament would be competent to legislate for the state. Two schedules were appended, listing the entries in the Union List, and those parts of the Constitution applicable to J&K.

The First Schedule,[19] which specified 35 entries relating to the heads of defence, foreign affairs and communications, also had two entries pertaining to the railways and audit. This excluded the State and Concurrent Lists, and left all residuary powers with J&K.

The Second Schedule[20] set out the parts/articles of the Constitution that would be applicable to J&K, in addition to Articles I and 370:[21]

> 1. Part V—pertaining to the union executive—was applied with some modifications. One of these, limited the jurisdiction of the Supreme Court to appellate matters, and barred the jurisdiction of the Comptroller and Auditor General.
>
> Articles 80 and 81 were modified to provide that J&K's representatives, in Parliament, would be appointed by the president, in consultation with the state.
>
> 2. Part XI—dealing with centre-state relations—was made applicable, with modifications and exceptions, as set out in the first schedule to the order.
>
> Article 257—concerning control of the union over states—in certain cases, was excluded. This meant that the centre could not issue orders to J&K to comply with union laws or directions. But there was an assurance by the state that such a contingency would not be allowed to arise.
>
> 3. In Part XII—concerning financial relations—the provisions of Articles 66 and 267, regarding the consolidated fund, public accounts, and the contingency fund, were to be restricted to the funds and accounts of the union.
>
> 4. The application of Part XV (elections), was limited to presidential and vice-presidential elections.
>
> 5. Part XVI—pertaining to special classes—was limited to the only relevant category, namely, scheduled castes.
>
> 6. The official language provisions of Part XVII, were limited to the proceedings of the Supreme Court.
>
> 7. Minor modifications were made with regard to Part XIX (miscellaneous).
>
> Article 365—empowering the president to declare an emergency should the state fail to comply with, or give effect, to directions by the union—was not to be applied to J&K.

Article 368—setting out the procedure for amending the union Constitution—was modified in relation to J&K, to make consultations with, and the consent of, the state government mandatory, as set out in Article 370.

Only five of the nine schedules to the Constitution were made applicable, namely, Schedules One (listing the territories of India), Two (the emoluments of certain high dignitaries), Three (oaths), Four (allocation of Rajya Sabha seats) and Eight (official language).

Among parts of the Constitution that did not apply were: Part III (fundamental rights), Part IV (directive principles), Part XIV (services under the union and the states) and Part XVIII (emergency provisions, subject to a modified application of Article 352 pertaining to a proclamation of emergency). Some of these exceptions were intended to avoid impairing the freedom of the proposed J&K constituent assembly to consider these issues. Nevertheless, the 1950 order did extend central powers beyond those surrendered to the union under the Instrument of Accession.

J&K went to the polls in August 1951, and the constituent assembly was convened in October. Early decisions were taken on the abolition of large estates without compensation, an elected Sadr-i-Riyasat to replace the hereditary ruler, and having a state flag. 'Reasoned conclusions regarding accession and the future of the State'[22] were remitted to the drafting committee.

Delhi Agreement, 1952

Some basic decisions having been taken by the constituent assembly, it was necessary to ensure central concurrence. The negotiations that followed resulted in the Delhi Agreement of 24 July 1952.[23]

- The major heads affirmed that residuary powers would vest in the state; under Article 5 of the Constitution, all those domiciled in J&K would be citizens of India; but state subjects—including those who had left the state and returned thereafter—would enjoy special rights and privileges;
- Articles 52 to 62 of the Constitution, pertaining to the president, would apply to the state. So also the president's power to grant pardons and remission of sentences;
- The state would have its own flag alongside the national flag;

- Though the Sadr-i-Riyasat would be elected by the state legislature, he would be a person acceptable to the centre, and be recognized by the president;
- It was left to be determined whether the fundamental rights chapter of the Indian Constitution should apply, subject to such modifications as necessitated—for example, by the abolition of big landed estates without compensation—or whether these should be incorporated in the state's Constitution;
- The Supreme Court would enjoy only appellate jurisdiction 'for the time being', in view of the existence of the Board of Judicial Advisers in the State;
- With regard to the centre's emergency powers, these were limited to defence against external aggression under Article 352, but with a proviso that in regard to internal disturbances its promulgation would be 'at the request, or with the concurrence, of the government of the State' .

On 24 July 1952, Jawaharlal Nehru announced in Parliament the signing of an agreement with Sheikh Abdullah.

1954 Presidential Order [24]

Sheikh Abdullah was dismissed on 8 August 1952.

The J&K constituent assembly continued its deliberations and, having adopted the report of its drafting committee ratifying accession to India, resolved that these matters and the Delhi Agreement be suitably incorporated in the Indian Constitution. The customs barrier between J&K and the rest of the country was removed on 13 April 1954, and the president promulgated the Constitution (Application to Jammu and Kashmir) Order on 14 May 1954.

The 1954 order provided that the following provisions of the Indian Constitution would apply to J&K:

A. The preamble.

B. A proviso was added to Article 3, to the effect that the area and boundaries of the state would not be altered without the consent of the state legislature.

C. Part II (citizenship) shall be deemed to have applied from 26 January 1950, with a proviso protecting migrant state subjects returning from Pakistan under a permit.

D. Part III (fundamental rights) would apply subject to such 'reasonable restrictions' as the state legislature might deem reasonable.

Further, freedom of assembly, association, movement and residence would be subject to restrictions in the interests of the security of the state.

In Article 22, preventive detention would be regulated by laws passed by the state legislature.

In Articles 31 (since deleted) and 31A, regarding protection of laws relating to compulsory acquisition of property, various provisos were to be omitted or substituted in their application to the state.

In Article 32 (constitutional remedies) the state court was empowered, in addition to the Supreme Court, to issue directions and writs.

E. A new Article 35A was inserted by Section 2(4) (j) of the 1954 order, saving laws defining permanent residents and their rights and privileges and, conversely, imposing upon other persons any restrictions with respect to government employment, acquisition of immovable property in the state, settlement in the state and the right to scholarships and other forms of aid as the state government might provide. Further, no state law in regard to any of these matters 'shall be void on the ground that it is inconsistent with or takes away or abridges any right conferred on other citizens of India by any provisions of this part', that is, Article 19. The state's laws also recognize companies as permanent residents for certain purposes.

F. Part V (the union) was to apply with the proviso that J&K's parliamentary representation would be by presidential appointment, on the recommendation of the state legislature.

G. Part VI (the states) was virtually rendered non-applicable.

H. In Part XI (relations between the union and the states), Article 246 was amended to limit the union's legislative powers to Lists I and II with certain modifications or exceptions. The exceptions to union initiatives are the barring of the Central Bureau of Investigation from exercising jurisdiction in J&K; the application of central preventive detention laws, though not the Foreigner's Act; the regulation of industry or mines in the public interest; film censorship; legislation pertaining to ancient monuments and archaeological sites; inter-state migration in relation to J&K; and state elections in J&K.

As for Article 248, Parliament was stripped of all residuary powers save that of making laws with respect to:

> disclaiming, questioning or disrupting the sovereignty and territorial integrity [...] cession [...] or secession of part of the

territory of India from the Union or causing insult to the Indian national flag, the Indian national anthem or this Constitution.

In Article 249, in clause (1), for the words 'any matter enumerated in the State List specified in the resolution', the words 'any matter specified in the resolution, being a matter which is not enumerated in the Union List or in the Concurrent List' shall be substituted.

To Article 253 (legislation for giving effect to international agreements) was added a proviso that:

[...] no decision affecting the disposition of the State of Jammu and Kashmir shall be made by the Government of India without the consent of the Government of that State.

Article 255 (providing that no union law shall be invalidated if duly assented to, merely because some recommendation or sanction constitutionally required was not given) was omitted.

Art 256, pertaining to obligations of the states and the union, was expanded to provide that:

The state of Jammu and Kashmir shall so exercise its executive power as to facilitate the discharge by the Union of its duties and responsibilities under the Constitution in relation to that State; and in particular, the said State shall, if so required by the Union, acquire or requisition property on behalf and at the expense of the Union, or if the property belongs to the State, transfer it to the Union on such terms as may be agreed, or in default of agreement, as may be determined by an arbitrator appointed by the Chief Justice of India.

I. Article 312 in Part XIV was amended to bring J&K within the purview of the all-India services.

J. Part XVII (official language) was to be limited to the official language of the Union, for inter-State or State-Union communication, and in relation to the proceedings of the Supreme Court.

K. Part XVIII (emergency provisions) was applied with modifications. Under Article 352, no proclamation of emergency made on grounds only of internal disturbance, shall have effect in J&K, unless made at the request or with the concurrence of the state government.

Article 356 (President's rule) was only to apply in case of a breakdown in the State Constitution.

Article 360 (financial emergency) was omitted.

L. In Part XX, in Article 368 (amendment of the Constitution) was conditioned by a new proviso:

Provided further that no such amendment shall have effect in relation to the State of Jammu and Kashmir unless applied by order of the President under clause (1) of Article 370.

M. Under Part XXII, the schedules were to be applied in accordance with the Delhi Agreement, with consequential modification in the Seventh Schedule (especially pertaining to the Concurrent List), and Ninth Schedule (adding J&K land reform laws to the list of protected legislation).

Further Extension of Union Powers

The J&K Constitution came into force on 26 January 1957. Over the ensuing years, Union powers were extended. Financial arrangements included listing J&K as a special category state, entitled to 90 per cent grant (earlier 70), and 10 per cent loan (earlier 30). A state cadre of IAS/IPS officers was created and the jurisdiction of the auditor and comptroller general, election commission and Supreme Court was fully extended in 1958, 1959 and 1960 respectively. The permit system that restricted the entry of Indian nationals from other parts of the country into J&K, was abolished on 1 April 1959.

Some forty-three Constitution (Application to J&K) Orders have been issued since 1954, incorporating these and other changes, many of them of a routine nature. Following the Moe-e-muqaddas (Prophet's Hair) agitation in the Valley, in 1964, a presidential order extended Articles 356 (which empowers the president to impose president's rule in the states) and 357 (which deals with the exercise of legislative powers under the proclamation issued under Article 356) to J&K. A year later, the state enacted a legislation changing the title Sadr-i-Riyasat to governor, and that of Wazir-e-Azam to chief minister. The governor would no longer be elected, but would be appointed by the president as in all other states. The appointment and tenure of judges of the high court were similarly brought on par with that prevailing in all other high courts in the country. The form of oath was also amended to include an affirmation to 'uphold the sovereignty and integrity of India'.

A significant change made in 1985 restored the union's residuary

powers under Article 248[25] and entry 97 ('residuary entry') of the
Union List. This enabled extension of TADA (Terrorist and
Disruptive Activities [Prevention] Act) to J&K.

In 1985, again, Articles 339 and 342 were made applicable, with
modifications, enabling the president to appoint a commission to
report on the welfare of scheduled castes, and list the tribes to be
included as scheduled tribes within the state. This followed the
Gujjar demand to be declared a tribal people.

In 1986, Article 249 was made applicable whereunder the Rajya
Sabha may, by a two-thirds majority, resolve that Parliament may,
in national interest, make laws listed in the state list.

In 1989, the Tenth Schedule pertaining to the defection law was
made applicable to J&K. Article 356 was amended, more than
once, to extend president's rule in J&K beyond the stipulated
maximum of two years.

Application of Union Laws

A number of union laws have been made applicable to J&K over
the years. Most of these are quite innocuous in terms of state
autonomy, and a commission set up by Sheikh Abdullah in 1975
did not find them objectionable up to that time.

These laws were, illustratively, in relation to opium, press and
registration of books, negotiable instruments, trade unions,
pledging of child labour, the Reserve Bank of India, payment of
wages, agriculture produce (grading and marking), insurance,
employers' liability, motor vehicles, drugs and cosmetics, industrial
disputes, coal mines, labour welfare, minimum wages, the Dentists'
Act, the National Cadet Corps, employees' state insurance, banking
companies, chartered accountants, the Indian Standards Institution
(certification marks), the Cinematograph Act (limited application),
commissions of inquiry, forward contracts, working journalists
(conditions of service), citizenship, companies, the UGC, LIC/life
insurance (emergency provisions), standards of weights and
measures, the Indian Medical Council, the suppression of immoral
trafficking of women, copyright, ancient monuments and
archaeological sites and remains, employment exchange
(compulsory notification of vacancies), the rice milling industry
(regulation), trade and merchandise marks, the Raj Committee,

advocates, air (prevention of pollution), narcotic drugs and psychotropic substances, destructive insects and pests, the Indian Red Cross, armed forces (special powers), TADA, and all-India services.

1974 Accord

The original jurisdiction over J&K, as vested in the centre under the Instrument of Accession, was confined to the three heads of defence, foreign affairs and communications. It was gradually extended through the mechanism of Article 370. Some felt that central jurisdiction was enlarged by undemocratically elected J&K governments or through the arbitrary exercise of the governor's power to erode the state's autonomy. This was Abdullah's own position prior to his restoration in 1975.

The six-point accord the Sheikh negotiated with Indira Gandhi in 13 November 1974:[26]

1. reaffirmed Article 370;
2. vested residuary powers in the state, with Parliament remaining empowered to make laws to protect the sovereignty and integrity of India;
3. stipulated that any Indian constitutional provisions applied to the state with modifications might be altered or repealed on merits if so requested; however, those provisions already applied, without modification would be unalterable;
4. provided that, given the state's right to legislate on welfare, culture, social security, personal laws and legal procedures, it would be entitled to review and propose amendments to, or a repeal of, laws made by Parliament, or extend these to the state after 1953 in matters relating to the Concurrent List; further, the state would be consulted with regard to an extension of such central laws to it in the future;
5. required the president's assent for any state legislation or constitutional amendment impinging on:
   (a) the appointment, powers, functions, duties, privileges and immunities of the governor; and
   (b) the following matters relating to elections, namely, the superintendence, direction and control of elections by the Election Commission of India, eligibility for inclusion in the electoral rolls without discrimination, adult suffrage and composition of the Legislative Council;

6. disagreed on restoring the nomenclatures Sadr-i-Riyasat and Wazir-e-Azam.

The matter was referred back to the principals, namely Sheikh Abdullah and Mrs Gandhi, by their representatives, Mirza Afzal Beg and G. Parthasarathy, to whom the review had been entrusted. The Sheikh reportedly found little to retract, especially with respect to welfare laws, though Beg would have preferred to press for certain modifications. Indira Gandhi would not countenance the usage of Sadr-i-Riyasat, but was agreeable to a restoration of the term, Wazir-e-Azam through an appropriate amendment to the J&K Constitution.

Issues in Contention

The question now before the State Autonomy Commission was—what if any of the provisions of the Constitution of India were to roll back, or what if specific central laws were to rescind in order to 'restore autonomy'? Some current issues could be listed as 'infringing' autonomy or threatening national integration. Some of these had little substance but were, nevertheless, of emotional significance—such as the nomenclatures given to the governor and chief minister, and symbols like the state flag.

The major issues of contention for Kashmiris are probably Article 356 and other emergency laws, the role and powers of the governor, the central services, the jurisdiction of the Supreme Court, Election Commission and the Comptroller and Auditor General of India (CAG), the restoration to the state of concurrent and residuary powers (Article 248) and Article 249 (which empowers Parliament to legislate with respect to a state subject in the national interest). As against this, the financial dependence of the state on the centre, and the importance of the Indian market for J&K in every respect, suggests the necessity of central assistance and support—not least in matters of inter-state trade and commerce, including investment and tourism.

Critics of Article 370, on the other hand, are uncomfortable with the 'protection' given to state subjects, and the 'discrimination' this entails against other Indians. Some of the protective barriers—as with regard to the ban on purchase of property by non-state subjects—are essentially aimed at safeguarding the interests of a relatively less advanced state, and preventing affluent Indians from outside the state from purchasing prime real estate. Time could be a solvent with respect to some of these matters. Himachal Pradesh has a similar bar on transfer of property to outsiders. Tribal lands, too, cannot be alienated anywhere in India.

Many provisions of the Indian Constitution do not formally apply to the state, as they are incorporated in the state's own Constitution, and vice versa. Some provisions of the J&K Constitution are perhaps in advance of the Indian Constitution. The J&K land reforms have, for instance, been far more radical and successful—at least in the Valley—than in the rest of the country, because the state is empowered to acquire large estates without payment of compensation. The rights of women and children are likewise more strongly enunciated in the J&K Constitution, and every permanent resident is entitled to free education up to the university level. The J&K Constitution extends the fundamental rights written into the Indian Constitution to all state subjects, and reproduces many of the directive principles from the latter.

What difference does any of this really make? The Indian penal code does not apply to J&K, but its 'Ranbir penal code' (RPC) is a close copy of the former. Does that make for more or less autonomy or integration? Some in Kashmir might feel that the jurisdiction of the Supreme Court, Election Commission, CAG, and even the all-India services, are an imposition. But others privately confess that some, or all, of these institutions are in the best democratic interests of the state. The wise course would be to let the people of the state decide, try out their own alternatives, and then determine which option to finally adopt. Greater autonomy could promote integration. Long back, Sheikh Abdullah said Kashmir wanted freedom before accession. That remains a good recipe.

Autonomy Committee

According to minister for finance and Ladakh affairs, Abdul Rahim Rather, in 1995, Narasimha Rao announced that he:

> [...] would be prepared to consider autonomy 'short of independence' for J&K. Dr. Farooq Abdullah had welcomed the

statement and asked the Union government to issue an order under Article 370, to restore the State's autonomy in terms of the Delhi agreement of 1952. And when this did not happen, the National Conference boycotted the parliamentary election in 1996.[27]

Following his resumption of office as chief minister, Sheikh Abdullah accordingly constituted two autonomy committees in November 1996.The first, Regional Autonomy Committee (RAC), headed by Balraj Puri, was mandated to make recommendations with regard to regional autonomy:

[...It had the power] to examine the possibilities of promoting better involvement and participation of people in different regions for balanced political, social and cultural development and evolving of instrumentalities, like local organs of power, at all levels. The committee had been assigned the task of examining the powers that such organs needed to be vested with for achieving the objectives and finding whether any change in the state constitution was required.[28]

The second committee, State Autonomy Panel, under Mohiuddin Shah, public works minister (originally headed by Dr Karan Singh, until his resignation in July 1997), was asked to

examine and recommend measures for the restoration of autonomy [...] consistent with the Instrument of Accession, the Constitution Application Order, 1950, and the Delhi Agreement. [It was further asked] to recommend safeguards for incorporation in the Union/State Constitution, to ensure that the constitutional arrangement finally evolved [...] is inviolable [and recommend measures] to ensure a harmonious relationship for the future between the State and the Union.[29]

The Delhi Agreement was implemented partly through enactment of the state Constitution, and partly through the 1954 presidential order. Both followed Sheikh Abdullah's dismissal and detention. But in 1974, the Sheikh agreed that the provisions of the Indian Constitution, already applied without modification, were unalterable.

In addition to such constitutional issues, there are certain powers that the centre has assumed through administrative and planning processes, and its financial and regulatory powers. Licensing of industries, foreign exchange and import-export control, plan approvals, matching grants, and matters such as determination of royalties and allocation of small savings, have resulted in some erosion of the states' rights. This is not peculiar to J&K, but has been a grievance that all states share. Some of these matters have been dealt with by the Finance Commission and the Planning Commission, but all the outcomes are seen as products of central discretion.

Many of these issues have been agitated by the states generally, and the Sarkaria Commission dealt with some of them. They concern federal relations as a whole, and are not an exclusive J&K issue. Some of these constraints have eased—or altogether disappeared—with deregulation, liberalization and privatization. Now, the states do enjoy a growing measure of economic initiative, and are beginning to exercise these newfound rights. Directly negotiating foreign investment is certainly one new trend.

Responding to a questionnaire issued by the Sarkaria Commission, the J&K government did indeed make a number of submissions on centre-state relations. It favoured greater state control over the all-India services, and maintained that the inter-state council would better serve the purpose of reducing friction and eliminating misunderstandings between the centre and states. It expressed reservations about the overbearing role of the Planning Commission, and the centre's excessive dependence on the concept of public interest to bring large areas of industry under the union.

Pushing autonomy beyond a point can, however, prove financially unviable for smaller and less-developed states, and those confronted by the difficulties imposed by a mountainous terrain and harsh climatic conditions. J&K is financially, even now, a special-category state, and will continue to be heavily dependent on the centre for infrastructure development over far-flung areas.

J&K can, however, make a claim on the centre in one respect. The Indus Treaty, signed in 1960, was dictated by national interest. This allocated the waters of the three eastern rivers to India (essentially to Punjab, Haryana, Rajasthan and Delhi, with only a modicum of potential benefit to J&K). This was in lieu of the apportionment of the three western rivers, Chenab, Jhelum and Indus, to Pakistan—curtailing J&K's rights on the upper reaches of all three, for purposes of even non-consumptive hydro-electric storage and diversions within these basins. Central assistance in developing hydro potential and storages, permissible under the treaty, would be appropriate compensation.

The issues in contention have been listed. Nothing is lost by viewing these demands with sympathy, as the essential problem is more a crisis of confidence than anything else. Once people in J&K know that autonomy under several heads is being repatriated, local and regional opinion might well favour a continuation of many aspects of the existing dispensation. Even otherwise, J&K is constitutionally different, and there need be no excessive fear of a domino effect on the rest of the country.

Suggestions for Action

Nevertheless, J&K's State Autonomy Committee was charged with 'restoring autonomy'. How far should one have gone? The mandate was to act consistently with the Instrument of Accession, with the 1950 Constitution (Application to Jammu & Kashmir) Order, and the Delhi Agreement, 1952. The 1950 order went beyond the bare Instrument of Accession. The Delhi Agreement, in turn, left over the question of fundamental rights and financial arrangements for detailed examination. The Constitution (Application to Jammu & Kashmir) Order, 1954, accordingly, went beyond the Delhi Agreement, on the basis of the views and recommendations of the state's constituent assembly. The fact that this order has been in operation for more than four decades—and no great objection to it was articulated during a review under the 1974 Agreement—carries a certain message. Nevertheless, there is no reason why certain adjustments cannot be contemplated.

The principle of the state legislature selecting the Sadr-i-Riyasat or governor, by whatever nomenclature, can be restored if the resident were to submit a name which the legislature might endorse. The president could then appoint the 'Governor that is Sadr-i-Riyasat' (on the analogy of 'India that is Bharat') and the latter would hold office at his pleasure.

The jurisdiction of the Supreme Court, the Central Election

Commission and the CAG should present little difficulty. Since the court's jurisdiction, in any case, extends to fundamental rights—matters listed under Article 131 (which pertains to the original jurisdiction of the Supreme Court) and implicitly all other heads with respect to which the union's authority has been accepted—it would be both logical and convenient to extend it to all other matters.

The impartiality of the Central Election Commission has come to be respected in J&K, despite certain past electoral aberrations. Even so, if necessary, power may be taken under Article 324 (4)[30] to appoint a regional election commissioner to assist the Central Election Commission in the conduct of elections in J&K. This appointment could be made by the president on the recommendation of the state government/legislature prior to each election.

Since the union government has been generous in devolving funds on J&K (as a special-category state), it is only appropriate that the CAG continue to perform his duties and exercise his powers as heretofore. The reports of the CAG, relating to the accounts of each state, are in any case presented to the governor and laid before the legislature, under Article 151.

Part XIV of the Constitution, pertaining to services under the union and the states, did not initially apply to J&K. But the provisions of Article 312, relating to all-India services, were extended to it in 1958. Under the scheme, entry is both by direct examination, and through selection by the UPSC (Union Public Service Commission) of promotees from the state civil service. In most states, the promotee quota has been around 33 per cent; in the case of J&K this has been 50 per cent.

The bulk of direct recruits to the all-India services comes from just about a dozen colleges/universities in India. There is every reason to expect that, as elsewhere, with improvements in the quality of education in J&K, the number of direct recruits from the state will increase in the years ahead. Even otherwise, consideration may be given to increasing the J&K selection quota on merit, and perhaps also making available a J&K quota in certain other central services, and in the public sector. This may be considered in view of the disruption of education in the state, at times, on account of disturbed conditions.

The misuse of Article 356 is a matter that has caused widespread concern in all states. The matter was considered by the inter-state council, and some agreed modifications and safeguards did emerge. In the days ahead, the J&K legislature may also be invited to recommend any further safeguards for consideration. Correspondingly, or otherwise, this may be done via the state Constitution by suitably amending Section 92 (which deals with a breakdown of the constitutional machinery).

Regional Factors

One ticklish problem is that Jammu and Ladakh might prefer less 'autonomy' and more 'integration' at one level, and more regional autonomy from Kashmir at another. Regional rivalries have long been evident in J&K, not surprisingly, in view of the divergent histories and socio-cultural backgrounds of the territories in question. The Glancy Commission was appointed by the maharaja in 1931 to address regional and communal imbalances in the state. It recommended that all state-service appointments should be advertised, and steps taken to ensure fair representation for all communities. At the district level, appointments should go to local people.

The regional and political balance changed after 1947. Following the 1962 conflict with China, a Ladakh Development Commission was set up, but proved ineffective. Following a few communal incidents in 1969 and worried of being consigned to a minority status, the Buddhist Action Committee asked for scheduled tribe status for Ladakhis; the settlement of Tibetan refugees in Ladakh; the Bodhi language to be made compulsory till high school; the construction of a rest house in Kargil; and Ladakhi representation in the state ministry at the cabinet level.

Subsequent discontent, in Jammu in particular, resulted in the appointment of the Gajendragadkar Commission in 1967 to look into regional disparities. It recommended the establishment of statutory development boards for Jammu, Kashmir and Ladakh respectively; and, detecting a sense of political neglect in Jammu and Ladakh, urged the government to take steps to counter such sentiments. It proposed an equable sharing of resources, regionally, so as to convey a feeling of balanced participation in the integrated development of the state. The commission favoured equal cabinet representation for J&K, and suggested that if the chief minister was from one region, the deputy chief minister should be drawn from the other.

The state administration's unwillingness to accept or implement the recommendations led to further agitation, which compelled the government to appoint the Sikri Commission in 1978. But before that, Sheikh Abdullah had convened a convention that proposed a five-tier federal structure for J&K—from the gram sabha, through the block samiti and zila parishad, to regional councils for the three provinces, and the state government at the apex.

The Sikri Commission submitted its report in 1980. It recommended the establishment of a state development board with some MLAs under the chief minister; and a new formula for regional financial allocations based on population, area, natural resource endowments and relative stage of development. It did not favour reservation in government services on the basis of community, caste or district. The report was again largely disregarded. In 1986, Farooq Abdullah, Sheikh Abdullah's son, appointed Balraj Puri to head a new regional autonomy committee, but did not persevere with this commitment after the 1987 elections.

As resentment in Jammu simmered, an All-party Action Committee was set up in Ladakh in 1980, to demand regional autonomy. The state government responded by appointing a ministerial sub-committee. This proved infructuous and the Ladakhis did not believe that the earlier established ministry of Ladakh affairs, in Srinagar, would be able to accomplish anything. Ladakhi representatives subsequently met Prime Minister Indira Gandhi to again press for regional autonomy, tribal status for the Buddhists, a parliamentary seat for Leh and greater representation in the state assembly.

A parallel Kargil Action Committee, in turn, sought provincial status for the two districts of Ladakh, namely, Kargil and Leh. (Those in Kargil were worried about being included along with the Buddhists of Ladakh.) The state government cited divided counsel for inaction. Scheduled tribe status for all Ladakhis was, however, conceded, though not for the Arguns, a small community of some six hundred Sunni Kashmiri trading families long settled in Ladakh. They were born of mixed marriages between these Kashmiri traders and local Ladakhi women. Their exclusion has potential for misunderstanding, though the Ladakh Buddhist Association sees the Arguns as exploiters.

The Ladakh Autonomous Hill Development Council Act, which came into effect in 1995, envisages an autonomous hill development council (AHDC) for each district of the region. It was adopted in Leh. Kargil rejected the proposal, since it believed that the council mirrored the priorities of Buddhist leadership, but it has the option to change its mind. Both would be sub-units of the Ladakh AHDC, which is designated the apex, coordinating body. The councils have development functions, and can raise local revenues, but have no police powers. The fact that the Leh Hill Council is controlled by the Congress, while the Ladakh Affairs minister is from the National Conference, has been a source of tension.

Sub-regional Identities

There has been an emergence of sub-regional identities, too, related to geo-political, religious and linguistic factors. The Buddhists of Leh, and the Shia Muslims of Kargil, have been caught up in rivalry. Citing discrimination by the district majority, and being cut off from the rest of the region for more than half the year by impassable mountain barriers, the Zanskar Buddhist Council has demanded a separate hill council within the Kargil district.

The Gujjars in J&K account for around 8 to 9 per cent of the population, though they claim double that number. They were granted tribal status by the Chandrashekhar government soon after this was conceded to the Ladakhis. This has stimulated the growth of a Pahari identity in parts of Doda, Rajouri and Poonch. Emulating the Gujjar and Bakerwal Welfare Board (established in 1975) and the impetus given to education within the community as a consequence, Pahari Speaking People (PSP)—embracing a somewhat wider ambit—is seeking scheduled tribe status for this community. This appears problematic as the Paharis include Rajputs, Brahmins, and other relatively advanced communities. The Paharis, however, emphasize the backward-area criterion.

The Kashmiri Pandits, who have a distinct identity, were largely forced out of the Valley in 1990 by Islamist militant groups who had little use for Kashmiriyat. Some 49,000 families are registered in migrant camps in Jammu, Delhi, and elsewhere, which makes a total population of around 2,00,000. Some of the more embittered among them have advocated a homeland within the Valley, Panun Kashmir. Most Kashmiri Muslims, however, want them back in their midst, and a section may have been emboldened to return to their former homes. But the Sangampora massacre in March 1997 of some Pandits who had preferred to remain in the Valley, and the targetted killings of isolated Hindu families in early 1998 at Wandhama and Parankote have engendered new fears.

The government was earlier reportedly working on a Rs 2,800-crore employment and rehabilitation package to bring the Pandits back with honour and dignity, and restore their livelihoods. A ban has been imposed on the sale of immigrant property, and a stay ordered on suits for recovery of dues from them by banks and financial institutions. The appointment of a protector-general of migrant property has been proposed, along with the establishment of three self-contained transit settlements for returning migrants, in Srinagar, Anantnag and Baramulla.

Panun Kashmir, however, is a flawed and unrealizable concept. Creating communal enclaves in the Valley—possibly necessitating the ouster of innocent majority-community residents—cannot be a solution. The answer, more probably, lies in the creation of small industrial townships in the Valley, where returning migrants and others could be rehabilitated and given employment after due training.

Jammu and Srinagar are the winter and summer capitals of the state, respectively, and the government (or durbar) shuttles between them. This is time consuming and wasteful, though it has been a convention since 1870, providing a seasonal stimulus to the local economy. It is possibly also a symbolic bond between the J&K regions. In October 1987, Farooq Abdullah cancelled the durbar move from Srinagar, which provoked a storm of protest in Jammu. The order had to be rescinded within weeks, to end Jammu's sense of deprivation.

Jammu nurses other grievances: discriminatory delimitation of constituencies that gives it fewer seats and larger constituencies, than is the case in Kashmir; skewed personnel policies that place it at a disadvantage in the administration; the presence of a disproportionately small number of state-level institutions; and a lesser range and volume of incentives. Another grudge has been the refusal to create more districts in the region.

In 1972, the Kadri Commission turned down the demand for the creation of new districts in either Jammu or Kashmir provinces. Nevertheless, in 1979, the state government carved out three new districts in Kashmir: Badgam, Pulwama and Kupwara, and Kargil in Ladakh. Jammu was outraged. To assuage feelings, the government appointed the Wazir Commission to review the matter. This reported in 1984, favouring the creation of Kishtwar, Samba and Reasi districts in Jammu, and another district—Bandipur—in the Valley. The recommendations were ignored.

What comes through quite clearly is that inter-regional and even intra-regional rivalries and sentiments will need to be kept in mind in any consideration of autonomy for J&K. Sub-regional identities, too, have perhaps begun to cloud regional demands. In Ladakh, the fact that the Leh Hill Council preceded the Ladakh Autonomous Hill Development Council has created a gulf between Ladakh and Kargil that remains to be bridged. Likewise, the rise of Gujjar, Pahari, Doda and Kargil identities, and the Zanskari Buddhist sub-identity within Kargil, could give rise to a revival of the Greater Kashmir idea which would bring together all contiguous Muslim-majority areas around the Valley. Any such move could swamp the Valley's Kashmiriyat tradition into a larger Muslim identity, and convert Jammu into a primarily Dogra entity.

Such a development would be unfortunate and could perhaps be avoided were sub-regional identities enabled to find expression in panchayati raj. J&K amended its panchayat law in 1989, three years before the enactment of the 73rd and 74th Amendments, which in any case only provided a model for the states to adopt. The panchayati raj law in J&K envisages a three-tier structure, with direct elections confined to basic halqa units.[31] The block development councils and district planning and development boards are to be indirectly elected, and will have a nominated element. The district board chairman will be nominated by the government, and the block development officer and village-level worker will, ex-officio, be member secretaries at the two lower levels. The members of the panchayat adalat are also to be nominated by the government.

Women will enjoy one-third reservation through a nomination by the government, to the extent of any deficit in their representation through the electoral process. Unlike elsewhere, there is no provision for a state finance commission—enfeebling the panchayati bodies financially, and making them dependent on governmental largesse. The list of transferred subjects, too, is limited. Finally, these institutions may be superseded by the government, but there is a mandatory requirement to hold fresh elections within six months.

Panchayati polls were mooted in the autumn of 1998 after the harvest. But Sheikh Abdullah's earlier vision of a five-tier federal continuum in J&K, as a means of devolution and participatory governance, would appear to have been diluted. This is a pity, as meaningful devolution in accordance with the 73rd and 74th Amendments (through which local self-governance was introduced in rural and urban India) could provide useful building blocks for dealing with regional and sub-regional identities and aspirations.

The state government would do well to upgrade the panchayat structure through suitable amendments, including empowering the halqa sabhas; mandating one-third electoral reservation for women; subjecting supercession to endorsement by a high-level, impartial advisory committee; and making the district planning and development boards also elective, rather than nominated bodies. Such reforms would fulfil the stated purpose of the Act, which is to make panchayati raj 'an instrument of vigorous local self government to secure the effective participation of the people [...].'[32]

Entrustment through Articles 258/258A

Regional differences on the degree of extension or rolling back of union laws and heads of intervention—as between Jammu and Ladakh on the one hand, and Kashmir on the other—could pose delicate problems. The Constitution of India does, however, have a mechanism that could perhaps be used to overcome such differential political equations. This is contained in Articles 258 and 258A.

Article 258 provides that:

> [...] the President may, with the consent of the Government of a
> State, entrust either conditionally or unconditionally to that
> Government or to its officers functions in relation to any matter
> to which the executive power of the Union extends.

The related administrative and financial costs will also be defrayed
by the union in any such case.

Conversely, Article 258A provides that:

> [...] the Governor of a State may, with the consent of the
> Government of India, entrust either conditionally or
> unconditionally to that Government or to its officers functions
> in relation to any matter to which the executive power of the
> State extends.

This constitutional power of entrustment, from centre to state and
vice versa, has probably never been used thus far. It could enable
the centre to devolve greater autonomy specifically to Kashmir—
not necessarily by process of constitutional amendment, but by
entrustment—while at the same time, permitting the J&K
government to entrust certain state functions to the centre in
relation, specifically, to Jammu and Ladakh. Given the consent of
the centre, the states and the regions concerned, one could
presumably structure differential levels of 'autonomy', 'accession'
or 'integration'. These differentials could be fine-tuned in the light
of experience and emerging circumstances—in a more flexible
and less cumbersome manner—than would be the case were
constitutional amendments, with a two-thirds majority, necessary
every time.

Article 258 (2) also provides that:

> A law made by Parliament which applies in any State may,
> notwithstanding that it relates to a matter with respect to which
> the Legislature of the State has no power to make laws, confer
> powers and impose duties, or authorise the conferring of powers
> and the imposition of duties, upon the State or officers and
> authorities thereof.

These provisions must be read with Article 154 (2) (b) which, in
relation to the executive powers of a State, '[...] prevent Parliament

or the Legislature of the State from conferring by law functions on any authority subordinate to the Governor.'

Discussing the scope and ambit of Article 258, the Sarkaria Commission argued that it

> [...] provides a tool, by the liberal use of which co-operative federalism can be substantially realised in the working of the system. We, therefore, recommend a more extensive and generous use of this tool [...] for progressive decentralisation of powers to the Governments of the states and/or their officers and authorities. [33]

The creative use of Articles 258 and 258A will propel the deconstruction and restructuring of centre-state and regional relationships in J&K.

Karbi Anglong and NC Hills Autonomy Model

The entrustment mechanism has been used particularly in the Northeast, to enable states to transfer certain powers to autonomous district councils to fulfil the demands for regional autonomy. There has been a growing accretion of entrusted powers over the years, with the Karbi Anglong Autonomous Council and North Cachar Hills Autonomous Council in Assam now representing the most advanced form of regional autonomy in the country.

Under a memorandum of understanding (MoU) signed in 1995,[34] these two autonomous councils are now entrusted with forty-four heads, in respect of which, the executive power of the state government has been statutorily delegated to them. Additionally, these autonomous councils may enact legislation on matters falling within the Concurrent List of the Constitution with the proviso that such laws shall be reserved for the consideration and approval of the president.

The Sixth Schedule is also to be amended, to enable the governor of Assam to consult the district council, in respect of subjects entrusted to these councils, instead of mandating him to act purely on the advice of his council of ministers. While law and order remains a state responsibility, a mechanism is to be evolved for consultation with the chief executive member of the councils regarding the posting of senior police and civil officers up to the rank of SP (superintendent of police) and DCP (deputy commissioner of police) and the writing of their confidential reports.

Under the MoU, officers of the councils are also to be included in state delegations sent to discuss the finalization of the annual plans with the Planning Commission. The state government will, before the commencement of each financial year, indicate to the councils the overall financial allocations that they might expect. Each council will thereafter prepare and pass its own budget, and forward it to the state government for inclusion in the overall state budget. The councils will be consulted and provided an explanation in the event of any change.

The Karbi Anglong and NC Hills Autonomous Council model is still getting into gear, but it offers an illustration of the innovative manner in which federal and sub-federal relations can be structured.

Implementing the Autonomy Package

It is unfortunate that the two autonomy committees were not set up sooner in J&K, and have not worked more expeditiously. Delay could entail loss of political credibility and queer the pitch. However, both committees are expected to submit their reports to the state government within the next few months.

It would be desirable to elicit public opinion on the recommendations contained in the two reports. This would be best done by laying them on the table of the assembly, and publishing them for wide distribution in the major state languages. Debate should be encouraged, and all political parties and sections of the people should be invited to proffer their views. None, not even the Hurriyat, should be excluded from this interactive exchange. The state government should then make such amendments as may be necessary, before initiating negotiations with the centre for a final determination and settlement of the centre-state package.

The regional autonomy package could, in turn, build upwards on the panchayati raj structure—which would be a good way to mediate between sub-regional and regional aspirations—and accommodate both without injury to either. The consensus reached here would need to be incorporated in the J&K Constitution.

Two of the terms of reference of the centre-state autonomy committee merit emphasis. The first is to keep in mind the need to maintain 'harmonious' relations with the centre. The other is to ensure the 'inviolability' of the final settlement. The former suggests a relationship of mutual trust and cooperation; the latter would require constitutional entrenchment of the agreement, so that there can be no reneging on it either way. This could be done by a mutual declaration, embodied in a new article, that specifies the agreement as part of the unamendable basic structure of the Indian Constitution.

The centre should, meanwhile, elicit opinion within the national parties, consult the inter-state council and, maybe, the national integration council, in order to secure a wider consensus. The views of all interests and sections of opinion should be fully taken into consideration. Apprehensions that a discussion on autonomy for J&K—let alone its actual implementation—will have a domino effect in other parts of India are exaggerated. An educative debate will help remove many misunderstandings and defuse possible tensions that could otherwise develop in the future.

Setting a four- to six-month timetable for such a consultative process would be appropriate. The matter has some urgency and a crisp schedule or deadline would help concentrate the mind.

The procedure for actual implementation of the final formulation might take many forms. Some adjustments may be made through administrative decisions; others might require constitutional amendments, both of the union and J&K Constitutions. However, a constitutional amendment may not be necessary in all cases, as a presidential order can be issued as in the past, in terms of Article 370 (l)(d). Other changes may be brought about through the entrustment mechanism under Articles 258 and 258A; or even through a Rajya Sabha resolution under Article 249, where appropriate (or as a bridging mechanism), but again, only with the concurrence of the state.

The Other Side of the Hill

No consideration of the future of J&K will be complete without reference to the constitutional status of AJK and the Northem Areas that are under the control of Pakistan.

Following the tribal invasion of the maharaja's dominion, the Muslim Conference announced the formation of an AJK provisional government under Sardar Ibrahim Khan on 24 October 1947 with its headquarters at Muzaffarabad. It claimed jurisdiction over all of J&K. There was no question of accession. Separately, on 28 October, the Gilgit Scouts led by an Englishman, Major William Brown, staged a coup and eventually arrested the Dogra governor of the Gilgit Wazarat, Brigadier Ghansara Singh. On 3 November 1947, Major Brown hoisted the Pakistani flag in the Scout Lines; the Northern Areas administration was handed over to the provisional AJK government. Pakistan flew in a representative to Gilgit on 14 November, and, thereafter, the feudatory chiefs of Hunza and Nagar 'acceded' to Pakistan—something quite beyond their power.

On 28 April 1949, a tripartite agreement was concluded between the government of Pakistan, the president of AJK and the president of the AJK Muslim Conference, in Karachi, defining their respective areas of jurisdiction in AJK. Pakistan took over defence, foreign affairs, publicity, relations with the UNCIP, refugee rehabilitation, plebiscite arrangements, civil supplies, etc. It was also temporarily handed over—or took complete control of—Northern Areas affairs, as the AJK government pleaded its inability to immediately administer and police that far-flung region.

The Northern Areas have ever since been totally controlled by the government of Pakistan. In March 1963, Pakistan ceded the Shaksgam Valley, across the Karakoram, to China. Pakistan's first Constitution of 1956, defined the constitutional link between itself and Azad J&K (AJK)/the Northern Areas. That Constitution was soon abrogated but subsequent constitutions, including Article 257 of the current 1973 Pakistan Constitution, adopted similar language:

> When the people of the State of Jammu and Kashmir decide to accede to Pakistan, the relationship between Pakistan and that State shall be determined in accordance with the wishes of the people of that State.

'Azad' J&K

AJK originally had no constitution of its own, and was from 1948 administered by the Azad Kashmir government rules of business.

These were revised in 1950. In 1960, limited franchise was introduced under the Azad Jammu and Kashmir Basic Democracies Act. The electoral college included the democrats, J&K refugees and the J&K diaspora in Pakistan. An executive council was set up, but the president and ministers were nominated by the Pakistan government. The power behind the throne was the minister for Kashmir affairs in Karachi/Islamabad. Earlier, in 1958, the rules had been changed, to vest authority in a chief adviser, appointed by the government of Pakistan, and ultimately responsible to the minister for Kashmir affairs.

The Azad Jammu and Kashmir Government Acts of 1964 and 1968 were followed by another amendment in 1970, which introduced adult suffrage, direct elections to a twenty-five-member legislative assembly (with proportional representation for AJK refugees living in Pakistan) and the presidential system.

The parliamentary system was restored with the Azad Kashmir Interim Constitution Act, 1974. The Constitution states that:

> [...] in the discharge of its responsibilities under the UNCIP Resolutions, the Government of Pakistan has approved of the proposed repeal and re-enactment of the said Azad Jammu and Kashmir Government Act, 1970, and authorized the president of Azad Jammu and Kashmir to introduce the present Bill in the Legislative Assembly of Azad Jammu and Kashmir [...][35]

The AJK Constitution stipulates that Islam shall be the state religion. Further, it states that:

> [Fundamental rights...] shall not apply to any law relating to the members of the defence services or of the forces charged with the maintenance of public order for the purpose of ensuring proper discharge of their duties or the maintenance of discipline among them.[36]

Freedom of association is subject to the proviso that:

> No person or political party in Azad Jammu and Kashmir shall be permitted to propagate against, or take part in activities prejudicial or detrimental to, the ideology of the State's accession to Pakistan.[37]

This obviously also curtails freedom of expression. Freedom of speech is made subject to 'any reasonable restrictions imposed by law in the interest of the security of Azad Jammu and Kashmir, friendly relations with Pakistan, public order [...]'[38]

The oath prescribed for official functionaries and legislators enjoins them to '[...] remain loyal to the country and the cause of accession of the State of Jammu and Kashmir to Pakistan [...]'[39]

The Azad Jammu and Kashmir Council requires the presence of the federal minister of state for Kashmir affairs and northern affairs as an ex-officio member of the council. [40]

The Azad Jammu and Kashmir Council

The AJK council is chaired by the prime minister of Pakistan and consists of the AJK president, five members nominated by the prime minister of Pakistan from among federal ministers or MPs, the federal minister for Kashmir affairs (ex-officio), the AJK prime minister or his nominee, and six elected members of the AJK assembly.

The executive authority of the council shall be exercised directly by the chairman or through the council secretariat consisting of a federal minister and not more than three advisers appointed by the chairman.

The AJK legislative assembly shall consist of forty-one members, elected on the absis of adult franchise. They in turn shall co-opt five women, a representative of the ulema, a J&K state subject residing abroad and a technocrat or professional. Both the assembly and the council enjoy legislative powers and may make laws for AJK and state subjects. However, neither body is empowered to legislate in matters concerning:

> (a) the responsibilities of Government of Pakistan under UNCIP resolutions; (b) the defence and security of Azad Jammu and Kashmir; (c) the current coin or the issue of any bills, notes or other paper currency; or (d) the external affairs of Azad Jammu and Kashmir including foreign trade and foreign aid.[41]

The reference to Pakistan's responsibilities 'under UNCIP resolutions' is an amusing fig leaf, as those resolutions by the United Nations Commission for India and Pakistan require Pakistan to vacate the state!

The AJK council has exclusive powers to legislate with respect to matters set out in the council's legislative list. Council bills do not require the assent of the AJK president but must be authenticated by the chairman of the council. The council controls the 'council consolidated fund' and must prepare and adopt a council budget each year. The assembly adopts a separate annual budget and controls the AJK assembly consolidated fund.

The chief justices and justices of the AJK Supreme Court and High Court, the chief election commissioner and the auditor-general are appointed by the president on the advice of the council.

A proclamation of emergency shall be issued by the president if so advised by the chairman of the council.

The constitutional provisions cited above are indicative of the extensive budgetary, legislative and personnel powers enjoyed by the AJK council which is chaired by the prime minister of Pakistan and run by a secretariat in Islamabad answerable to him.

The council's legislative list includes, among other things, nationality, citizenship, migration; P&T, telephones, broadcasting and other forms of communication; public debt and borrowings; banking, insurance, stock exchanges; railways; oil, natural gas and electricity; taxes on income other than agricultural income; tourism; jurisdiction and powers of all courts and offences against laws with respect to matters enumerated in the council list; and ancillary matters.[42] All other matters shall be within the legislative competence of the AJK assembly.

Northern Areas

The mountainous terrain of the Northern Areas (now Gilgit-Baltistan) has been reorganized into the five districts of Gilgit, Skardu, Diamir, Ghizer and Ghanche. They were virtually annexed by Pakistan under the Karachi Agreement of 1949.

The Northern Areas were politically and constitutionally part of the maharaja's kingdom, as mentioned in 'Treaties, Engagements and Sanads'[43] and other British records, and were recognized as such by the UN. Pakistan has, at various times, sought to maintain that the Northern Areas were never part of J&K, but has been unable to sustain this fiction. Further, Pakistan has sought to separate the Northern Areas from AJK, deliberately reinforcing its unclear constitutional status, hoping to integrate the Northern

Areas with Pakistan in the event of a pebescite during which the Kashmiris might vote for independence or self-determination.

First, however, let's consider the recent history of the Northern Areas. Following the rebellion of the Gilgit Scouts and the liberation of the Northern Areas in October 1947, a short-lived provisional government under Shah Rais was established. Shah Rais, in turn, handed over power to the Pakistan government. After taking over the control of the Northern Areas, the government of Pakistan enforced the colonial law of Frontier Crimes Regulations (FCR) across whole area; accordingly, a civil servant exercised all judicial and administrative powers. The political agent in Gilgit, in the meantime, was placed under the political resident of the NWFP, which was another attempt to include the area into administrative control of a province of Pakistan. Subsequently, political control was removed from the NWFP governor and handed over to the ministry of Kashmir affairs. By 1952, the joint secretary in that ministry was appointed as the resident of the Northern Areas. Such remote administrative control ended in 1967, with the creation of the post of a resident of the Northern Areas in Gilgit. In 1971, a new political party—Tanzeem-e-Millat—demanded provincial status for the area. The ensuing agitation, and the refusal of the Gilgit Scouts to fire on the rebels, led to the disbandment of the Gilgit Scouts. It was replaced by the Chitral Scouts, a Sunni force. The FCR was withdrawn, jagirdars and the former feudal chiefdoms were abolished and newer districts carved out. The Tanzeem-e-Millat merged with the Pakistan Peoples Party.

The Northern Areas, being neither part of AJK nor Pakistan, were in constitutional limbo. The people were not citizens of either entity, nor did they have any constitutional status or apparatus of self-governance of their own. They did not enjoy fundamental rights, and had no representation in any assembly or parliament—until Zia ul-Haq nominated three representatives to the Majlis-e-Shura in Islamabad, as observers in 1982. The observers were removed with the subsequent change in regime.

Governance by Federal Kashmir and Northern Areas Ministry

The governance of the Northern Areas is under the Kashmir and Northern Areas (KANA) division of the ministry of Kashmir affairs in Islamabad.

Until the 1995 reforms, the executive was headed by a chief commissioner who ruled through the Pakistan bureaucracy. The lower civil and criminal courts were under a judicial commissioner, who was the final appellate authority— but without writ jurisdiction—as no fundamental rights were applicable to the region.

The KANA division exercised the powers of a provincial government, and could extend the laws of Pakistan to the Northern Areas by notification. These laws, whether amended or applied directly, left the people with little or no judicial redress. The Northern Areas Council had virtually no powers and was headed by the KANA minister. Until 1993, there was no newspaper in the region; the weekly *K2* later began publication. The area was remote and poorly developed, until the opening of the Karakoram Highway to Xinjiang, across the Khunjerab Pass, in 1978. This brought trade and commerce but most of it was controlled by outsiders, mostly Pathans. Sectarian strife was endemic with periodic Shia-Sunni riots.

Development work, after 1982, was largely carried out under the aegis of the Aga Khan Rural Support Programme (AKRSP)— which earned much goodwill and respect, but then ran foul of the orthodoxy, which accused it of indulging in un-Islamic activities such as offering credit and employing female staff. Fatwas against the AKRSP reportedly brought its activities in Skardu and Shigar valleys virtually to a standstill. The Northern Areas earn the bulk of Pakistan's foreign tourist revenues and has gold and gemstone deposits that are being looked into, but need to be further explored. The grievance is that the revenues and the employment generated mostly go to outsiders.

The total ambiguity of their political status led a group of Northern Areas residents to petition the AJK High Court in 1990. The plea taken was that the Northern Areas are an integral part of J&K and, therefore, of AJK as well, and should accordingly be brought, administratively and politically, under AJK. They prayed for civil liberties and democratic rights. Delivering its judgement in 1993, the AJK High Court pronounced that the Northern Areas were part of the territory of Kashmir, and the administration should be in the hands of the AJK government. While the AJK government, under Abdul Qayyum Khan, was delighted with the judgement, the Pakistan government appealed to the AJK Supreme Court. This ruled, in 1994, that the Northern Areas were indeed part of J&K but were not administratively part of AJK when the Interim AJK Constitution was promulgated in 1974. Hence the AJK High Court had no jurisdiction and its order was accordingly quashed.

Dissatisfied with this judgement, another set of petitioners went to the Lahore bench of the Supreme Court, seeking full constitutional rights for the region. On 7 April 1997, the federal government counsel told the court that the Northern Areas did not form part of Pakistan, in terms of Article 1 (2) of the Constitution[44] and its status was linked with the Kashmir issue, which is under the consideration of the UN. Extending constitutional rights to the people of the area would be tantamount to a unilateral annexation of the region, in violation of Pakistan's stand before international fora.[45] The KANA ministry, it was said, extended federal laws to the area in the public interest in accordance with the provisions of the UNCIP resolutions.

Further, the counsel argued that the Northern Areas Council had since been made more representative, and the status of the judicial council had also been improved. He was referring to the so-called reform package put into effect in 1994,[46] as a sop to local sentiments aroused by the AJK court petition and appeal. Besides, the 1994 reforms, which were introduced by an amendment of the 1975 Legal Framework Order, increased the strength of the Northern Areas Council from 16 to 24 elected members, plus two nominated women. The chief executive's powers were exercised by the federal KANA minister. An elected member of the council, enjoying majority support, was made deputy chief executive with the rank of federal minister of state. He was supported by three to five councillors, to be appointed by the KANA minister, as advisers with the rank of provincial ministers. The commissioner was re-designated chief secretary and, with four other secretaries, ran the day-to-day administration. The post of judicial commissioner for the Northern Areas was abolished, and a three-member chief court established in its place under the chairmanship of a retired judge. Any senior judicial officer belonging to the federation or the provincial high court was eligible to be deputed as member of the chief court, whereas a district sessions judge from the Northern Areas was eligible to be its member. The Chitral Scouts were ordered to remain for at least two more years.

Elections to the new Northern Areas Council were held in November 1994, but gave little satisfaction to the local population, and evoked dismay in AJK. Matters came to a head with a former SSP (senior superintendent of police) and a resident of Gilgit—Amir Hamza—filing a petition before the Pakistan Supreme Court, in the name of the AI Jihad Trust, questioning the validity of Pakistan's occupation of the Northern Areas. A copy of the petition was sent to the UN Secretary-General.

Hamza and other youths had formed the Gilgit-Baltistan Jamhoori Mahaz in the late 1960s. The Northern Areas Council was given a trial but proved hollow, leading (in the 1980s) to the formation of the Karakoram Students' Organization, and the Baltistan Students Federation. Rising unemployment and charges of discrimination in public employment (in favour of outsiders) led to the formation of an Unemployed Action Committee in Gilgit, which, in turn, spawned the Balwaristan ('land of the high mountains') National Front (BNP) by Nawaz Khan Naji and Abdul Hamid Khan. The BNP sought self-determination for the Northern Areas, and even Ladakh, with whom the Baltis have much in common. A 1993 Gilgit-Baltistan National Conference brought together a number of larger and lesser organizations, and resulted in the formation of a Northern Areas United Front—to give voice to a number of political demands.

The 1994 reforms were deeply disappointing and triggered protest. On 22 June 1996, the Chitral Scouts opened fire on a demonstration of unemployed youth seeking enrolment in the new paramilitary force, the Northern Scouts. Soon after, 14 August 1997 witnessed an anti-Pakistan 'black jubilee' demonstration in Gilgit, while the rest of the country was celebrating the fiftieth Independence anniversary. It was led by the Karakorum National Movement (under Dr Muzaffar Reley) and the Pakistan Peoples Party-Shaheed Bhutto Group. The protest leaders were still awaiting trial, well into 1998, when last reports came in. The Muttahida Quami Party, under Major Hussain Shah (retired), in turn, sought the rights of the people as enshrined in the 13 August 1948 UN Resolution—namely, full autonomy for the Northern Areas outside of defence, foreign affairs and communications. Though relatively small, these organizations and fronts gained voice and influence in the struggle to preserve the Northern Areas' linguistic and cultural identity.

Free elections, democratic decentralization and wider autonomy for J&K within India could electrify both AJK and the Northern Areas. There is little doubt that an internal settlement of the J&K question will have a transforming effect on the Kashmir dimension of Indo-Pakistan relations.

19

Overcoming Partition

India did not seek Partition; Partition was virtually forced on it. The Congress found the two-nation theory deeply flawed and repugnant. But after Jinnah's call for direct action on 16 August 1946—which was no less than a call to civil war, resulting in pitched battles between Hindus and Muslims in Calcutta (now Kolkata)—the Congress went along with the two-nation proposition as an alternative to internal strife. The die was cast. A popular theory that Partition became inevitable after Nehru's 'betrayal'—when, after the 1937 elections, he refused to share power in the United Provinces with the Muslim League[1]—does not hold water. It may have been an irritant, but was not a breaking point.

While the Labour party in the UK was in some ways sympathetic to the Congress, the Conservatives were clearly inclined to support Jinnah. Correspondence, declassified by the UK, points to a close link between Jinnah and Churchill. The letters relate to 1946, when Churchill was leader of the opposition. He took on the role of adviser to Jinnah, and told him they should not meet in public. Instead, correspondence was to be addressed—care of Miss E.A. Gilliatt [his private secretary], at 6 Westminster Gardens, London. The letters reveal that Jinnah saw Churchill as an ally against 'caste Hindus'.[2]

In a letter dated 6 July 1946, Jinnah wrote:

> If power politics are going to be the deciding factor in total disregard for fair play and justice, we shall have no other course open to us except to forge our sanctions to meet the situation

which, in that case, is bound to arise. Its consequence, I need not say, will be most disastrous and a peaceful settlement will then become impossible.[3]

Less than six weeks later came the bloodbath of direct action.

Replying to Jinnah on 5 August, Churchill espoused the right of Muslims and the depressed classes to their 'fair share of life and power.'[4] Yet, the relationship between the two wasn't without some tension; indeed, on 3 August, Churchill had written to Jinnah:

> I was […] surprised to read all the insulting things that were said about Britain at the Moslem Congress in Bombay, and how the Moslems of India were described as undergoing British slavery. All this is quite untrue and ungrateful.[5]

Subsequently, on 12 December, a wary Churchill turned down a lunch invitation from Jinnah at the Claridges, advising that the two should not be associated publicly.[6]

Gandhi opposed Pakistan tooth and nail. But Nehru and the others saw Partition as a family parting that would heal; that in due course, the estranged siblings would come together, not as one country, but in friendship and cooperation.

This was not to be. To borrow a Churchillian phrase, the very iron had entered into Jinnah's soul. The Quaid-e-Azam or 'great leader' was defeated by his own two-nation logic and was compelled to partition Punjab and Bengal/Assam, to leave behind—what Zulfikar Ali Bhutto was to call— a 'moth-eaten' Pakistan. Bhutto, of course, wanted J&K, Junagadh, Hyderabad, Tripura, and still more.

Twenty-four years later, Pakistan fractured, with Bangladesh breaking away—a development that Maulana Azad had presciently foreseen. Today, it is a near-failed state which is learning that it must come to terms with India, or perish under the weight of its own follies and contradictions. More and more people see the writing on the wall. But not the military and the jihadis. Hafiz Saeed—proclaimed a terrorist by the US—was invited as chief guest at the Lahore High Court Bar Association on 11 July 2014, where he inveighed against India and the US, and called for their destruction.[7] The civil government under Nawaz Sharif remained silent, powerless to act against such blatant incitement to war and terror by a terrorist who masterminded the Mumbai attack of 26/11.

Nawaz Sharif, on his part, found himself in the middle of a storm, when through August and September 2014, he was under siege in Islamabad, with thousands of supporters of Imran Khan's Pakistan-i-Insaf, and a Pakistani-Canadian cleric, Tahirul Qadri, calling for his resignation and for fresh polls; this was on the belated charge that he had rigged the general election the previous year. The army intervened to keep the peace, gaining ascendancy in the bargain, and winning power with regard to the key issues of foreign policy and security—all without any accountability.

The final US pull out from Afghanistan could aggravate matters, as Pakistan seeks to consolidate its own position with the 'good' Taliban—more of whom may be diverted to India—with the added ideological impetus of a new Caliphate in the making.

Nonetheless, there are undercurrents of resistance and reform in Pakistan, which could be encouraged were the US to end its duplicitous policy of tolerating and funding soft terror in the country, as long as it continues to serve as a strategic asset.

*

The Kashmir question is often seen as a dangerous nuclear flashpoint, aggravated by the Afghanistan-Pakistan (AfPak) imbroglio. It has got so tangled in myth, malice and partisanship, that the many perceptions can scarce be reconciled with ground realities. Uniquely, the aggressor has been placed on the same pedestal as the victim, and even portrayed as the injured party. 'Kashmir' is a cancer, eating the vitals of Pakistan.

As I've pointed out earlier, post-Independence Pakistan, tragically, cast its identity in a resolutely negative mould, as India's 'other', with an unfolding narrative that found territorial expression in Kashmir. Today, an Islamist Pakistan, radicalized with Saudi money, stands opposed to the Shias, Aga Khanis, Sufis and other schools of Islam. The soft, humanistic Islam of South Asia—the largest and most advanced Muslim community in the world—is being called upon to 'save' Islam from Christian, Jewish and Hindu hegemony! In the process, Pakistan has mortgaged its soul to defend Islam and reclaim 'Kashmir' and has, instead, fallen prey to the military-mullah-feudal combine.

How and why did this come about? The 1857 uprising was a turning point, marking the end of 800 years of Muslim supremacy in India. The ensuing era of modernization and graduated democratic reform under the Raj saw Muslims retreat into a shell. An increasingly non-competitive Muslim minority feared being eclipsed—hence the sense of victimhood, and the demand for separate electorates and parity between the Muslim and Hindu 'nations', despite the vast disparity in relative numbers.

Syed Ahmed Khan realized the importance of modern education to liberate the Muslim Indians. Thus Aligarh Muslim University was born. But with apathetic Muslims losing out to educated Hindus and others in all branches of governance and law that were opening out for Indians, a hitherto secular Jinnah adopted the pernicious two-nation theory, to leverage equality between Pakistan and India, and the British pandered to this sentiment through a policy of divide and rule.

Jinnah was not unaware of the inherent contradictions in Pakistan's founding ideology, as it remained a plural state. With Pakistan won, addressing the inaugural session of the nation's constituent assembly in Karachi on 11 August 1947, he denounced the two-nation theory. However, it was too late. The dragon seed of mistrust and hate—sown with Jinnah's call to 'direct action' in 1946—had taken root; what followed was a harvest of communal horror, killing hundreds of thousands and, at final count, displacing some 20 million people both ways. When Jinnah's homily at the constituent assembly was repudiated by the new ruling elite of Pakistan, Jinnah reversed gear and, on 25 January 1948 told the Karachi Bar Association that the Constitution would be based on the Sharia 'to make Pakistan a truly great Islamic state'.[8]

In the meantime, planning had commenced to annex J&K. With official backing from the very top, tribal invaders—officered, armed and logistically supported by the Pakistan army—entered the state in October 1947. This perfidious story has been narrated in earlier chapters. The Kashmir jihad had commenced.

Britain had long back vested the Muslim League with veto powers. A series of post-war strategic studies undertaken in London favoured retaining influence over eastern and northwestern India in order to contain communism and leverage control over the

Gulf's oil resources. This is elaborated in Narendra Singh Sarila's *The Shadow of the Great Game: The Untold Story of Partition*[9] which details Britain's conceptualization of Pakistan as a western 'frontline' state.

Pakistan's adventure in J&K is also documented from declassified British archival papers, in Chandrashekhar Dasgupta's *War and Diplomacy in Kashmir*.[10] By 1949-50, America had written off India as a Soviet ally under the cover of non-alignment. By 1953, Pakistan had formally become a frontline military and strategic ally in the Cold War—granting the US an air base in Peshawar—and subsequently joining the CENTO and SEATO. The Security Council's consideration of the Kashmir question was vitiated by Cold War predilections. Indian appeals to principles, and Pakistan's aggression, went unheeded. What mattered was whose side you were on.

Owen Dixon, the UN representative for India and Pakistan, formally reported in September 1950, that:

> [...] when the frontier of the State of J&K was crossed, on I believe 20 October 1947, by hostile elements, it was contrary to international law, and that when, in May 1948 as I believe, units of the regular Pakistan forces moved into the territory of the State that too was inconsistent with international law.[11]

Howsoever politely stated, the finding was one of aggression against what was—from 15 August 1947—an independent sovereign state. In the meantime, the UNCIP, constituted in January 1948, called on both sides to report 'any material change'. The UNCIP arrived in the Indian subcontinent on 7 July 1948, and began consultations in Karachi, only to be greeted with a 'bombshell': three Pakistani brigades had entered J&K in May, allegedly to prevent the Indian spring offensive from spilling into Pakistan proper. Even as Josef Korbel of the UNCIP described this as a 'flagrant and contradictory admission',[12] the Pakistan army thought nothing of knocking at the doors of Leh—hundreds of miles to the east—taking over a huge swathe of Baltistan in Ladakh!

A Security Council resolution of 13 August 1948, described in earlier chapters, proposed a ceasefire (Part I) that would bar any augmentation of armed forces, regular or irregular; followed by a truce (Part II), calling for a wholesale withdrawal of all Pakistani forces and tribal invaders from J&K. The territory so evacuated was to be administered by the local authorities of the state under the surveillance of UNCIP, with such Indian military assistance as might be considered necessary by the commission. After this phase was satisfactorily completed, the bulk of the Indian forces would be withdrawn from the state, subject to such numbers as would be required to safeguard law and order. Thus India's legal right to be in J&K (and its de facto sovereignty) was not questioned. Nevertheless, after implementation of parts I and II of the resolution, steps would be taken under Part III to ascertain the will of the people as subsequently elaborated in a further UN resolution, dated 5 January 1949.

However, far from implementing parts I and II of the 13 August 1948 UN Resolution, Pakistan brazenly consolidated its administrative and military position in J&K, and entered into a military alliance with the US. The conditions for a plebiscite were never fulfilled, and Part III of the 1948 Resolution remained a dead letter. It was, in the course of time, rendered effete by political and demographic changes, and Pakistan's unilateral and illegal cession of Shaksgam (in northern J&K) to China in 1963.

Post-independence India, in its chequered history with Pakistan, witnessed Operation Gibraltar, the liberation of Bangladesh, the 1971 war with Pakistan and the Shimla Accord. Bangla (cultural) nationalism had triumphed over Islamic nationalism, leaving the two-nation theory in tatters. Notwithstanding the Shimla Accord, Pakistan next attempted cartographic aggression against Siachen and beyond, to the Karakoram Pass.

This was climaxed by Pervez Musharraf's brazen Kargil operation in 1999, after the Indian prime minister, Atal Bihari Vajpayee had taken a 'friendship bus' to Lahore to meet Nawaz Sharif and initiate a new peace process. Pakistan's gambit failed; the country was roundly defeated along the Kargil heights, and its malafides and dangerous adventurism exposed. Naked but unashamed, soon after the Kargil war, Musharraf staged a coup.

In 1999, two days after the Pakistan army embarked on its Kargil misadventure, Lieutenant General Mahmud Ahmed gave a 'crisp and to the point' briefing to a group of senior army and air force officers. Kaiser Tufail, then director of operations, Pakistan air force, who attended this meeting, wrote that they were told that it was nothing more than a defensive manoeuvre and the Indian air force will not get involved at any stage. 'Come October, we shall walk into Siachen—to mop up the dead bodies of hundreds of Indians left hungry, out in the cold,' General Mahmud told the meeting. He had casually sought PAF air support, if necessary, from an astonished air command who had, like others, been kept out of the loop.[13]

An even more detailed account of Musharraf's Kargil war comes, first hand, from Lieutenant General Shahid Aziz, in his Urdu biography published in Lahore.[14] As a major general, he served as head of the analysis wing of the ISI that oversaw the Kargil operations and its aftermath. What does the general say? He identifies 'the hate that is being sown […] and the hands sowing these seeds'[15]. As chief of general staff, in 2002, he initiated a research study to see what lessons could be derived from that war. Musharraf was furious and ordered the study stopped immediately. But then Aziz had realized that the operations were planned by no more than a handful of top army officers. It was a charade. The assumptions made, the justifications given, were 'astonishing'.

> I was in charge of the ISI, keeping an eye on all Indian activities. There was not a single activity from their side suggesting that they had intentions to undertake any aggressive actions […] From their side there was no preparation for an attack on us, nor was there any intention that could be discerned. It [Kargil] was entirely an offensive operation. It was unprovoked […] In this entire battle the Mujahideen did not have any part at all… Dead bodies were not taken back. Even the numbers of dead were not declared.

What could be more authoritative, more telling, more shameful, than that?

Despite Kargil, India resumed the peace process. However, the Red Fort in Delhi, the J&K Assembly in Srinagar, the Indian parliament, the Bombay stock exchange, and carefully selected economic, scientific and communally sensitive targets elsewhere were the subjects of continuing jihadi terror strikes from Pakistan, combined with unabated infiltration into J&K. Earlier, the Indian Airlines flight IC-814 was hijacked, en route, from Kathmandu to Delhi, and diverted to Kandahar where—after the killing of one passenger—the rest were traded for three top jihadis incarcerated in India. The hijack was believed to have been overseen by Mullah Omar, head of the Pakistan Taliban. Latter depredations were masterminded by the LeT led by Hafiz Saeed. The Indian embassy in Kabul was also, twice, bombed by Taliban elements close to Pakistan.

No sooner was the LeT listed as a terror organization by the UN than it changed its name to JuD, and declared itself a charitable body. Hafiz Saeed was arrested, nominally tried, and discharged, only to continue plotting against India—culminating in the horrendous 26/11 terror attack on Mumbai. Pakistan has dragged its feet in investigating this dastardly crime—starting with denials, and then pleading lack of hard evidence and receipt of mere 'literature' from India. Hafiz Saeed is at large and periodically leads marches in major cities, spitting venom and threatening nuclear war against India.

For a time it seemed that Musharraf—his options closing after 9/11—might be willing to talk peace. After initially grandstanding at Agra, he moved forward on a back-channel peace plan, in concert with Manmohan Singh, the outlines of which became public knowledge. The emerging deal envisaged the LoC as an international boundary. But the boundary was to be rendered 'irrelevant', by conversion into a soft or open border—to facilitate people-to-people and cultural exchange, trade and commerce, regular trans-LoC bus services, phased demilitarization, and so forth, concurrently with a settlement of other outstanding Indo-Pakistan issues.

Mutual management of these cross-border issues could spawn joint councils and consultative bodies at various levels, which could be institutionalized over a period of time. Thus, some kind of confederation of two sets of autonomous J&Ks might duly emerge, binding the two sides of the current LoC within Indian and Pakistani sovereignties. Internal autonomy for its jurisdiction, within J&K, would be left to each side to determine. Manmohan Singh hoped that the two armies would face outwards, and J&K's

historic, cultural and commercial relationship with Central Asia would be restored. He even hinted at joint management of further Indus water development so as to ensure optimality in terms of Article VII 'Future Cooperation' under the Indus Treaty.

Such a confederal J&K had, in fact, been mooted by Nehru and Abdullah in 1964, and indeed, such a solution would give both sides more than what they have, reunite all of J&K, and open a new chapter of good neighbourly and fraternal relations between India and Pakistan.

SAARC-2020, envisioned by expert groups and endorsed by the heads of state, also envisaged this body—including Afghanistan, and even Iran and Myanmar—moving towards a South Asian Economic Union or South Asian Community with a common currency. It is principally the Indo-Pakistan imbroglio that has impeded progress.

Musharraf sought a pause in the fast-moving back-channel discussions between India and Pakistan in 2007, on account of his own growing political difficulties at home. The Pakistan Taliban and other radical elements accused him of selling out to India. The talks froze entirely after 26/11, with the Pakistan Peoples Party in office, but power back in the hands of the army chief, General Kayani, and the ISI.

The new US AfPak policy and war in Afghanistan had, by now, spilled over into Pakistan. The US and NATO increasingly found themselves militarily and politically at loggerheads with Islamabad, which was found playing both sides, securing vast amounts of US military and civil aid but using much of this to frustrate the war on terror, while assisting it at other times, making plain that its military-strategic posture was India-centric. The busting of the Osama bin Laden hideout in the garrison town of Abbotabad on 2 May 2011 finally brought out the ugly truth of Pakistan's complicity with terror, its incredible and contradictory denials notwithstanding. The terror attack on the Mehran naval base near Karachi, later that same month, gives cause for concern regarding the safety of Pakistan's nuclear assets.

Despite Musharraf backing away from his out-of-the-box Kashmir solution, the threads were picked up in subsequent back-channel talks between Satish Lambah of India and Tariq Aziz of

Pakistan, both special envoys to their respective heads of government. They, too, came within an ace of success before the fall of Manmohan Singh's government.

*

Where do we go from here? It is a fact that once Pakistan begins to shed its permanent enmity with India it will discover its own inherently rich personality and place in the sun, and regain its soul.

The US, on its part, claims to be part of the solution in Afghanistan and Pakistan, but is in fact part of the problem. Over the years it has propped up Pakistan's unreasoning malice towards India—a sentiment not shared by its hapless people who have become the victims of savage jihadi killings, the medieval barbarism of jihadi Islamism and the military-mullah-feudal overlordship. Democracy has not been given a chance and civil society remains fragmented, with even the judiciary lauding the appalling public murders of the Punjab governor[16] and the minister for minorities[17] for speaking against the brutal tyranny of blasphemy laws.

> Few know that the Pakistan military controls about 20-40 percent of the Pakistan economy, and large chunks of the best agricultural land, through various foundations manned by serving and retired military personnel, and land grants to them. This constitutes a huge vested interest, which would be jeopardizsed if the military lost its raison d'être without a make-believe Kashmir 'dispute' and an ever-present enemy—India. The military-mullah nexus is also mutually self-serving.

Most Pakistanis are secular liberals who wonder what the 'ideology of Pakistan' is about and for whose benefit, when all they want is to get on with their lives rather than flounder in a failing state. They want an out.

Pakistan's democratic roots have, hopefully, not altogether withered. However, despite its knowledge of Islamabad's perfidy, the US believes that any loosening of ties could destabilize Pakistan and jeopardize the safety of its nuclear facilities—hence the continuing alliance and aid, and cultivation of the military to keep the war on terror in Afghanistan going. The real answer would be to curtail both civil and military aid, to compel Pakistan to abandon terror as an instrument of state policy. The fear that China will immediately fill the breach is exaggerated. The Pakistan economy is on drip and Western/UN pressure could encourage a transfer of power from the military to the people.

A regional settlement in Afghanistan—as a stable and neutral member of SAARC—through a policy of reconciliation and development, could get America off the hook and bring reassurance all around. The new post-Karzai Afghan government of Ashraf Ghani Ahmadzai and Abdullah Abdullah offers hope of new initiatives.

The only practical solution to the Indo-Pak standoff has to be some variant of the Manmohan-Musharraf formula, combined with internal autonomy reforms within J&K and Pakistan-Gilgit-Balistan.

The recent aberrant and unprecedented September 2014 floods on both sides of the LoC, with the Jhelum and Chenab in spate after horrendous rains, has a lesson. It has undoubtedly heightened the need to build counter-measures against climate change impact, stretching across the Himalayan-Karakoram belt, and across into Tibet as well. But equally, it is apparent that the devastating Chenab floods could have been mitigated if India and Pakistan could optimize dam development in that basin, which would provide many times more irrigation storage, flood moderation and hydel production than permissible under the treaty. The need for further integrated development of the Indus basin, from the Karakoram range to the sea, under the rubric of the Indus Treaty's mandate of 'Future Cooperation' (Article VII), has been discussed in an earlier chapter.

Talk of restoring the Pandits to their former homes in the Valley could only result in ghettoes and permanent estrangement. The alternative would be to build new employment hubs along the Baramulla-Srinagar-Jammu rail, and a new all-weather highway with the Banihal range being pierced at a lower elevation. This transport corridor—linked to an activated Srinagar International Airport and a parallel optic-fibre link—could be converted into a multi-nodal industrial belt with new townships and training facilities to attract unemployed youth and whosoever is looking for better opportunities.

Some of these projects are at an advanced stage and could be completed within the next two to three years. The new facilities planned could include cold storages linked to proposed new 1,000-2,000 MW power augmentation, fruit and agro-processing centres, floriculture and herbiculture, and IT-enabled services. If land is available on long-term lease, and there's a waiver of self-defeating state-subject rules for bona-fide investors and workers, domestic and foreign investors would come pouring in. Tourism would increase manifold.

Earlier chapters detail how a parallel trans-Karakoram corridor from Xinjiang to Karachi would be mutually reinforcing, especially if the Srinagar-Baramulla line were pushed to Uri and Muzaffarabad to join the Pakistan system. At another level, Leh could be opened up to trade with Tibet and Central Asia—given the quietus along the Line of Actual Control—and an early boundary settlement could be reached.

These proposals entail big ifs. The petty, compartmentalized thinking that has governed policy thus far will simply not work. We need to think big in order to achieve big results.

The fugitive hope surrounding Partition was that India and Pakistan would separate to come together in time, as fraternal friends and partners in a larger South Asian Union. That time has come. Kashmir is not the 'core problem'. It can be shared. This will not undo Pakistan. Reconciliation could make it whole.

Notes

Preface

1. G. Allana, *Pakistan Movement Historical Documents* (Karachi: Department of International Relations, University of Karachi, 1969), pp. 407-11.
2. *The Constitution of the Islamic Republic of Pakistan*, in <http://www.pakistani.org/pakistan/constitution>, accessed on 14 October 2014.
3. The idea of Islamic 'ideological frontiers' is often attributed to General Zia ul-Haq. See, for example, Zahid Hussain, *Frontline Pakistan: The Struggle with Militant Islam* (USA: Columbia, 2007), p. 18. In truth, it was voiced by General Yahya Khan. See Husain Haqqani, *Pakistan: Between Mosque and Military* (USA: Carnegie Endowment for International Peace, 2005), p. 51.
4. B.G. Verghese, *A J&K Primer: From Myth to Reality* (New Delhi: India Research Press, 2007), p. 44.
5. Taha Siddiqui, 'Pakistan Textbooks Raise Debate about "Curriculum of Hate"', *The Christian Science Monitor*, 28 February 2013, in <http://www.csmonitor.com/World/Asia-South-Central/2013/0228/Pakistan-textbooks-raise-debate-about-curriculum-of-hate/(page)/2>, accessed on 14 October 2014.
6. *India-Pakistan Relations 1947-2007: A Documentary Study*, edited by Avtar Singh Bhasin, 10 Volumes (New Delhi: Geetika Publishers, 2012).
7. See, for instance, Bruce Riedel, *Deadly Embrace: Pakistan, America, and the Future of the Global Jihad* (USA: Brookings Institution Press, 2011), p. xviii. The author says, 'For reasons good and bad, successive U.S. Presidents from both parties have pursued narrow short-term interests in Pakistan that have contributed to its instability and radicalization, and thereby created fertile ground for global jihad.'
8. Edward Lear, 'The Akond of Swat', *Complete Nonsense* (UK: Wordsworth Editions Ltd, 1994), pp. 192-94.
9. *Encyclopaedia Britannica*.

HISTORICAL CHURNINGS

1. Blood and Mistrust

1. In *India-Pakistan Relations 1947-2007: A Documentary Study*, edited by Avtar Singh Bhasin, 10 Volumes (New Delhi: Geetika Publishers, 2012).

2. *Ibid.*
3. See *Security and Defence Related Treaties of India*, edited by V.P. Malhotra (New Delhi: Vij Books, 2010), pp. 15-23.
4. Zulfikar Ali Bhutto, *The Myth of Independence* (UK: Oxford University Press, 1969).
5. See Brahma Chellaney, 'Military is the Problem', *The Times of India*, 3 January 2008.
6. *Dawn*, 8 February 1850.
7. 'Indo Pak Press Code', *Dawn*, 12 June 2010. The article states: 'The editors were asked to "observe voluntary restraint […] by avoiding dissemination of news calculated to undermine relations between the majority and minority communities in the two countries; by refusing to give currency to mischievous opinion of individuals […]; by excluding rigorously from the press of each country opinion directed against the territorial sovereignty of the other […]; by avoiding alarming headlines for reports of communal incidents […]; by examining objectively outstanding problems between the two countries […]; by confining comment to the merits of the problem" and not making such problems "the basis of a general attack on the two governments"; by eschewing personal, "contumacious or scurrilous attacks on the respected leaders of either country or the religion, culture and faith of the people of both countries; and by avoiding historical controversies which may create or revive bitterness between the two countries."'
8. See Husain Haqqani, *Pakistan: Between Mosque and Military* (USA: Carnegie Endowment for International Peace, 2005), p. 51.
9. See Kulwant Rai Gupta, *India-Pakistan Relations with Special Reference to Kashmir* (New Delhi: Atlantic Publishers, 2003), pp. 813-16.
10. See Suhail Alam, 'Secular Ideology', *Scribed*, 16 August 2014, in <https://www.scribd.com/doc/236978643/Secular-Ideology>, accessed on 14 October 2014.
11. *India-Pakistan Relations 1947-2007: A Documentary Study*, edited by Avtar Singh Bhasin, 10 Volumes (New Delhi: Geetika Publishers, 2012).
12. *Ibid.*
13. *Ibid.*
14. Jawaharlal Nehru to Liaquat Ali Khan, 4 August 1951. In *Selected Works of Jawaharlal Nehru*, 1st Series, edited by Sarvepalli Gopal (New Delhi: Orient Longman, 1972), p. 351.

2. Integration: Bahawalpur, Kalat

1. See David Syiemlieh, *On the Edge of Empire: Four British Plans for North East India* (New Delhi: Sage, 2014).
2. Penderel Moon, *Divide and Quit* (London: Chatto & Windus, 1961).
3. *Ibid.*
4. *Jinnah Papers—The States: Historical and Policy Perspectives and Accession to Pakistan*, Volume VIII, edited by Z.H. Zaidi (Pakistan: Government of Pakistan, 2003).

5. *Ibid.* Also see Naseer Dashti, *The Baloch and Balochistan: A Historical Account from the Beginning to the Fall of the Baloch State* (USA: Trafford, 2012), pp. 330-31.
6. *Ibid.*
7. *The Transfer of Power*, Volume XII, edited by Penderel Moon (UK: Stationery Office, 1982).
8. *Reuters*, India and Pakistan Service, Karachi, 28 March 1948.
9. Baren Ray, 'The Pathanks and the Baluchis', *The Partition in Retrospect*, edited by Amrik Singh (New Delhi: Anamika Publishers, 2000), p. 84.

3. Doublespeak: Junagadh, Hyderabad

1. See V.P. Menon, *The Story of the Integration of the Indian States* (India: Orient Longman, 1956), p. 120.
2. *India-Pakistan Relations 1947-2007: A Documentary Study*, edited by Avtar Singh Bhasin, 10 Volumes (New Delhi: Geetika Publishers, 2012).
3. See A.G. Noorani, *The Kashmir Question* (Bombay: Manaktalas, 1964).
4. *Jinnah Papers—Pangs of Birth, 15 August-30 September 1947*, Volume 5, edited by Z.H. Zaidi (Pakistan: Government of Pakistan, 2003), pp. 609-10.
5. *Ibid.* Also see Srinath Raghavan, *War and Peace in Modern India* (UK: Palgrave Macmillan, 2010), p. 43.
6. *India-Pakistan Relations 1947-2007: A Documentary Study*, edited by Avtar Singh Bhasin, 10 Volumes (New Delhi: Geetika Publishers, 2012).
7. A press note issued by the Pakistani foreign minister, 13 November 1947.
8. V.P. Menon, *The Story of the Integration of the Indian States* (India: Orient Longman, 1956). Also see B. Krishna, *India's Bismarck: Sardar Vallabhbhai Patel* (Mumbai: Indus Source Books, 2007), p. 128.
9. *India-Pakistan Relations 1947-2007: A Documentary Study*, edited by Avtar Singh Bhasin, 10 Volumes (New Delhi: Geetika Publishers, 2012).
10. *Ibid.*
11. *Jinnah Papers—The States Historical and Policy Perspectives and Accession to Pakistan*, Volume VIII, edited by Z. H. Zaidi (Pakistan: Government of Pakistan, 2003), p.7.
12. *India-Pakistan Relations 1947-2007: A Documentary Study*, edited by Avtar Singh Bhasin, 10 Volumes (New Delhi: Geetika Publishers, 2012).
13. See V.P. Menon, *The Story of the Integration of the Indian States* (India: Orient Longman, 1956).
14. See R.P. Bhargava, *The Chamber of Princes* (Delhi: Northern Books, 1991), p. 302.
15. The Razakars were a private militia organized by Kasim Razvi to support the rule of the nizam and resist the accession of Hyderabad to India.
16. See A.G. Noorani, 'Lessons of Murree', *Frontline*, Volume 27, Issue 13, 19 June-2 July 2010.
17. A.G. Noorani, *The Destruction of Hyderabad* (New Delhi: Tulika Books, New Delhi, 2013).

4. The Kashmir Unfolding

1. Christopher Snedden, *Kashmir: The Untold Story* (India: HarperCollins, 2013), p. 1924.
2. In May 1946, Sheikh Abdullah launched the Quit Kashmir agitation against Maharaja Hari Singh; he was arrested and sentenced to three years' imprisonment.
3. Dr D.R. Sardesai, *India: The Definitive History* (USA: Westview Press, 2008), p. 396.
4. *India-Pakistan Relations 1947-2007: A Documentary Study*, edited by Avtar Singh Bhasin, 10 Volumes (New Delhi: Geetika Publishers, 2012).
5. See Sumantra Bose, *Kashmir: Roots of Conflicts, Paths to Peace* (USA: Harvard University Press, 2003), p. 38.
6. See B. Krishna, *India's Bismarck: Sardar Vallabhbhai Patel* (Mumbai: Indus Source Books, 2007), p. 202.
7. *India-Pakistan Relations 1947-2007: A Documentary Study*, edited by Avtar Singh Bhasin, 10 Volumes (New Delhi: Geetika Publishers, 2012).
8. Christopher Snedden, *Kashmir: The Untold Story* (India: HarperCollins, 2013).
9. *India-Pakistan Relations 1947-2007: A Documentary Study*, edited by Avtar Singh Bhasin, 10 Volumes (New Delhi: Geetika Publishers, 2012).
10. Akbar Khan, *Raiders in Kashmir* (Islamabad: Nation Book Foundation, 1975), p. 4.
11. *India-Pakistan Relations 1947-2007: A Documentary Study*, edited by Avtar Singh Bhasin, 10 Volumes (New Delhi: Geetika Publishers, 2012).
12. Akbar Khan, *Raiders in Kashmir* (Islamabad: Nation Book Foundation, 1975), p. 4.
13. *Ibid.*, p. 184.
14. *Ibid.*, p. 91.
15. C. Dasgupta, *War and Diplomacy in Kashmir* (New Delhi: Sage, 2002).

5. UN Scorned, Gilgit-Baltistan Seized

1. *India-Pakistan Relations 1947-2007: A Documentary Study*, edited by Avtar Singh Bhasin, 10 Volumes (New Delhi: Geetika Publishers, 2012).
2. *Ibid.*
3. The Gilgit Scouts was the name of a paramilitary force, originally raised in 1889 under the name 'Gligit Levies' by British Army Colonel Algernon Durand, headquartered in Gilgit (within the princely state of J&K). After Partition, the Gilgit Scouts joined the forces of the Pakistan army and fought the maharaja during the First Kashmir War.
4. See 'V.K. Krishna Menon's Marathon Speech Lasting for Eight Hours on Kashmir at the United Nations Security Council's Seven Hundred and Sixty Second Meeting, 23 January 1957', *India-Pakistan Relations with Special Reference to Kashmir*, edited by K.R. Gupta (New Delhi: Atlantic Publishers, 2006), p. 156.
5. *India-Pakistan Relations 1947-2007: A Documentary Study*, edited by Avtar Singh Bhasin, 10 Volumes (New Delhi: Geetika Publishers, 2012).

6. *Ibid.*
7. *Official Records of the Security Council, Third Year*, Nos. 7-15, 240th Meeting, p. 371.
8. See Sankar Ghosh, *Jawaharlal Nehru: A Biography* (Bombay: Allied Publishers, 1993), p. 187.
9. A letter dated 20 February 1949. *Selected Works of Jawaharlal Nehru*, Volume 5 (New Delhi: Jawaharlal Nehru Memorial Fund. 1987), p. 222.
10. *Ibid*, Volume 29.
11. *Pakistan Horizon*, Volume 10, No. 1, March, 1957, pp. 50-60.

6. New Factors and Options

1. *India-Pakistan Relations 1947-2007: A Documentary Study*, edited by Avtar Singh Bhasin, 10 Volumes (New Delhi: Geetika Publishers, 2012).
2. *Ibid.*
3. *Ibid.*
4. Letter from B.K. Nehru to Commonwealth secretary, Y. D. Gundevia, 24 September 1963. See A.G. Noorani, 'US & Kashmir', *Frontline*, Volume 26, Issue 26, 19 December 2009-1 January 2010.
5. The Sino-Pakistan agreement resulted in China ceding over 1,942 square kilometres to Pakistan and Pakistan recognizing Chinese sovereignty over hundreds of square kilometers of land in Northern Kashmir and Ladakh. The agreement is controversial and not recognized as legal by India.
6. See Victoria Schofield, *Kashmir in Conflict: India, Pakistan and the Unending War* (London: IB Tauris, 2003), p. 102.
7. On 8 August 1953, Sheikh Abdullah was dismissed as prime minister on the charge that he had lost the confidence of his cabinet. He was arrested and later jailed for eleven years, accused of espousing the cause of an independent Kashmir in the infamous Kashmir conspiracy case. On 8 April 1964, the state government dropped all charges, and Sheikh Abdullah was released.
8. D.N. Panigrahi, *Jammu and Kashmir, the Cold War, and the West* (New Delhi: Routledge, 2009), p. 242.

7. Division of J&K Spurned; War

1. In December 1963, the government of India had estimated the presence of three lakh Pakistani immigrants within Assam; this figure was considered to be an underestimation in some circles. See Bimal J. Dev and Dilip Kumar Lahiri, *Assam Muslims: Politics and Cohesion* (New Delhi: Mittal Publications, 1985).
2. M.C. Chagla, during his speech at the Security Council meeting in 1964, said: 'The basic principle of its [Pakistan's] international policy is opposition to India on every front and [...] Its desire is to use the forum of the Security Council to carry on its agitation against my Government and my country. [...Pakistan] wants to see discord and turmoil in India, and, as *The Times of London* recently observed, it wants India to be

politically and economically weakened so that it can get an opportunity to continue further its present illegal occupation of a part of territory which by Indian law is as much a part of Indian territory as Bombay or Delhi is.' See J.C Aggarwal and S.P. Agrawal, *Modern History of Jammu and Kashmir*, Volume 1 (New Delhi: Concept Publishing, 1995).

3. Altaf Gauhar, *Ayub Khan: Pakistan's First Military Ruler* (UK: Oxford University Press, 1993).

4. *Memoirs of Lt. Gen. Gul Hassan Khan* (UK: Oxford University Press: 1993), p. 179.

5. Abdul Ghafoor Bhurgri, *Zulfikar Ali Bhutto: the Falcon of Pakistan* (Pakistan: Szabist, 2002), p. 195.

6. On 26 December 1963, a hair of the Prophet Mohammed mysteriously vanished from the Hazratbal Mosque, which sparked mass protests and riots all across J&K. The Awami Action Committee was formed to find it, and Nehru addressed the nation. The sacred relic was eventually recovered on 4 January 1964.

7. See Hassan Abbas, *Pakistan's Drift into Extremism: Allah, the Army, and America's War on Terror* (USA: M.E. Sharpe, 2004), p. 49.

8. Operation Gibraltar

1. Prime Minister Shastri's message to the UN's secretary general, 4 September 1965,

2. *India-Pakistan Relations 1947-2007: A Documentary Study*, edited by Avtar Singh Bhasin, 10 Volumes (New Delhi: Geetika Publishers, 2012).

3. Altaf Gauhar, *Ayub Khan: Pakistan's First Military Ruler* (Lahore: Sang-e-Meel Publications, 1993).

4. *Ibid.*

5. See *Keesing's Record of World Events*, Volume 11, December 1965.

6. See *Pakistan Horizon*, Volume 18, Number 4, Fourth Quarter: 1965, pp. 394-431.

7. See *India-Pakistan Relations 1947-2007: A Documentary Study*, edited by Avtar Singh Bhasin, 10 Volumes (New Delhi: Geetika Publishers, 2012).

8. *Ibid.* See also Roedad Khan, *The British Papers: Secret and Confidential, India, Pakistan, Bangladesh Documents 1958-1969* (UK: Oxford University Press, 2002).

9. 'Notes, Memoranda and Letters Exchanged and Agreements Signed between The Governments of India and China', *White Paper XII*, January 1965-February 1966, Ministry of External Affairs, Government of India, in <http://www.claudearpi.net/maintenance/uploaded_pics/WhitePaper12.pdf>, accessed on 24 November 2014.

10. G.S. Bajpai, *China's Shadow over Sikkim: The Politics of Intimidation* (New Delhi: lancer Publishers, 1999), p. 151.

9. Tashkent and After

1. *50 Years of Indo-Pak Relations*, edited by Verinder Grover and Ranjana Arora (New Delhi: Deep & Deep Publications, 1999), p. 495.

2. *Tashkent Declaration in Perspective* (Pakistan: The Department of Films and Publications, Government of Pakistan, 1966), p 16.

3. 'Cease-fire Violations by India: Address to the Security Council, October 25, 1965', *Zulfikar Ali Bhutto*, in <http://www.bhutto.org/1957-1965_speech52.php>, accessed on 24 February 2015.

4. *India-Pakistan Relations 1947-2007: A Documentary Study*, edited by Avtar Singh Bhasin, 10 Volumes (New Delhi: Geetika Publishers, 2012).

5. See *Parliamentary Debate*, Volume 45, Issues 10-18, p. 2273.

6. Roedad Khan, *The American Papers: Secret and Confidential* (UK: Oxford University Press, 1999), p. 190.

7. *Asian Almanac*, Volume 4 (Malaysia: V.T. Sambandan, 1966), p. 1833.

8. *India-Pakistan Relations 1947-2007: A Documentary Study*, edited by Avtar Singh Bhasin, 10 Volumes (New Delhi: Geetika Publishers, 2012).

9. *Ibid.*

10. As stated by Zia ul-Haq. See Lal Khan, *Crisis in the Indian Subcontinent, Partition: Can It be Undone?* (New Delhi: Aakar Books, 2007), p. 173.

11. *India Quarterly*, Volume 27 (India: Indian Council of World Affairs, 1971), p. 143.

12. *50 Years of Indo-Pak Relations*, edited by Verinder Grover and Ranjana Arora (New Delhi: Deep & Deep Publications, 1999), pp. 509-10.

13. F.S. Aijazuddin, *The White House & Pakistan: Secret Declassified Documents, 1969-1974* (UK: Oxford University Press, 2003).

14. *Lok Sabha Debates* (India: Lok Sabha Secretariat, 1970), p. 54.

15. F.S. Aijazuddin, *The White House & Pakistan: Secret Declassified Documents, 1969-1974* (UK: Oxford University Press, 2003).

16. *India-Pakistan Relations 1947-2007: A Documentary Study*, edited by Avtar Singh Bhasin, 10 Volumes (New Delhi: Geetika Publishers, 2012).

10. Towards 1971 and 'Joy Bangla'

1. Christophe Jeffrelot, *Pakistan: Nationalism without A Nation* (New Delhi: Manohar Publishers, 2002), p. 21.

2. In Praveen Swami, *India, Pakistan and the Secret Jihad: The Covert War in Kashmir, 1947-2004* (UK: Routledge, 2007), p. 115.

3. In Ramachandra Guha, *India after Gandhi: The History of the World's Largest Democracy* (India: Picador, 2008), p. 99.

4. John Grenville and Bernard Wasserstein, *The Major International Treaties of the Twentieth Century* (UK: Routledge, 2001), p. 419.

5. *India-Pakistan Relations 1947-2007: A Documentary Study*, edited by Avtar Singh Bhasin, 10 Volumes (New Delhi: Geetika Publishers, 2012).

6. See the author's *First Draft: Witness to the Making of Modern India* (India: Tranquebar Press, 2010), p. 167.

7. *India-Pakistan Relations 1947-2007: A Documentary Study*, edited by Avtar Singh Bhasin, 10 Volumes (New Delhi: Geetika Publishers, 2012).

8. Srinath Raghavan, *1971: A Global History of the Creation of Bangladesh* (USA: Harvard University Press, 2013), pp. 103-104.

9. Fakhruddin Ahmed, *Critical Times: Memoirs of a South Asian Diplomat* (Bangladesh: University Press Limited, 1994), p. 62.

10. Tariq Ali, *The Duel: Pakistan on the Flight Path of American Power* (New York: Scribner, 2009).

11. *India-Pakistan Relations 1947-2007: A Documentary Study*, edited by Avtar Singh Bhasin, 10 Volumes (New Delhi: Geetika Publishers, 2012).

12. *Ibid.*

13. 'India, Pakistan and War', *The Pittsburgh Press*, 24 November 1971

14. Kalyani Shankar, *Nixon, Indira and India: Politics and Beyond* (New Delhi: Macmillan Publishers, 2010), p. 79.

15. *India-Pakistan Relations 1947-2007: A Documentary Study*, edited by Avtar Singh Bhasin, 10 Volumes (New Delhi: Geetika Publishers, 2012).

16. *Ibid.*

17. *Ibid.*

18. *Ibid.*

19. *Ibid.*

20. *Ibid.*

21. *Ibid.*

22. *Ibid.*

23. Dinesh Kumar, 'Give Words at the Heart of the Dispute', *The Tribune*, in <http://www.tribuneindia.com/2014/20140413/pers.htm> [accessed on 10 April 2015].

24. *India-Pakistan Relations 1947-2007: A Documentary Study*, edited by Avtar Singh Bhasin, 10 Volumes (New Delhi: Geetika Publishers, 2012).

25. *Ibid.*

26. Sudha Ramachandran, 'Drawing a Line on a Kashmir Solution', *Asia Times Online*, 20 May 2003, in <http://www.atimes.com/atimes/South_Asia/EE20Df01.html>, accessed on 10 April 2015.

27. *India-Pakistan Relations 1947-2007: A Documentary Study*, edited by Avtar Singh Bhasin, 10 Volumes (New Delhi: Geetika Publishers, 2012).

28. *Ibid.*

29. *Ibid.*

30. *Ibid.*

31. *Ibid.*

32. *Ibid.*

33. 'Rupture in South Asia', *UNHCR*, in <http://www.unhcr.org/3ebf9bab0.pdf>, accessed on 10 April 2015.

34. *Ibid.*

HANGING ISSUES

11. Siachen Follies

1. See Nitin Gokhale, 'The Siachen Saga', *The Diplomat*, 21 April 2014, in <http://thediplomat.com/2014/04/the-siachen-saga/>, accessed on 17 April 2015.

2. See Nitin Gokhale, 'Why Siachen Matters To India', *Journal of Indian Research*, Volume 2, Number 2, April-June 2014.

3. *India-Pakistan Relations 1947-2007: A Documentary Study*, edited by Avtar Singh Bhasin, 10 Volumes (New Delhi: Geetika Publishers, 2012).
4. *Ibid.*
5. See Nitin Gokhale, 'Why Siachen Matters to India', *Journal Of Indian Research*, Volume 2, Number 2, April-June 2014.
6. Also see Musharraf's memoir. Pervez Musharraf, *In the Line of Fire* (London: Free Press, 2006).
7. Dinesh Mathur, *Chinese Perceptions of Various Territorial Disputes*, in <http://www.claws.in/images/journals_doc/1102892486_DineshMAthur.pdf>, accessed on 17 April 2015.
8. More in the author's *First Draft: Witness to the Making of Modern India* (India: Tranquebar Press, 2010),
9. Robert Wirsing, *India, Pakistan and the Kashmir Dispute: On Regional Conflict and Its Resolution* (New Delhi: Rupa 1994).
10. *Ibid.*
11. See Jasjit Singh, *Kargil 1999: Pakistan's Fourth War for Kashmir* (New Delhi Knowledge World, 1999), p. 80.
12. *Kissinger Transcripts: The Top Secret Talks with Beijing and Moscow*, edited by William Burr (USA: Diane Pub Co, 1999).
13. *India Today: An Encyclopaedia of Life in the Republic*, Volume 1, edited by Arnold P. Kaminsky and Roger D. Long (USA: ABC-CLIO, 2011), p. 381.
14. 'Pak India Peace Process: An Appraisal', *Policy Perspectives*, Volume 4, Number 2.

12. Going Nuclear

1. Prime Minister Mohammad Nawaz Sharif on 28 May 1998 famously said, 'Today, we have settled a score and have carried out five successful nuclear tests'. See <http://nuclearweaponarchive.org/Pakistan/PakTests.html>, accessed on 22 June 2015.
2. Dr Rajesh Mishra, 'Pakistan's Nuclear Blackmailing: Spreading Fear of Nuclear Terror', *South Asia Analysis*, in <http://www.southasiaanalysis.org/paper482>, 20 September 2012, accessed on 23 June 2015.
3. Manu V. Mathai, *Nuclear Power, Economic Development Discourse and the Environment: The Case of India* (New York: Routledge, 2013), p. 75
4. See 'About NSAB', *National Security Advisory Board*, in <http://www.nsab.gov.in/?1001>, accessed on 20 June 2015.
5. 'Draft Report of the National Security Advisory Board on the Indian Nuclear Doctrine', *The Ministry of External Affairs*, in < http://mea.gov.in/in-focus-article.htm?18916/Draft+Report+of+National+Security+Advisory+Board+on+Indian+Nuclear+Doctrine>, 17 August 1999, accessed on 20 June 2015.
6. *From Surprise To Reckoning: The Kargil Review Committee Report* (New Delhi: Sage, 2000).
7. See Hiader K. Nizamani, *The Roots of Rhetoric: Politics of Nuclear Weapons in India and Pakistan* (New Delhi: India Research Press, 2001), p. 86.

8. 'CIA Asked Dutch Govt Bot to Act against A.Q. Khan: Report', *Zee News*, in <http://zeenews.india.com/home/cia-asked-dutch-govt-not-to-act-against-a-q-khan-report_240624.html>, 9 September 2005, accessed on 20 June 2015.

9. See Gordon Corera, *Shopping for Bombs: Nuclear Proliferation, Global Insecurity, and the Rise and Fall of the A.Q. Khan Network* (UK: Oxford University Press, 2009). Corera points out that 'the US officials involved at the time deny [Lubbers' claims…] and say that it was the Dutch who had Khan under surveillance, who failed to pick him up, and who never realized that he might flee'.

10. David Armstrong and Joe Trento, *America and the Islamic Bomb: The Deadly Compromise* (USA: Steerforth, 2007), p. 54.

11. Joop Boer, Henk van der Keur, Karel Kosterand and Frank Slimper, *A.Q. Khan, Urenco and the Proliferation of Nuclear Weapons Technology*, in <https://www.nirs.org/les/khanreportfinal29404.pdf>, May 2004, accessed on 20 June 2015.

12. See Gordon Corera, *Shopping for Bombs: Nuclear Proliferation, Global Insecurity, and the Rise and Fall of the A.Q. Khan Network* (UK: Oxford University Press, 2009).

13. 'Kuldip Nayar's Book Spills Pak Nuclear Bomb Secrets', *The Times of India*, 7 July 2012.

14. Seymour Hersh, 'On the Nuclear Edge', *New Yorker*, 29 March 1993, p. 59.

15. *China's Nuclear Exports and Assistance to Pakistan*, in <http://cns.miis.edu/archive/country_india/china/npakpos.htm>, accessed on 20 June 2015.

16. See Graham Hutchings, *Modern China: A Guide to a Century of Change* (UK: Penguin, 2000).

17. 'Britain Slaps Case against Customs Agent who Probed A.Q. Khan', *Indian Express*, 16 December 2007.

18. See *A.Q. Khan and Onward Proliferation from Pakistan*, in <http://sites.miis.edu/exportcontrols/files/2009/02/IISS-from-web.pdf>, accessed on 24 June 2015.

19. Adrian Levy and Catherine Scott-Clarke, *Deception: Pakistan, the United States and the Nuclear Weapons Conspiracy* (USA: Penguin, 2007).

20. See also Bruce Riedel, *Double Game Deepens*, in <http://www.brookings.edu/research/opinions/2012/04/06-double-game-pakistan-riedel>, 6 April 2012, accessed on 24 June 2015.

21. 'A Secret Nuke Offer?' *Newsweek*, 11 May 1998, p 11.

22. Pervez Musharraf, *In the Line of Fire* (USA: Simon & Schuster, 2006).

23. Anwar Iqbal, 'Dr Khan Asked Daughter to Leak N-Secrets', *Dawn*, 26 September 2006.

24. See David Albright, Paul Brannan, and Andrea Scheel Stricker, 'Detecting and Disrupting Illicit Nuclear Trade after A.Q. Khan', *The Washington Quarterly*, April 2010.

25. 'Musharraf Says Army Will Keep Control of Nukes', *Reuters*, 17 November 2007.

26. Adrian Levy and Catherine Scott-Clarke, *Deception: Pakistan, the United States and the Nuclear Weapons Conspiracy* (USA: Penguin, 2007).

27. See A. Subramanyam Raju, *Terrorism in South Asia: Views from India* (New Delhi: Inda Research Press, 2004).

28. See 'Musharraf Admits US Aid Diverted', *BBC*, in <http://news.bbc.co.uk/2/hi/south_asia/8254360.stm>, 14 September 2009, accessed on 20 June 2015.

13. The Indus: Waters of Unity

1. Post 9/11, Kashmir has—in jihadi jargon—been defined as part of an incipient 'Eastern Caliphate'.

2. In 1948, having consolidated their position in Kashmir, Indian military forces launched a spring offensive against tribal invaders.

3. Zulfiqar Ali Bhutto and Swaran Singh, the Indian foreign minister held multiple rounds of talks in 1962-63. The talks failed partially because of India's justifiable refusal to hand over the Kashmir Valley, and Pakistan's surrender of territory (Aksai Chin and the Shaksgam Valley) to China.

4. In 2014, too, Pakistan expressed concerns about treaty violations. 'India Accused of Violating Indus Water Treaty', *Dawn*, 25 August 2014.

5. *Water Resource Conflicts and International Security: A Global Perspective,* edited by Dhirendra K. Vajpeyi (USA: Lexington Books, 2012).

6. J. Allouche, *Water Nationalism: An Explanation of the Past and Present Conflicts in Central Asia, the Middle East and Indian Subcontinent*, Ph.D. thesis, University of Geneve, 2005.

7. When the province of Punjab was partitioned, two important head works, Madhopur on the River Ravi and Ferozepur on River Sutlej, went to India. However, East Punjab (India) and West Punjab (Pakistan) signed a Standstill Agreement on 20 December 1947, providing inter alia, that until the end of the present rabi crop on 31 March 1948, status quo would be maintained with regard to water allocation in the Indus Basin irrigation system. See Salman M.A. Salman and Kishor Uprety, *Conflict and Cooperation on South Asia's International Rivers* (The Hague: Kluwer Law International).

8. Chaudhury Mohammad Ali, *Emergence of Pakistan* (USA: Columbia University Press, 1967).

9. Ramaswamy Iyer, *Towards Water Wisdom: Limits, Justice and Harmony* (New Delhi: Sage Publications, 2007). 'In Pakistan, it is often argued that this represented an act of generosity on its part, as the portion of territory that went to India was historically using only 8 per cent of the Indus waters. Indian sources put it at a higher figure.'

10. Vijepal Singh Mann, *Troubled Waters of Punjab* (New Delhi: Allied Publishers, 2003).

11. 'Transboundary Waters', *Central Water Commission*, in <http://www.cwc.nic.in/main/downloads/Theme%20Paper%20WWD-2009.pdf>, 2009, accessed on 26 July 2015.

12. *India-Pakistan Relations 1947-2007: A Documentary Study*, edited by Avtar Singh Bhasin, 10 Volumes (New Delhi: Geetika Publishers, 2012).
13. *Ibid.*
14. *Ibid*
15. See Anupama Aira and Jayanth Jacob, 'Pakistan Writes to World Bank on Concerns over Sutlej Power Project', *Hindustan Times*, 25 May 2010.
16. The soil here has, since then, turned somewhat sour due to over-irrigation, over-fertilization and lack of diversification—a problem that is now being sought to be remedied.
17. 'Pakistan Wastes 1/3rd of Indus Water It Gets, admits Qureshi', *The Times of India*, 2 May 2010.
18. See Alok Bansal, *Baglihar and Kishanganga: Problems of Trust*
19. The Indus Waters Treaty, Section 15(3) of Part 3 (New run-of-river plants) of Annexure D, pertaining to 'generation of hydro-electric power by India on the western rivers'.
20. See 'Hague Court of Arbitration Rules in Indus Waters Kishenganga Arbitration (Pakistan v. India) (December 20, 2013)', *American Society of International Law*, in <http://www.asil.org/blogs/hague-court-arbitration-rules-indus-waters-kishenganga-arbitration-pakistan-v-india-december#sthash.IUyxO47M.dpuf>, accessed on 24 July 2015.
21. See 'Central Electricity Authority', Government of India, in <http://powermin.nic.in/whats_new/PFR/J-K/KIRU.pdf>, accessed on 27 July 2015.
22. See The Indus Waters Treaty, Preamble.
23. See Navnita Chadha Behera, *Demystifying Kashmir* (Washington: Brookings Institution, 2006).
24. *India-Pakistan Relations 1947-2007: A Documentary Study*, edited by Avtar Singh Bhasin, 10 Volumes (New Delhi: Geetika Publishers, 2012).
25. *India-Pakistan Relations 1947-2007: A Documentary Study*, edited by Avtar Singh Bhasin, 10 Volumes (New Delhi: Geetika Publishers, 2012).
26. N.D. Gulhati, *Indus Waters Treaty: An Exercise in International Mediation* (Mumbai: Allied Publishers, 1973).
27. See 'Kashmir Issue Can't Be Resolved In A Day: PM', *Hindustan Times*, 18 April 2005.
28. *PM's Speech on Launch of Amritsar-Nanaka Sahib Bus Service*, in <archivepmo.nic.in/drmanmohansingh/speech-details.php?nodeid=293>, 24 March 2006, accessed on 28 July 2015.
29. *International Cooperation*, in <www.archive.india.gov.in/sectors/water_resources/index.php?id=6>, accessed on 28 July 2015.

DECONSTRUCTING PAKISTAN

14. What is Pakistan? An Inconvenient Truth

1. *India-Pakistan Relations 1947-2007: A Documentary Study*, edited by Avtar Singh Bhasin, 10 Volumes (New Delhi: Geetika Publishers, 2012).
2. *Ibid.*

3. *Ibid.*
4. *Ibid.*
5. Zulfikar Ali Bhutto, *The Myth of Independence* (UK: Oxford University Press, 1969).
6. See also 'The Subtle Subversion: The State of Curricula and Textbooks in Pakistan', *Sustainable Development Policy Institute*, in <http://unesco.org.pk/education/teachereducation/reports/rp22.pdf>, accessed on 22 May 2015.
7. *Ibid.*
8. M.D Zafar, *A Textbook of Pakistan Studies*, Lahore, p. 4.
9. *Ibid.*, pp. 4-8.
10. *Ibid.*, pp. 9-23.
11. Muashrati Ulum, Class V, NWFP, Textbook Board, Peshawar, p. 9.
12. Zubeida Mustafa, 'The Continuing Biases in Our Textbooks', *Policy Brief: The Jinnah Institute*, in <http://jinnah-institute.org/wp-content/uploads/2014/02/ZubeidaPB.pdf>, 30 April 2012, accessed on 22 May 2015.
13. *Ibid.*
14. 'Creating National Memory: The Organisation of Social Knowledge in Pakistan'.
15. See 'The Communalization of Education: The History Textbooks Controversy', Delhi Historians' Group, in <http://www.friendsof southasia.org/textbook/NCERT_Delhi_Historians__Group.pdf>, December 2001, accessed on 22 May 2015.
16. *Ibid.*
17. See 'Modi @ Reliance Hospital Opening: "Plastic surgeon May Have Fixed Elephant's head on Ganesha"', *Rediff*, in < http://www.rediff.com/news/report/modi—reliance-hospital-opening-plastic-surgeon-may-have-fixed-elephants-head-on-ganesha/20141025.htm>, accessed on 22 May 2015.

15. Flawed at Birth

1. *India-Pakistan Relations 1947-2007: A Documentary Study*, edited by Avtar Singh Bhasin, 10 Volumes (New Delhi: Geetika Publishers, 2012).
2. See 'The Fantastic India-Pakistan Battle', *Multiversity*, in <http://vlal.bol.ucla.edu/multiversity/Nandy/Nandy_indpak.htm>, accessed on 29 May 2015.
3. 'Ajmal Kasab, the only attacker who was captured alive, later confessed upon interrogation that the attacks were conducted with the support of Pakistan Government's intelligence agency ISI…' '… disclosed that the attackers were members of Lashkar-e-Taiba among others. Pakistan initially contested this attribution, but agreed this was the case on 7 January 2009'. In *The New York Times*, 7 January 2009; *Dawn*, 7 January 2009, respectively.
4. 'Federation Administered Tribal Areas'—a semi-autonomous tribal region, or proposed province of Pakistan in the northwestern region.

5. See 'The Subtle Subversion: The State of Curricula and Textbooks in Pakistan', *Sustainable Development Policy Institute*, in <http://unesco.org.pk/education/teachereducation/reports/rp22.pdf>, accessed on 22 May 2015.

6. 'Muhammad Ali Jinnah's first Presidential Address to the Constituent Assembly of Pakistan', 11 August 1947, *G. Allana, Pakistan Movement Historical Documents* (Karachi: Department of International Relations, University of Karachi, nd [1969]), pp. 407-411.

7. *The Hindu,* 12 June 2012, (International Section): '… according to historian Mubarak Ali, the speech was censored because it caused great discomfort within the Muslim League and the bureaucracy […] After Jinnah's death, the direction given in that speech was replaced with the Objectives Resolution that laid the foundations of an Islamic state. […] Former Prime Minister Zulfiqar Ali Bhutto claimed that attempts were made to burn the speech and a concerted effort was made during the regime of military dictator Zia ul-Haq to remove all reference to that historic address from textbooks.'

8. See 'Pakistan: Revisiting the Munir Committee Report', *The Siasat Daily*, in <http://www.siasat.com/english/news/pakistan-revisitng-munir-committee-report>, 1 January 2015, accessed on 1 June 2015.

9. In *Social Studies for Class VI* (Sindh Textbook Board, 1997). See also 'The Subtle Subversion: The State of Curricula and Textbooks in Pakistan', *Sustainable Development Policy Institute*, in <http://unesco.org.pk/education/teachereducation/reports/rp22.pdf>, accessed on 22 May 2015. Also Yvette Claire Rosser, *Curriculum as Destiny: Forging National Identity in India, Pakistan and Bangladesh*, The University of Austin, Texas, in <https://www.lib.utexas.edu/etd/d/2003/rosseryc036/rosseryc036.pdf>, August 2003, accessed on 1 June 2015.

10. *Ibid.*

11. Founded in 1964, an economic union in which the three countries agreed to develop ties in trade, commerce and industry. See M.B. Bishku, 'In Search of Identity and Security: Pakistan and the Middle East', 1947-77, *Conflict Quarterly*, Volume 12, Number 3, Summer 1992, p. 36.

12. *The Making of Pakistan* (Pakistan: Jumhoori Publications, 2013).

13. 'West Pakistan Established as One Unit', *The Story of Pakistan*, in <http://storyofpakistan.com/west-pakistan-established-as-one-unit/>, accessed on 1 June 2015.

14. C. Christine Fair, *Fighting to the End: The Pakistan Army's Way of War* (UK: Oxford University Press, 2014).

15. General Headquarters of the Pakistan army in Rawalpindi.

16. Inter-Services Intelligence, Pakistan's premier intelligence agency.

17. In relation to 'the Pakistani Army's support to terror groups, and the management of the nuclear weapon and related missile capability' which are 'under the sole control of the Pakistan Army', see <nationalinterest.org/commentary/sharif-must-square-the-circle-8468>, accessed on 2 June 2015.

18. See Qamar Zaman, 'Budget Debate: 'N' Demands Greater Military Accountability, *Tribune,* 19 June 2011.
19. Nirupama Subramanian, 'Military Inc. It's Big Business in Pakistan', *The Hindu,* 19 April 2007. See also Sudha Ramachandran, 'Pakistan's Military Minds Its Own Business', *Asia Times Online,* in <http://www.atimes.com/atimes/South_Asia/FI10Df03.html>, 10 September 2004, accessed on 1 June 2015.
20. See Ayesha Siddiqa's *Military Inc,* (UK: Pluto Press, 2007).
21. Leslie Wolf-Phillips, 'Constitutional Legitimacy: A Study of the Doctrine of Necessity', *Third World Quarterly,* Volume 1, Number 4, October, 1979, p.98.
22. 'An agenda of Islamisation, and a new series of penal laws based on Islam, introduced by Zia ul-Haq on 2 February 1979', *Pathways to Power: The Domestic Politics of South Asia,* edited by Arjun Guneratne and Anita M. Weiss (USA: Rowman & Littlefield Publishers, 2013).

16. A Warrior State

1. The Great Game refers to the strategic rivalry and conflict between the British Empire and the Russian Empire for supremacy in Central Asia, running approximately from 1813 to 1907.
2. T.V. Paul, *The Warrior State: Pakistan in the Contemporary World* (USA: Oxford University Press, 2014).
3. See Rajendra Prasad, *India Undivided* (New Delhi: Penguin, 2010), p. 27.
4. M.S. Golwalkar, *We, Our Nationhood Defined* (India, Bharat Publications, 1939).
5. Kanti Bajpai, 'India and China: Can the Giants of Asia Cooperate?', *Institute for Defence Studies and Analyses,* in <http://www.idsa.in/event/IndiaandChinaCantheGiantsofAsiaCooperate30.11.html>, 30 November 2011, accessed on 15 June 2015.
6. Imran Khan, *Pakistan: A Personal History* (UK: Transworld, 2011).
7. See also *South Asia and Afghanistan: The Robust India-Pakistan Rivalry,* in <http://file.prio.no/Publication_files/Prio/Tadjbakhsh,%20S%20(2011)%20South%20Asia%20and%20Afghanistan%20(PRIO%20Paper).pdf>, accessed on 15 June 2015.
8. T.V. Paul, *The Warrior State: Pakistan in the Contemporary World* (USA: Oxford University Press, 2014), p. 196.
9. See also Ishtiaq Ahmed, *The Pakistan Military in Politics: Origins, Evolution, Consequences* (New Delhi: Amaryllis, 2013), which serves as another good example.
10. In a letter to Pir of Manki Sharif, November 1945, cited in *Constituent Assembly of Pakistan Debates,* Volume 5, 1949, p. 46.
11. For serious scholars of the Radcliffe Award it would be interesting to note that it corresponded exactly to the Breakdown Plan which Viceroy Wavell had sent as a top secret document to London on 7 February 1946. Also in Ishtiaq Ahmed, 'The Battle for Lahore and Amritsar', *The News,* 25 August 2007.

12. S.K. Malik, *The Quranic Concept of War* (Lahore: Wajidalis, 1979).
13. Hasan Suroor, 'Islam and its Interpretations', *The Hindu*, 29 September 2014.
14. *Ibid.*
15. *Ibid.*
16. Abbottabad Commission of Enquiry Report, in *Al Jazeera* <http://www.aljazeera.com/indepth/spotlight/binladenfiles/2013/07/201378143927822246.html>, accessed on 15 June 2015.
17. See 'Pakistan is a Failing State, ISI Chief Tells Abbottabad Commission', *Business Standard*, 9 July 2013.
18. Abbottabad Commission of Enquiry Report, in *Al Jazeera* <http://www.aljazeera.com/indepth/spotlight/binladenfiles/2013/07/201378143927822246.html>, accessed on 15 June 2015.
19. *Ibid.*
20. In one commentary, *The New York Times* reporter Carlotta Gall comes close to confirming that the US had information about the ISI knowing of the whereabouts of bin Laden. See *The Wrong Enemy: America in Afghanistan, 2001-14* (USA: Houghton Mifflin Harcourt, 2014).
21. See Rana Banerji, 'Pakistan: The Abbottabad Commission of Enquiry', *IPIS Review*, in <http://www.ipcs.org/article/peace-and-conflict-database-pakistan/pakistan-the-abbottabad-commission-of-enquiry-4027.html >, 9 July 2013, accessed on 15 July 2015.
22. Heraldo Munoz, *Getting Away With Murder* (USA: Norton, 2014).
23. 'Report of the United Nations Commission of Inquiry into the Facts and Circumstances of the Assassination of Former Pakistani Prime Minister Mohtarma Benazir Bhutto', *United Nations*, in <http://www.un.org/News/dh/infocus/Pakistan/UN_Bhutto_Report_15April2010.pdf>, accessed on 16 June 2015.
24. 'Munoz's investigation revealed that the black Mercedes car that was assigned to Bhutto's security detail on Dec 27, one that was supposed to rescue her in case of an untoward incident, had also mysteriously disappeared and failed to show up. Instead, the SUV in which Bhutto had been travelling (and which had three blown tyres) continued to try and drive the severely injured leader to a hospital and away from the scene of the bombing.' See Rafia Zakaria, 'Truth and Assasination', *Dawn*, in <http://www.dawn.com/news/1167224>, 4 March 2015, accessed on 16 June 2015.
25. 'Report of the United Nations Commission of Inquiry into the Facts and Circumstances of the Assassination of Former Pakistani Prime Minister Mohtarma Benazir Bhutto', *United Nations*, in <http://www.un.org/News/dh/infocus/Pakistan/UN_Bhutto_Report_15April2010.pdf>, accessed on 16 June 2015.
26. Khaled Ahmed, 'Man of the Year: General Raheel Sharif', *Newsweek*, 31 December 2014.
27. Malala Yousafzai Delivers Defiant Riposte to Taliban Militants With Speech to the UN General Assembly, *The Independent*, 12 June 2013.

17. Pakistan@In-denial.com

1. See Farzana Shaikh, *Making Sense of Pakistan* (London: Hurst, 2009).
2. *Indian Independence Act, 1947*, see <http://www.legislation.gov.uk/ukpga/1947/30/pdfs/ukpga_19470030_en.pdf>, accessed on 22 June 2015.
3. On the other hand, as we know from preceding chapters, Kalat was forcibly annexed by Pakistan in 1948. Pakistan also claimed Hyderabad, Junagadh and other non-Muslim states.
4. B.G. Verghese, *A J&K Primer: From Myth to Reality* (New Delhi: India Research Press, 2007).
5. See Dipankar De Sarkar, 'Lines on a Map? Time to Unleash South Asian Energies', *Mint*, 30 May 2014.
6. Power of the Union to confer powers, etc. on States in certain cases—
   (1) Notwithstanding anything in this Constitution, the President may, with the consent of the Governor of a State, entrust either conditionally or unconditionally to that Government or to its officers functions in relation to any matter to which the executive power of the Union extends
   (2) A law made by Parliament which applies in any State may, notwithstanding that it relates to a matter with respect to which the Legislature of the State has no power to make laws, confer powers and impose duties, or authorise the conferring of powers and the imposition of duties, upon the State or officers and authorities thereof
   (3) Where by virtue of this article powers and duties have been conferred or imposed upon a State or officers or authorities thereof, there shall be paid by the Government of India to the State such sum as may be agreed, or, in default of agreement, as may be determined by an arbitrator appointed by the Chief Justice of India, in respect of any extra costs of administration incurred by the State in connection with the exercise of those powers and duties
7. Power of the States to entrust functions to the Union—Notwithstanding anything in this Constitution, the Governor of a State may, with the consent of the Government of India, entrust either conditionally or unconditionally to that Government or to its officers functions in relation to any matter to which the executive power of the State extends.

SEEKING SOLUTIONS

18. Autonomy, Restructuring and Peaceful Resolution

1. The manifesto announced a programme of 'freedom, equality and democracy for the people'. See Mohan C. Bhandari, *Solving Kashmir* (New Delhi: Lancer, 2006).
2. See 'Hurriyat's Geelani Sets Down Conditions for Dialogue on Kashmir Issue', *Zee News*, in <http://zeenews.india.com/news/nation/hurriyats-geelani-sets-down-conditions-for-dialogue-on-kashmir-issue_652122.html>, 1 September 2010, accessed on 29 July 2015.

3. See 'Demilitarise. Repeal Black Laws. Talk To Pakistan. Have A Referendum. Remember That Kashmiris Are Not Indians', *Tehelka*, Volume 7, Issue 34, 28 August 2010.

4. See 'Pak Wants Composite Dialogue Covering Kashmir Issue', *The Hindu*, 11 February 2010.

5. Prime Minister P.V. Narasimha Rao's announced in Burkina Faso in 1995 that the 'sky is the limit' with respect to the quantum of autonomy that J&K could get within the framework of the Constitution.

6. *Delhi Agreement 1952*, in <http://jklaw.nic.in/delhi1952agreemnet.pdf>, accessed on 29 July 2015.

7. See Tony Karon, 'After Mumbai, Can the US Cool India-Pakistan Tension?', *Time*, 4 December 2008.

8. See 'Miliband Accused of Creating Diplomatic Storm over Kashmir Comments,' *The Guardian*, 21 January 2009. Miliband also belatedly disowned the Bush administration's ' War on Terror' (in Afghanistan and Iraq), so strenuously supported by his government, which continues more truly to fuel Islamic radicalism and jihadi terror worldwide.

9. See 'Lashkar Offers to End Jihad', *The Hindu*, 19 January 2009.

10. Thomas Bruce Millar, *The Commonwealth and the United Nations* (Australia: Sydney University Press, 1967), p.26.

11. See Harish Khare, 'Time for a New Compact in Kashmir', *The Hindu*, 12 July 2000.

12. *J&K Constitution*, in <jklegislativeassembly.nic.in/Constitution_of_J&K.pdf>, accessed on 31 July 2015.

13. *Ibid.*

14. Happymon Jacob, 'Kashmir Needs a Political Package', *The Hindu*, 23 September 2010.

15. Article 246 states:
    • Notwithstanding anything in clauses (2) and (3), Parliament has exclusive power to make laws with respect to any of the matters enumerated in List I in the seventh Schedule (in this Constitution referred to as the 'Union List').
    • Notwithstanding anything in clause (3), Parliament, and, subject to clause (1), the legislature of any State also, have power to make laws with respect to any of the matters enumerated in List III in the Seventh Schedule (in this Constitution referred to as the "Concurrent List").
    • Subject to clauses (1) and (2), the Legislature of any State has exclusive power to make laws for such State or any part thereof with respect to any of the matters enumerated in List II in the Seventh Schedule (in this Constitution referred to as the 'State List').
    • Parliament has power to make laws with respect to any matter for any part of the territory of India not included in a State notwithstanding that such matter is a matter enumerated in the State List.

16. The Seventh Schedule allocates powers and functions between the union and the states.

17. *Ibid*

18. *Ibid*
19. See The Constitution (Application to Jammu and Kashmir) Order, 1950, in <http://india.gov.in/sites/upload_files/npi/filescoi_appendix.pdf>, accessed on 12 August 2015.
20. Speech of Sheikh Mohammed Abdullah in the constituent assembly, 1951.
21. See Delhi Agreement, 1952, in <-jklaw.nic.in/delhi1952agreemnet.pdf>, accessed on 13 July 2015.
22. See Constitution (Application to Jammu and Kashmir) Order, in <http://jklaw.nic.in/constitution_jk.pdf>, accessed on 13 September 2015.
23. Article 248 affirms residuary powers of legislation
    (1) Parliament has exclusive power to make any law with respect to any matter not enumerated in the Concurrent List or State List; (2) Such power shall include the power of making any law imposing a tax not mentioned in either of those Lists.
24. *The Kashmir Accord*, in <http://www.jammu-kashmir.com/documents/kashmiraccord.html>, accessed on 19 August 2015.
25. 'Restore Autonomy to Bring Peace in J-K: Ruling NC to Centre', *India Today*, 17 June 2012.
26. M.L. Kak, 'J&K: Yet Another Pandora's Box', *The Tribune*, in <www.tribuneindia.com/2000/20000326/spectrum/main1.htm>, 26 March 2000, accessed on 10 August 2015.
27. See *The Politics of Autonomy: Indian Experiences*, edited by Ranabir Samaddar (New Delhi: Sage, 2005).
28. This states: 'Before each general election to the House of the People and to the Legislative Assembly of each State, and before the first general election and thereafter before each biennial election to the Legislative Council of each State having such Council, the President may also appoint after consultation with the Election Commission such Regional Commissioners as he may consider necessary to assist the Election Commission in the performance of the functions conferred on the Commission [...]'
29. 'Halqa' means the area comprising a village or such contiguous number of villages as may be determined by the government from time to time.
30. See Directorate of Rural Development in Kashmir, in <http://www.drdk.nic.in/righttry2.htm>, accessed on 20 August 2015.
31. Sarkaria Commission, *Scribed*, in <http://www.scribd.com/doc/49034978/SARKARIA-COMMISSION#scribd>, accessed on 24 August 2015.
32. Memorandum of Understanding—Administrative Reforms, in <http://artassam.nic.in/Hills%20Areas%20Deptt/Office%20Memorandum.pdf>, accessed on 24 August 2015.
33. *The All Pakistan Legal Decisions*, Volume 27, Part 4, 1975.
34. *The Azad Jammu and Kashmir Interim Constitution Act, 1974*, in <http://

www.ajkassembly.gok.pk/AJK_Interim_Constitution_Act_1974.pdf>, accessed on 25 August 2015.

35. *Ibid.*
36. *Ibid.*
37. *Ibid.*
38. *Ibid.*
39. *Ibid.*
40. *Ibid.*
41. C.U. Aitchison, *A Collection Of Treaties Engagements And Sanads* (New Delhi: Government of India, 1909).
42. This holds that 1[(2) The territories of Pakistan shall comprise—(a) the Provinces of Balochistan, the Khyber Pakhtunkhwa, the Punjab and Sindh; (b) the Islamabad Capital Territory, hereinafter referred to as the Federal Capital; (c) the Federally Administered Tribal Areas; and (d) such States and territories as are or may be included in Pakistan, whether by accession or otherwise.
43. See Navnita Chadha Behera, *Demystifying Kashmir* (USA: Brookings Institute, 2006).
44. 'Islamabad announced a reforms package for the Northern Areas in April 1994, the implementation of which turned the contested territory into a de facto fifth province of Pakistan.' See *Prospects for Peace in South Asia*, edited by Rafiq Dossani and Henry S. Rowen (USA: Stanford University Press, 2005).

19. Overcoming Partition

1. Nehru, it is said, wriggled out of a pre-election agreement with the Muslim League to share power in the United Provinces government after learning that the Congress had won a majority on its own. This 'betrayal', some say, led to a demand for Pakistan.
2. Sudhi Ranjan Sen, 'Did Jinnah Betray Congress to UK in the 1946 Riots', *The Indian Express*, in <http://expressindia.indianexpress.com/news/fullstory.php?newsid=52299>, 8 August 2005, accessed 26 August 2015.
3. *Ibid.*
4. *Ibid.*
5. *Ibid.*
6. *Ibid*
7. 'Days After Declared Terror Outfit, LeT Founder Hafiz Saeed Spews Venom against India, US', *The Indian Express*, in < http://indianexpress.com/article/world/asia/days-after-us-declares-terror-outfit-let-founder-hafiz-saeed-addresses-seminar-in-lahore-court/#sthash.NIws1tTV.dpuf>, 11 July 2014, accessed on 26 August 2015.
8. Ayesha Jalal, *State of Martial Rule* (UK: Cambridge University Press, 2007).
9. Narendra Singh Sarila, *The Shadow of the Great Game: The Untold Story of Partition (New Delhi: HarperCollins, 2009).*

10. Chandrashekhar Dasgupta's *War and Diplomacy in Kashmir* (New Delhi: Sage, 2002).
11. See Sayyid Mîr Qâsim, *My Life and Times* (New Delhi: Allied Publishers, 1992).
12. See *India Today: An Encyclopedia of Life in the Republic*, edited by edited by Arnold P. Kaminsky and Roger D. Long (California: ABC-CLIO, 2011).
13. See Mohammad Hanif, 'Pakistan's General Problem', *Open Magazine*, 11 June 2011; also see V.R. Raghavan, *Internal Conflicts—A Four State Analysis: India-Nepal-Sri Lanka-Myanmar* (Chennai: Centre for Security Analysis, 2013).
14. Lieutenant General Shahid Aziz, *Yeh Khamoshi Kahan Tak? Aik Sipahi ki Dastan-e-Ishq o Junoon [English: How Long Will You Remain Silent? A Soldier's Saga of Love and Passion]* (Islamabad: Seven Springs Publishers, 2013).
15. *Ibid.*
16. In 2011, the governor of Punjab, Salmaan Taseer, a very outspoken critic of the blasphemy law, was fatally wounded by his own police guard for defending a poor Christian woman, Asia Bibi, who had been sentenced to death. His killer has since been celebrated as a hero by many who consider his actions to be in compliance with the Quran.
17. Pakistani Minorities Minister Shahbaz Bhatti had told the BBC in January 2011 that he would defy the death threats he had received from Islamist militants for his efforts to reform the blasphemy law. However, eventually, in March 2011, he was shot dead by gunmen who ambushed his car in broad daylight in the capital, Islamabad. See 'Pakistan Minorities Minister Shahbaz Bhatti Shot Dead', *BBC*, in <http://www.bbc.com/news/world-south-asia-12617562>, accessed on 4 September 2015.

Index